MINOTAUR PRESS, A TOP COW PRODUCTIONS COMPANY, PRESENTS...

THE TANK

CREATED BY
MATT HAWKINS
&
RAHSAN EKEDAL

published by
Top Cow Productions, Inc.
Los Angeles

THINK TANK ™

MATT HAWKINS
CO-CREATOR & WRITER

RAHSAN EKEDAL
CO-CREATOR & ARTIST

TROY PETERI
LETTERER

COVER ART BY
RAHSAN EKEDAL
& BILL FARMER

EDITED BY
BETSY GONIA

BOOK DESIGN AND LAYOUT BY
ADDISON DUKE

 To find the comic shop
nearest you, call:
1-888-COMICBOOK

Want more info? Check out:
www.topcow.com
for news & exclusive Top Cow merchandise!

888-COMICBOOK
888-266-4226

 TOP COW PRODUCTIONS, INC.
Marc Silvestri - CEO
Matt Hawkins - President & COO
Betsy Gonia - Managing Editor
Elena Salcedo - Operations Manager
Ryan Cady - Production Assistant

IMAGE COMICS, INC.
Robert Kirkman – Chief Operating Officer
Erik Larsen – Chief Financial Officer
Todd McFarlane – President
Marc Silvestri – Chief Executive Officer
Jim Valentino – Vice-President

Eric Stephenson – Publisher
Ron Richards – Director of Business Development
Jennifer de Guzman – Director of Trade Book Sales
Kat Salazar – Director of PR & Marketing
Jeremy Sullivan – Director of Digital Sales
Emilio Bautista – Sales Assistant
Branwyn Bigglestone – Senior Accounts Manager
Emily Miller – Accounts Manager
Jessica Ambriz – Administrative Assistant
Tyler Shainline – Events Coordinator
David Brothers – Content Manager
Jonathan Chan – Production Manager
Drew Gill – Art Director
Meredith Wallace – Print Manager
Monica Garcia – Senior Production Artist
Jenna Savage – Production Artist
Addison Duke – Production Artist
Tricia Ramos – Production Assistant
IMAGECOMICS.COM

THINK TANK Volume 3
ISBN: 978-1-60706-851-8
March 2014. FIRST PRINTING.

3 2508 13278 0754

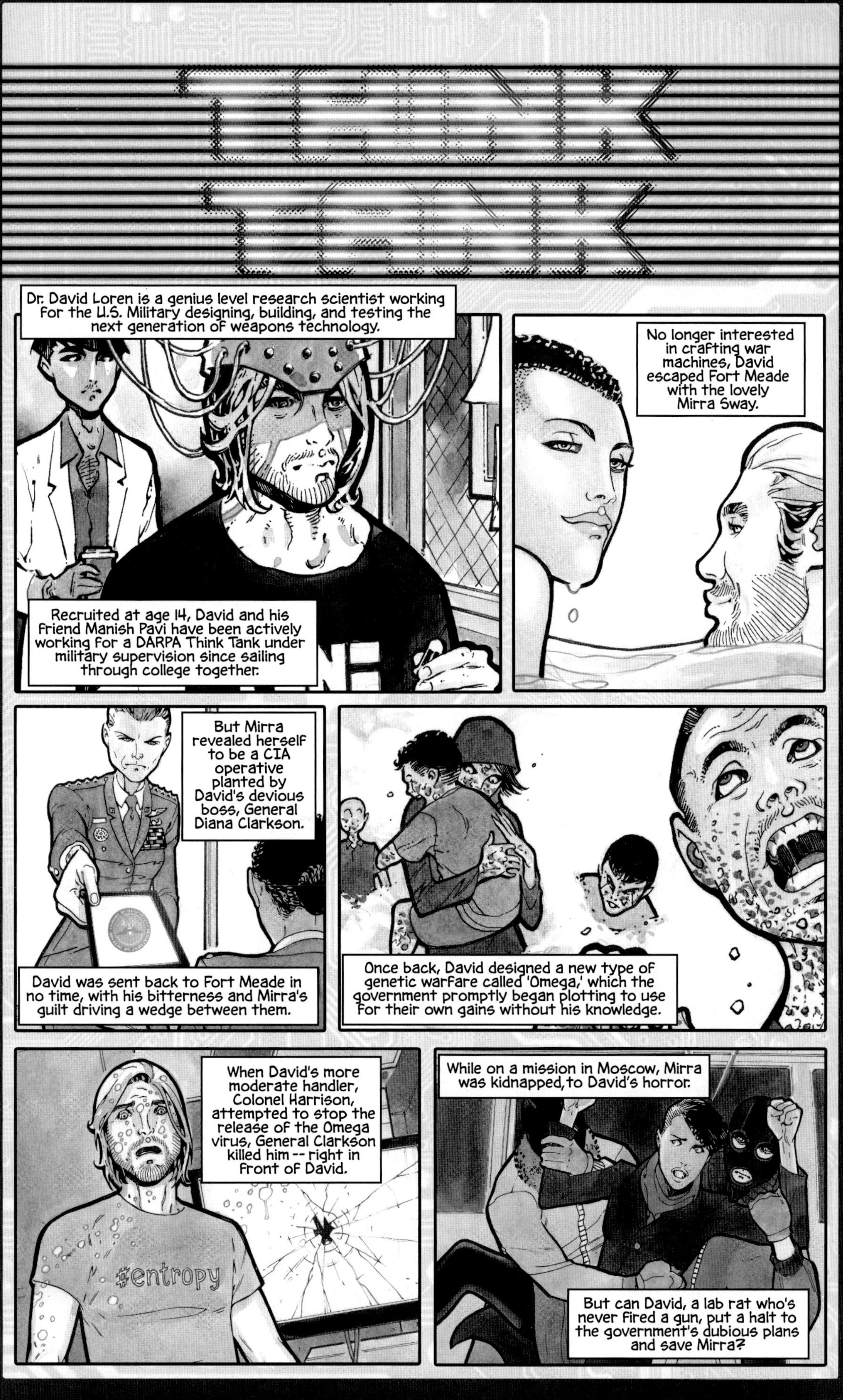
THINK TANK
Dr. David Loren is a genius level research scientist working for the U.S. Military designing, building, and testing the next generation of weapons technology.
Recruited at age 14, David and his friend Manish Pavi have been actively working for a DARPA Think Tank under military supervision since sailing through college together.
No longer interested in crafting war machines, David escaped Fort Meade with the lovely Mirra Sway.
But Mirra revealed herself to be a CIA operative planted by David's devious boss, General Diana Clarkson.
David was sent back to Fort Meade in no time, with his bitterness and Mirra's guilt driving a wedge between them.
Once back, David designed a new type of genetic warfare called 'Omega,' which the government promptly began plotting to use for their own gains without his knowledge.
When David's more moderate handler, Colonel Harrison, attempted to stop the release of the Omega virus, General Clarkson killed him -- right in front of David.
#entropy
While on a mission in Moscow, Mirra was kidnapped, to David's horror.
But can David, a lab rat who's never fired a gun, put a halt to the government's dubious plans and save Mirra?

CHAPTER ONE

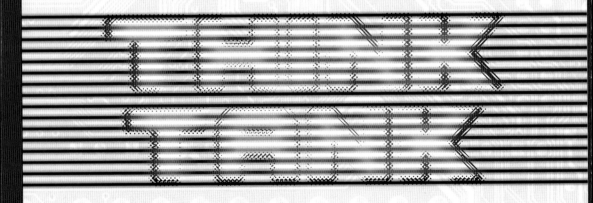

$$\oint \vec{E} \cdot d\vec{A} = \frac{1}{\varepsilon_0} q_{in} \qquad \oint \vec{B} \cdot d\vec{A} = 0 \qquad \oint \vec{E} \cdot d\vec{x} = -\frac{d}{dt} \int \vec{B} \cdot d\vec{A}$$

$$\oint \vec{B} \cdot d\vec{l} = \mu_0 I_{in} \qquad \vec{F} = q(\vec{v} \times \vec{B} + \vec{E}) \qquad i = \frac{dq}{dt}$$

point charge $\quad E = \frac{1}{4\pi\varepsilon_0} \frac{q}{r^2} \qquad V = \frac{1}{4\pi\varepsilon_0} \frac{q}{r} \qquad p = qd$

$$V_f - V_i = -\int_i^f \vec{E} \cdot d\vec{s} \qquad E_x = -\frac{\partial V}{\partial x} \qquad \vec{\tau} = \vec{p} \times \vec{E}$$

$$C = \frac{Q}{V} \qquad U_E = \frac{1}{2} QV = \frac{1}{2} CV^2 = \frac{1}{2} \frac{Q^2}{C} \qquad C = \varepsilon_0 \frac{A}{d}$$

$$R = \frac{V}{i} \qquad P = Vi \qquad P = i^2 R = \frac{V^2}{R} \qquad R = \rho \frac{L}{A}$$

$$R_{eq} = R_1 + R_2 + \cdots$$

"WAR DOES NOT DETERMINE WHO IS RIGHT—ONLY WHO IS LEFT."

BERTRAND RUSSELL

$$\frac{1}{R_{eq}} = \frac{1}{R_1} + \frac{1}{R_2} + \cdots \qquad \frac{1}{C_{eq}} = \frac{1}{C_1} + \frac{1}{C_2} + \cdots$$

$$d\vec{B} = \frac{\mu_0}{4\pi} \frac{i \, d\vec{s} \times \hat{r}}{r^2} \qquad B = \frac{\mu_0}{2\pi} \frac{i}{r} \qquad B = \mu_0 n i \qquad \vec{\tau} = \vec{\mu} \times$$

$$\varepsilon = -\frac{d\Phi}{dt} \qquad \mathcal{E} = -N\frac{d\Phi}{dt} \qquad L = \frac{|\varepsilon|}{\left|\frac{di}{dt}\right|} = \frac{N\Phi}{i}$$

$$u_E = \frac{1}{2} \varepsilon_0 E^2 \qquad u_B = \frac{1}{2} \frac{B^2}{\mu_0} \qquad U_B = \frac{1}{2} Li^2$$

$$q = q_0 e^{-t/\tau_c} \qquad q = C\mathcal{E}(1 - e^{-t/\tau_c}) \qquad i = i_0 e^{-t/\tau_L} \qquad i = \frac{\mathcal{E}}{R}(1 - e^{-t/\tau_L})$$

$$\tau_L = \frac{L}{R} \qquad \tau_c = RC \qquad \mu = NiA \qquad \frac{1}{4\pi\varepsilon_0} = 9 \times 10^9 \qquad \frac{\mu_0}{4\pi} = 10^{-7}$$

M means 10^6 $\qquad$ μ means 10^{-6}

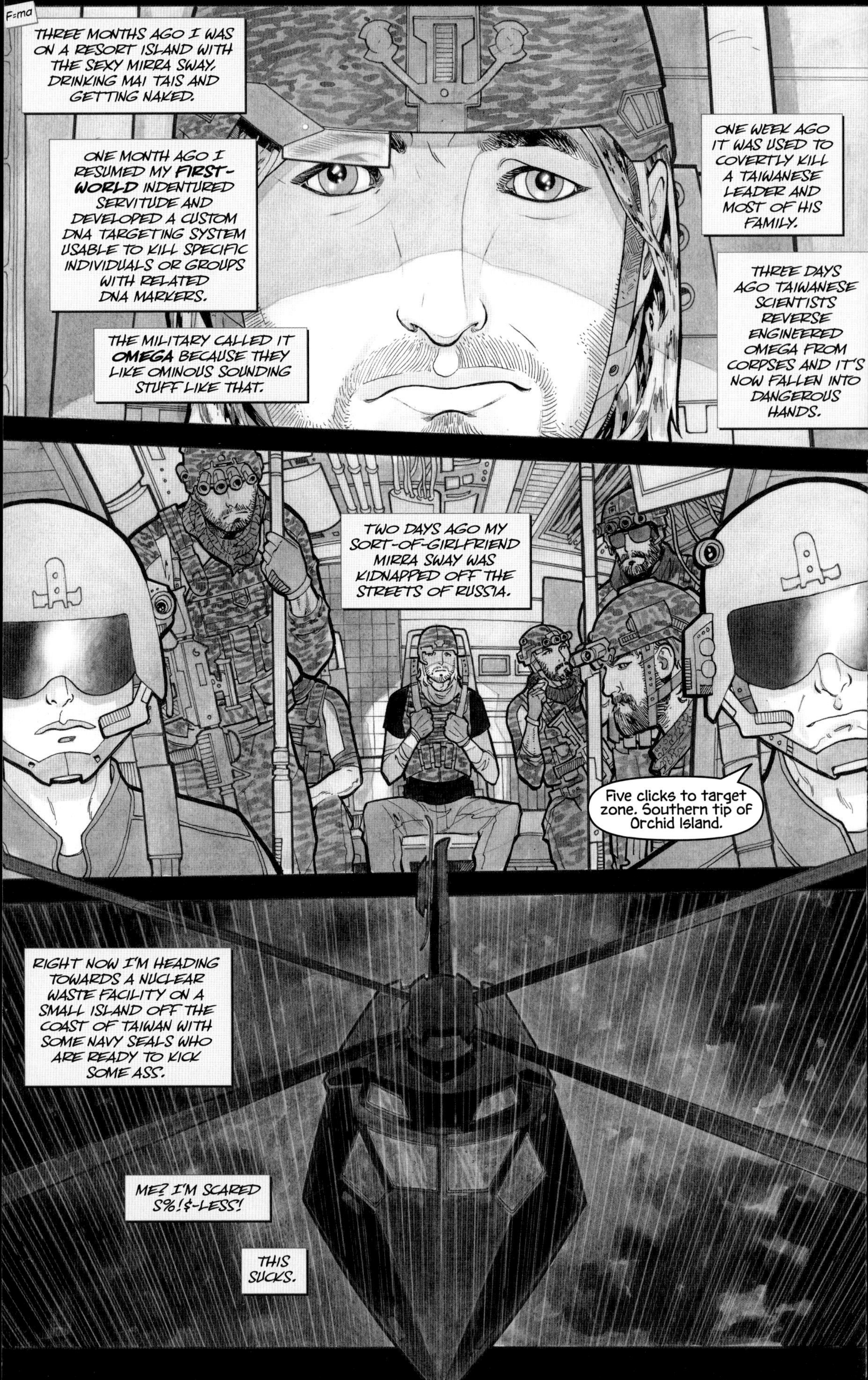
F=ma
THREE MONTHS AGO I WAS ON A RESORT ISLAND WITH THE SEXY MIRRA SWAY, DRINKING MAI TAIS AND GETTING NAKED.
ONE MONTH AGO I RESUMED MY FIRST-WORLD INDENTURED SERVITUDE AND DEVELOPED A CUSTOM DNA TARGETING SYSTEM USABLE TO KILL SPECIFIC INDIVIDUALS OR GROUPS WITH RELATED DNA MARKERS.
THE MILITARY CALLED IT OMEGA BECAUSE THEY LIKE OMINOUS SOUNDING STUFF LIKE THAT.
ONE WEEK AGO IT WAS USED TO COVERTLY KILL A TAIWANESE LEADER AND MOST OF HIS FAMILY.
THREE DAYS AGO TAIWANESE SCIENTISTS REVERSE ENGINEERED OMEGA FROM CORPSES AND IT'S NOW FALLEN INTO DANGEROUS HANDS.
TWO DAYS AGO MY SORT-OF-GIRLFRIEND MIRRA SWAY WAS KIDNAPPED OFF THE STREETS OF RUSSIA.
Five clicks to target zone. Southern tip of Orchid Island.
RIGHT NOW I'M HEADING TOWARDS A NUCLEAR WASTE FACILITY ON A SMALL ISLAND OFF THE COAST OF TAIWAN WITH SOME NAVY SEALS WHO ARE READY TO KICK SOME ASS.
ME? I'M SCARED S%!$-LESS!
THIS SUCKS.

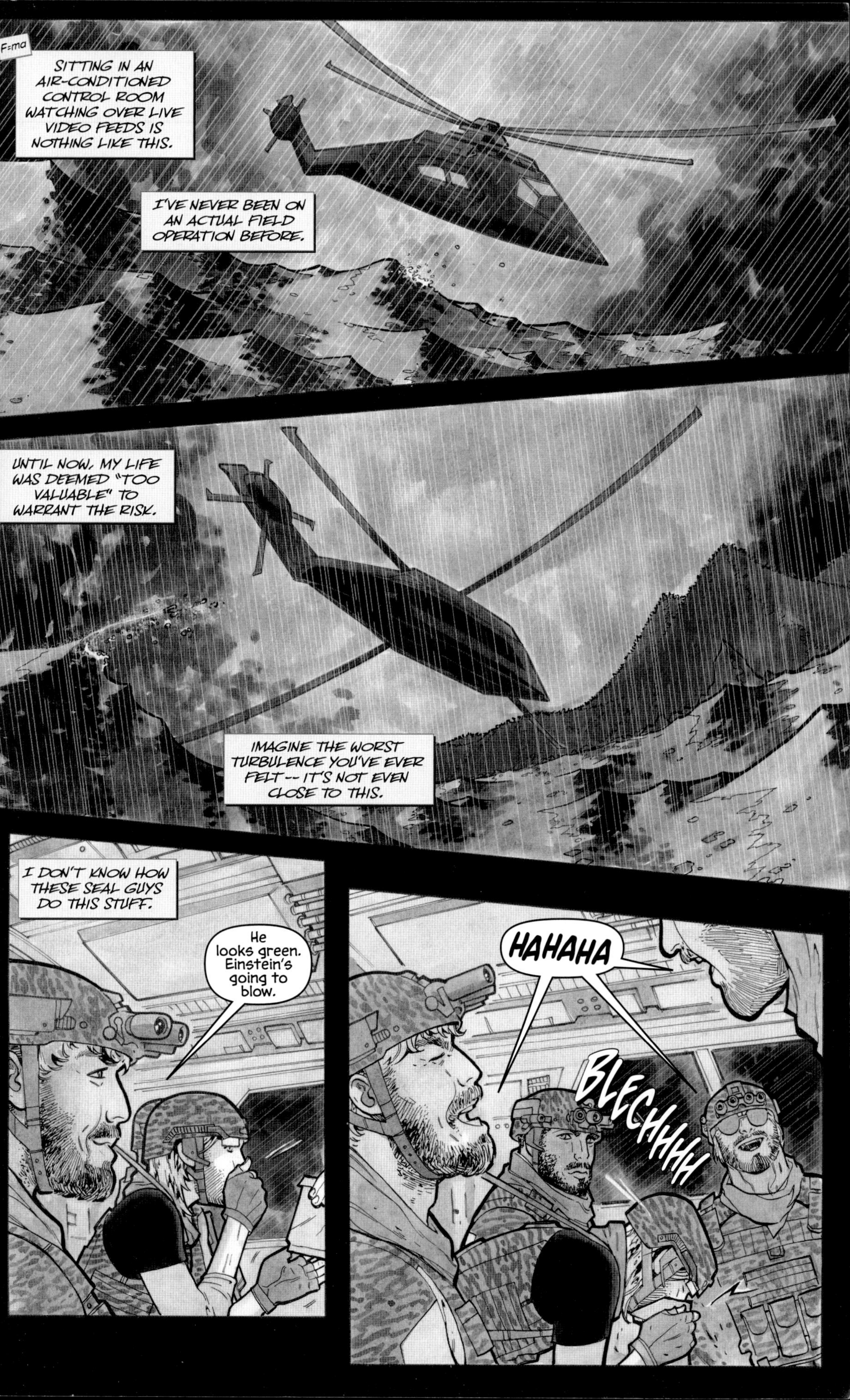
F=ma
SITTING IN AN AIR-CONDITIONED CONTROL ROOM WATCHING OVER LIVE VIDEO FEEDS IS NOTHING LIKE THIS.
I'VE NEVER BEEN ON AN ACTUAL FIELD OPERATION BEFORE.
UNTIL NOW, MY LIFE WAS DEEMED "TOO VALUABLE" TO WARRANT THE RISK.
IMAGINE THE WORST TURBULENCE YOU'VE EVER FELT -- IT'S NOT EVEN CLOSE TO THIS.
I DON'T KNOW HOW THESE SEAL GUYS DO THIS STUFF.
He looks green. Einstein's going to blow.
HAHAHA
BLECHHHH

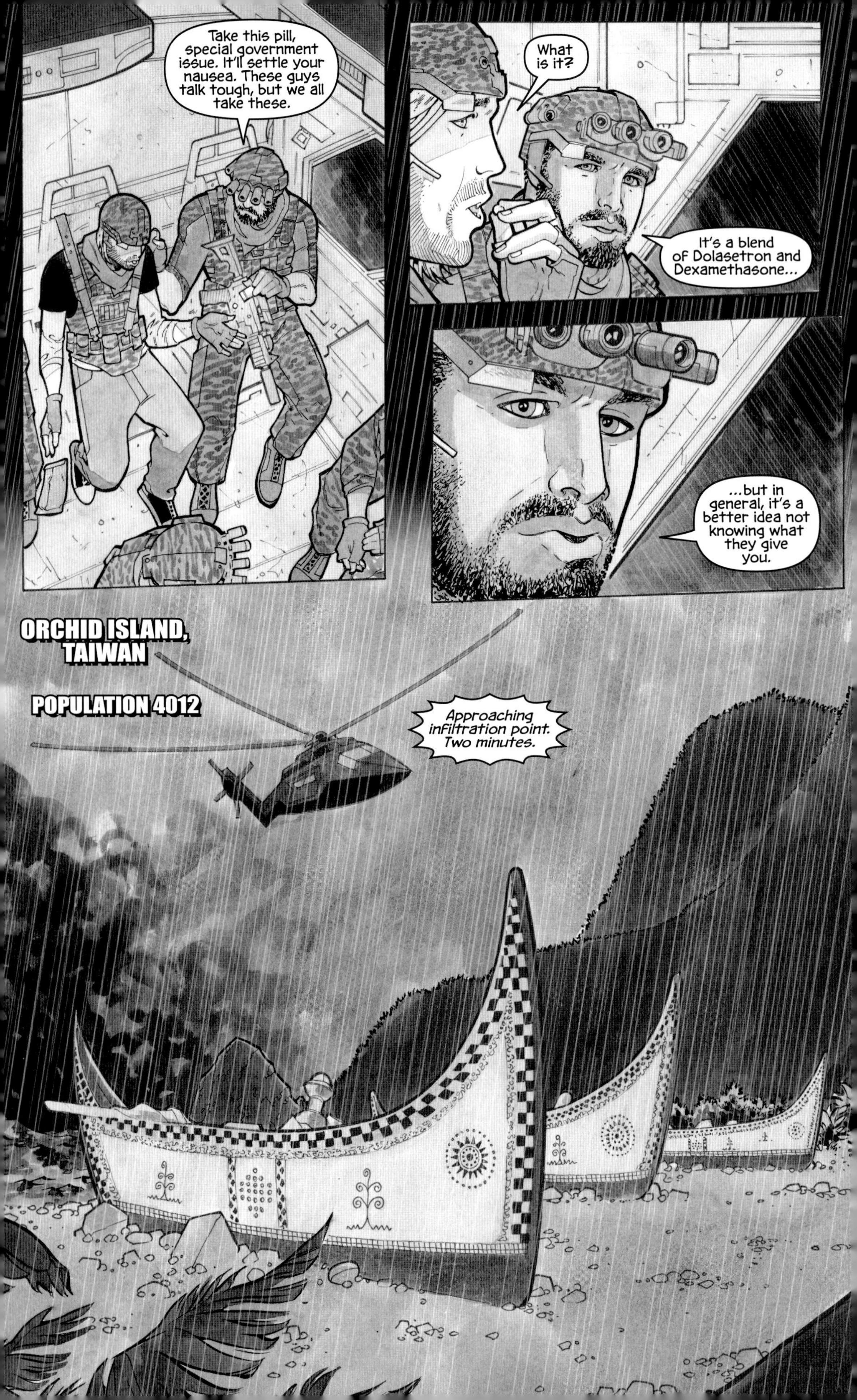
Take this pill, special government issue. It'll settle your nausea. These guys talk tough, but we all take these.
What is it?
It's a blend of Dolasetron and Dexamethasone...
...but in general, it's a better idea not knowing what they give you.
ORCHID ISLAND, TAIWAN
POPULATION 4012
Approaching infiltration point. Two minutes.

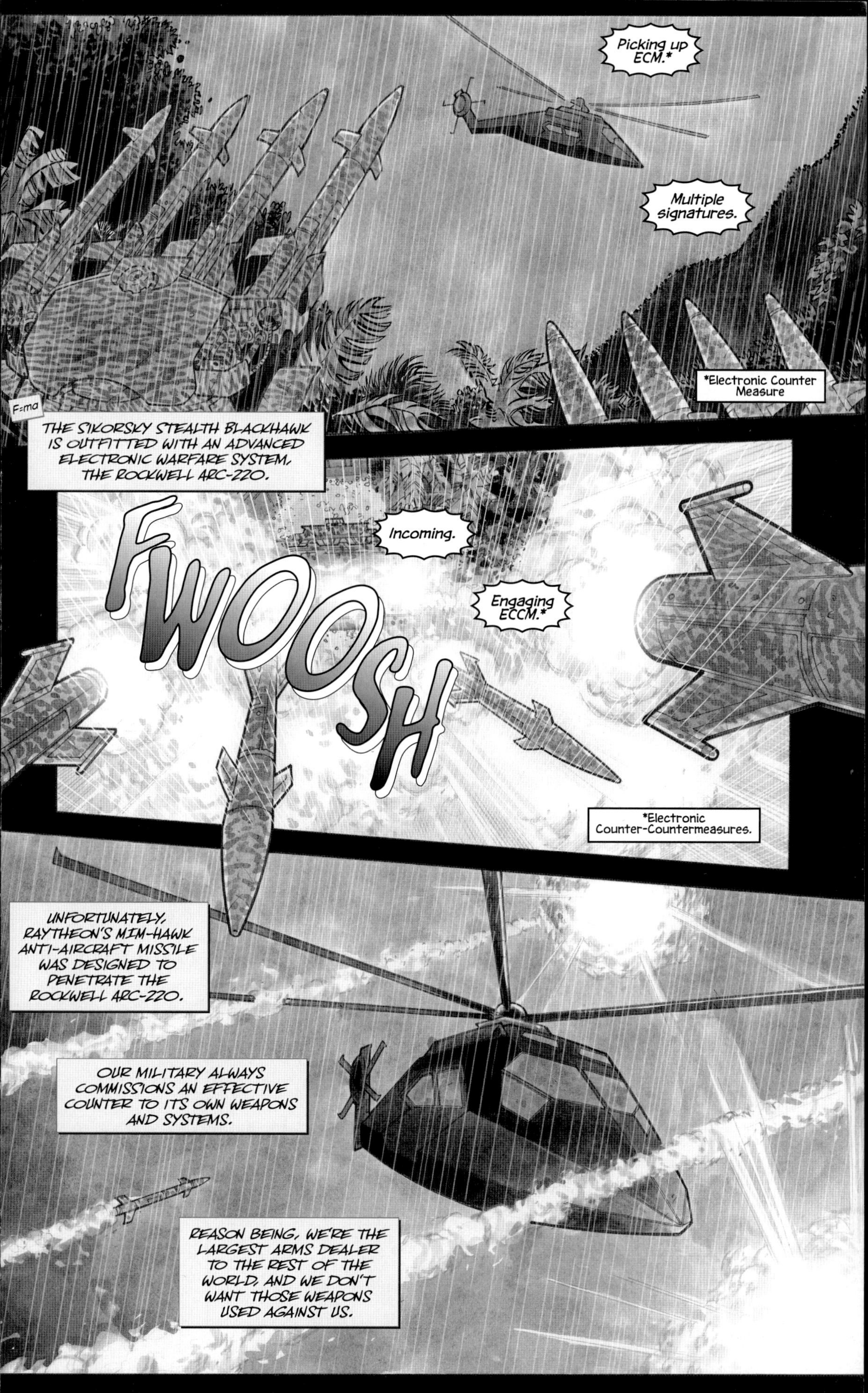
Picking up ECM.*
Multiple signatures.
*Electronic Counter Measure
F=ma
THE SIKORSKY STEALTH BLACKHAWK IS OUTFITTED WITH AN ADVANCED ELECTRONIC WARFARE SYSTEM, THE ROCKWELL ARC-220.
FWOOSH
Incoming.
Engaging ECCM.*
*Electronic Counter-Countermeasures.
UNFORTUNATELY, RAYTHEON'S MIM-HAWK ANTI-AIRCRAFT MISSILE WAS DESIGNED TO PENETRATE THE ROCKWELL ARC-220.
OUR MILITARY ALWAYS COMMISSIONS AN EFFECTIVE COUNTER TO ITS OWN WEAPONS AND SYSTEMS.
REASON BEING, WE'RE THE LARGEST ARMS DEALER TO THE REST OF THE WORLD, AND WE DON'T WANT THOSE WEAPONS USED AGAINST US.

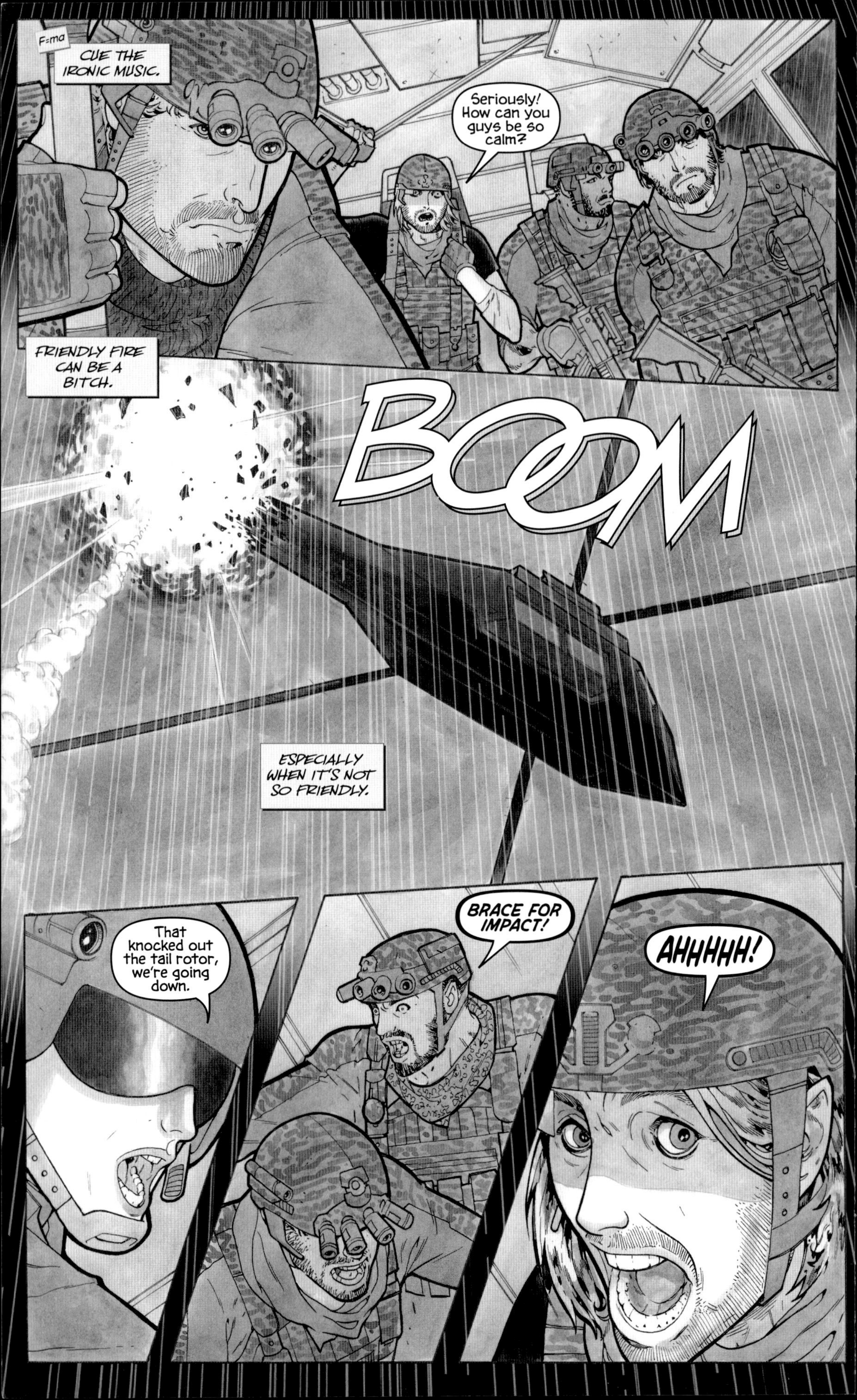
F=ma
CUE THE IRONIC MUSIC.
Seriously! How can you guys be so calm?
FRIENDLY FIRE CAN BE A BITCH.
BOOM
ESPECIALLY WHEN IT'S NOT SO FRIENDLY.
That knocked out the tail rotor, we're going down.
BRACE FOR IMPACT!
AHHHHH!

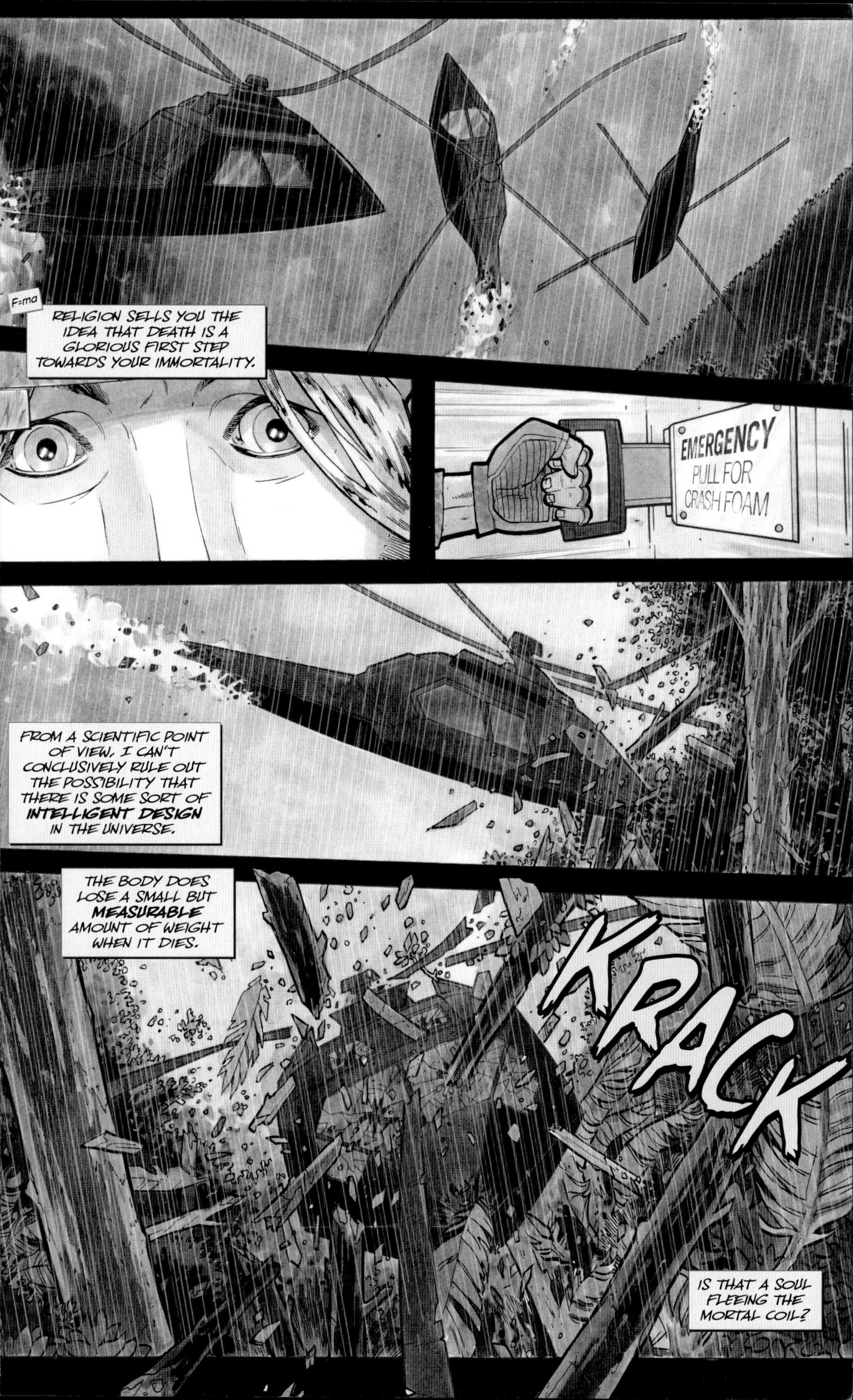
F=ma
RELIGION SELLS YOU THE IDEA THAT DEATH IS A GLORIOUS FIRST STEP TOWARDS YOUR IMMORTALITY.
EMERGENCY PULL FOR CRASH FOAM
FROM A SCIENTIFIC POINT OF VIEW, I CAN'T CONCLUSIVELY RULE OUT THE POSSIBILITY THAT THERE IS SOME SORT OF INTELLIGENT DESIGN IN THE UNIVERSE.
THE BODY DOES LOSE A SMALL BUT MEASURABLE AMOUNT OF WEIGHT WHEN IT DIES.
KRACK
IS THAT A SOUL FLEEING THE MORTAL COIL?

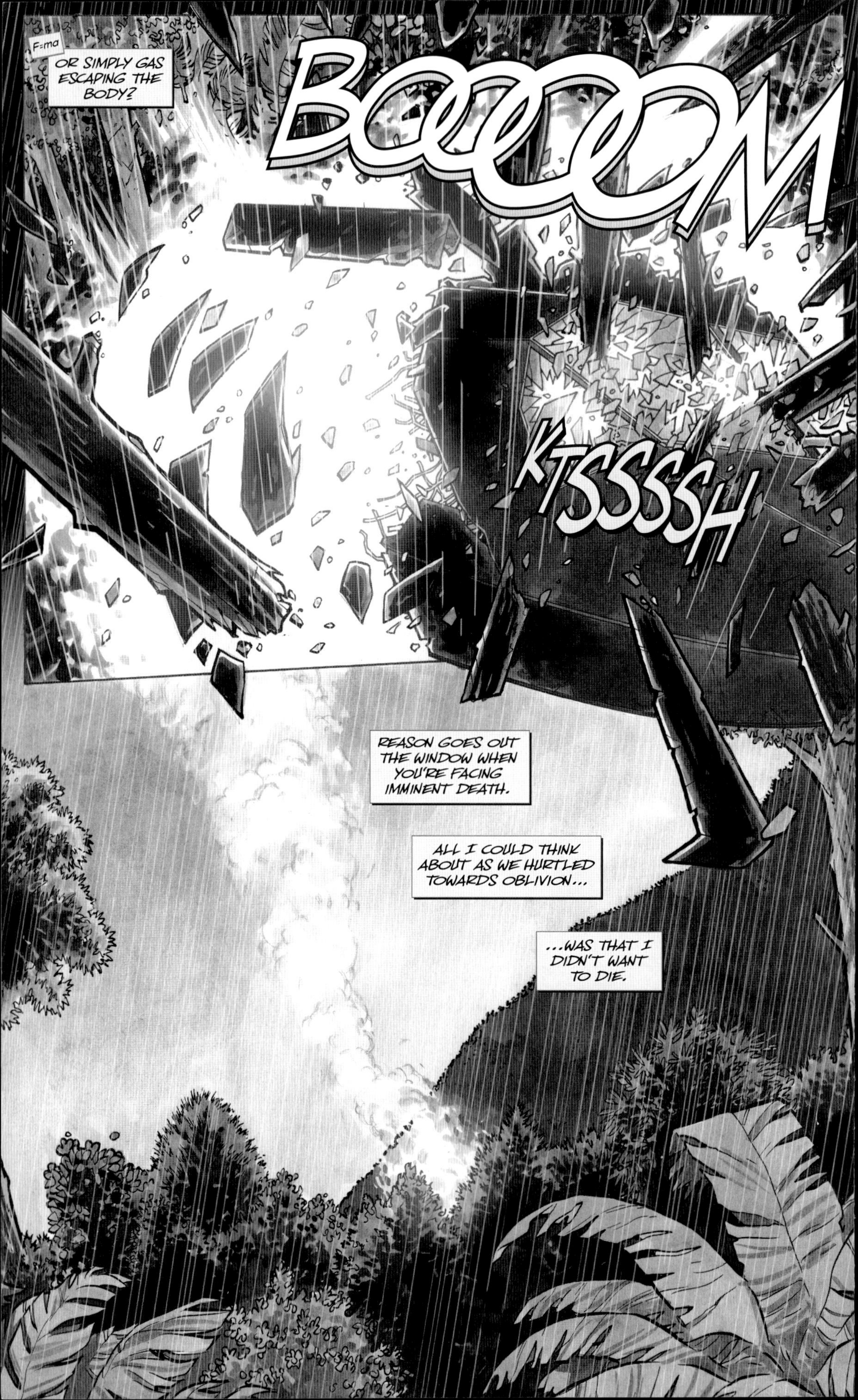
F=ma
OR SIMPLY GAS ESCAPING THE BODY?
BOOOOM
KTSSSSH
REASON GOES OUT THE WINDOW WHEN YOU'RE FACING IMMINENT DEATH.
ALL I COULD THINK ABOUT AS WE HURTLED TOWARDS OBLIVION...
...WAS THAT I DIDN'T WANT TO DIE.

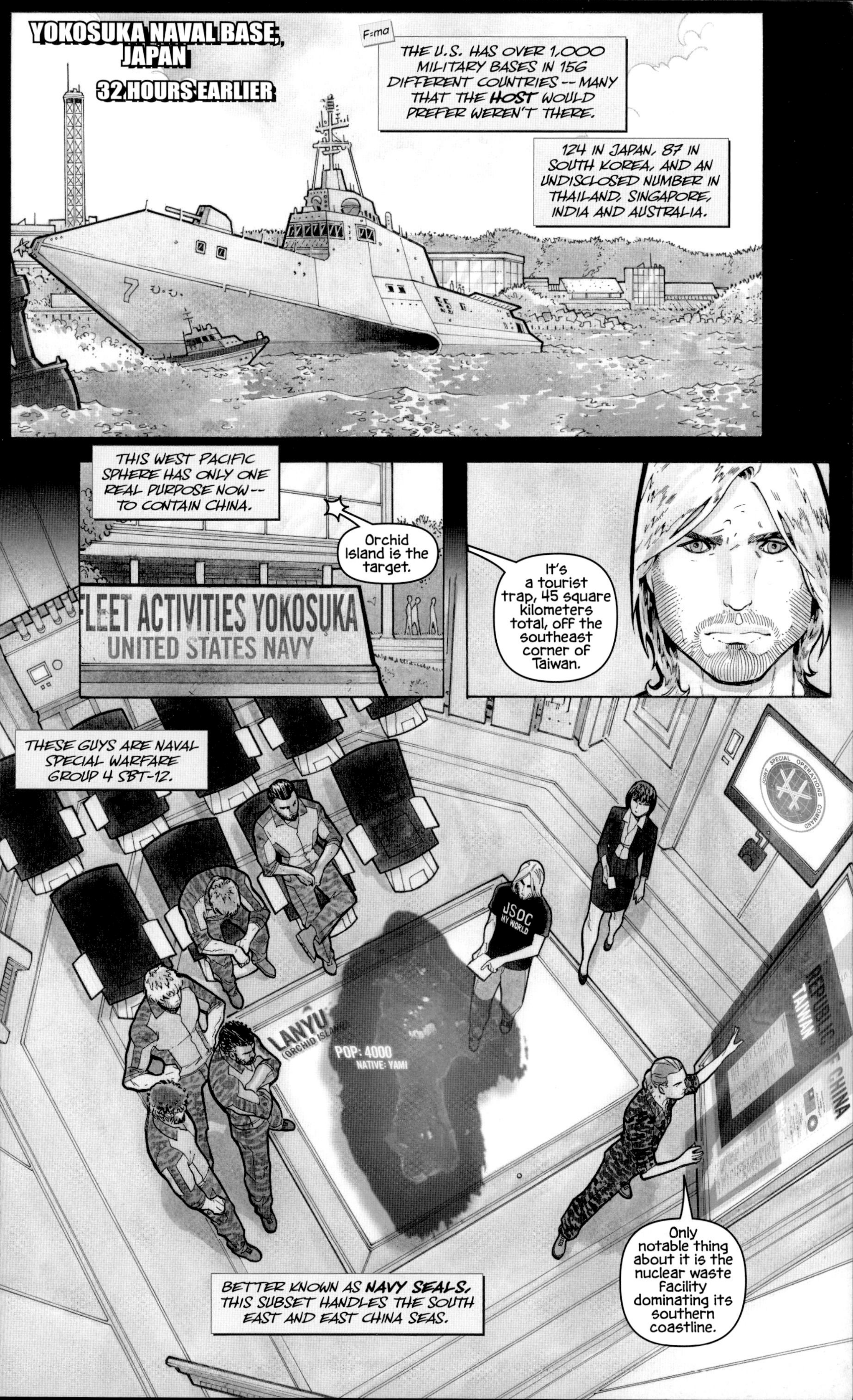
YOKOSUKA NAVAL BASE, JAPAN
32 HOURS EARLIER
F=ma
THE U.S. HAS OVER 1,000 MILITARY BASES IN 156 DIFFERENT COUNTRIES -- MANY THAT THE HOST WOULD PREFER WEREN'T THERE.
124 IN JAPAN, 87 IN SOUTH KOREA, AND AN UNDISCLOSED NUMBER IN THAILAND, SINGAPORE, INDIA AND AUSTRALIA.
7
THIS WEST PACIFIC SPHERE HAS ONLY ONE REAL PURPOSE NOW -- TO CONTAIN CHINA.
Orchid Island is the target.
FLEET ACTIVITIES YOKOSUKA
UNITED STATES NAVY
It's a tourist trap, 45 square kilometers total, off the southeast corner of Taiwan.
THESE GUYS ARE NAVAL SPECIAL WARFARE GROUP 4 SBT-12.
JOINT SPECIAL OPERATIONS COMMAND
JSOC MY WORLD
LANYU (ORCHID ISLAND)
POP: 4000
NATIVE: YAMI
REPUBLIC OF CHINA TAIWAN
BETTER KNOWN AS NAVY SEALS, THIS SUBSET HANDLES THE SOUTH EAST AND EAST CHINA SEAS.
Only notable thing about it is the nuclear waste facility dominating its southern coastline.

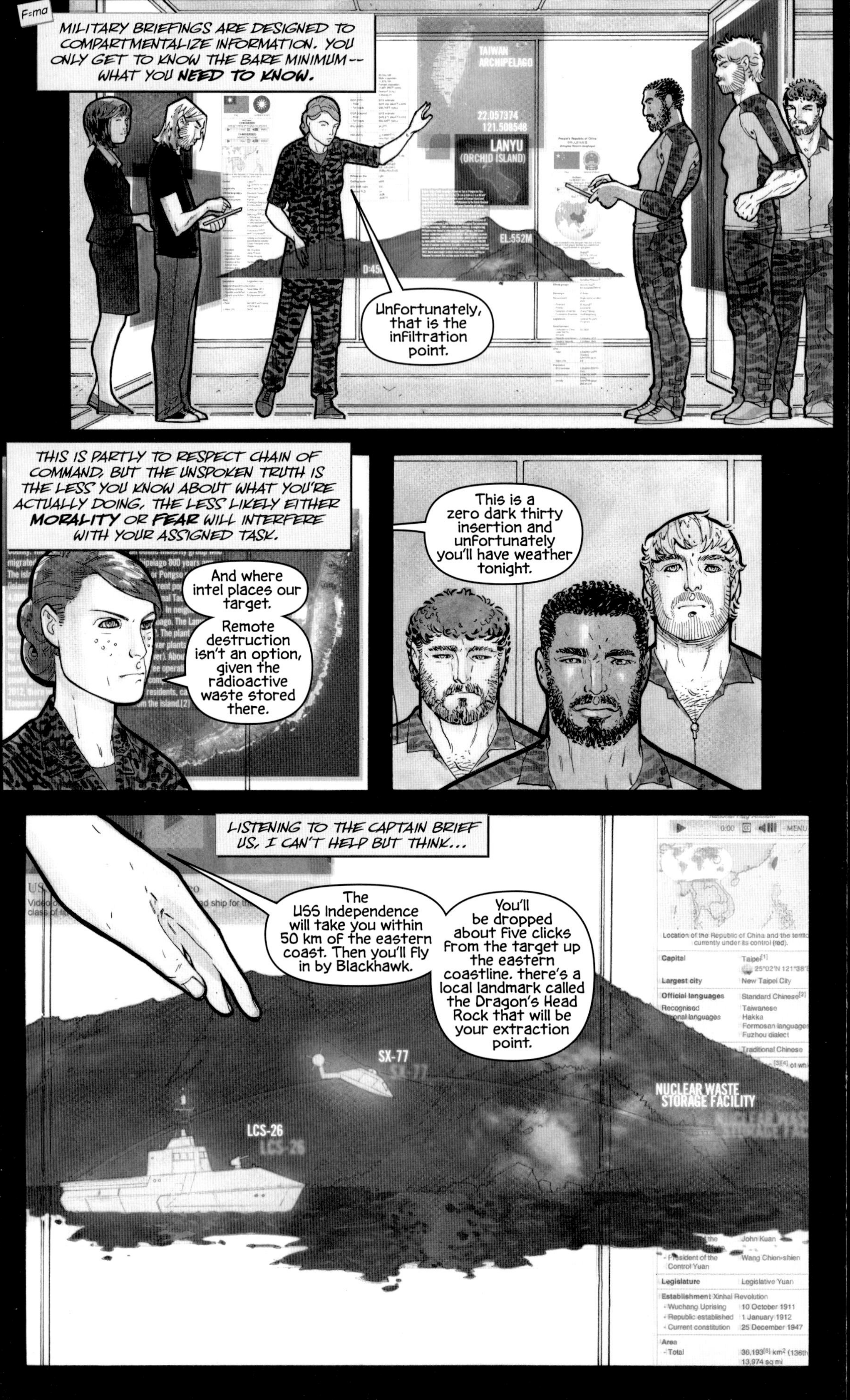
F=ma
MILITARY BRIEFINGS ARE DESIGNED TO COMPARTMENTALIZE INFORMATION. YOU ONLY GET TO KNOW THE BARE MINIMUM-- WHAT YOU **NEED TO KNOW.**
TAIWAN ARCHIPELAGO
22.057374
121.508548
LANYU
(ORCHID ISLAND)
EL:552M
Unfortunately, that is the infiltration point.
THIS IS PARTLY TO RESPECT CHAIN OF COMMAND, BUT THE UNSPOKEN TRUTH IS THE LESS YOU KNOW ABOUT WHAT YOU'RE ACTUALLY DOING, THE LESS LIKELY EITHER **MORALITY** OR **FEAR** WILL INTERFERE WITH YOUR ASSIGNED TASK.
And where intel places our target.
Remote destruction isn't an option, given the radioactive waste stored there.
This is a zero dark thirty insertion and unfortunately you'll have weather tonight.
LISTENING TO THE CAPTAIN BRIEF US, I CAN'T HELP BUT THINK...
The USS Independence will take you within 50 km of the eastern coast. Then you'll fly in by Blackhawk.
You'll be dropped about five clicks from the target up the eastern coastline. there's a local landmark called the Dragon's Head Rock that will be your extraction point.
SX-77
LCS-26
NUCLEAR WASTE STORAGE FACILITY
Location of the Republic of China and the territory currently under its control (red).
Capital
Taipei
Largest city
New Taipei City
Official languages
Standard Chinese
Taiwanese
Hakka
Formosan languages
Fuzhou dialect
Traditional Chinese
John Kuan
President of the Control Yuan
Wang Chien-shien
Legislature
Legislative Yuan
Establishment Xinhai Revolution
Wuchang Uprising
10 October 1911
Republic established
1 January 1912
Current constitution
25 December 1947
Area
Total
36,193 km²
13,974 sq mi

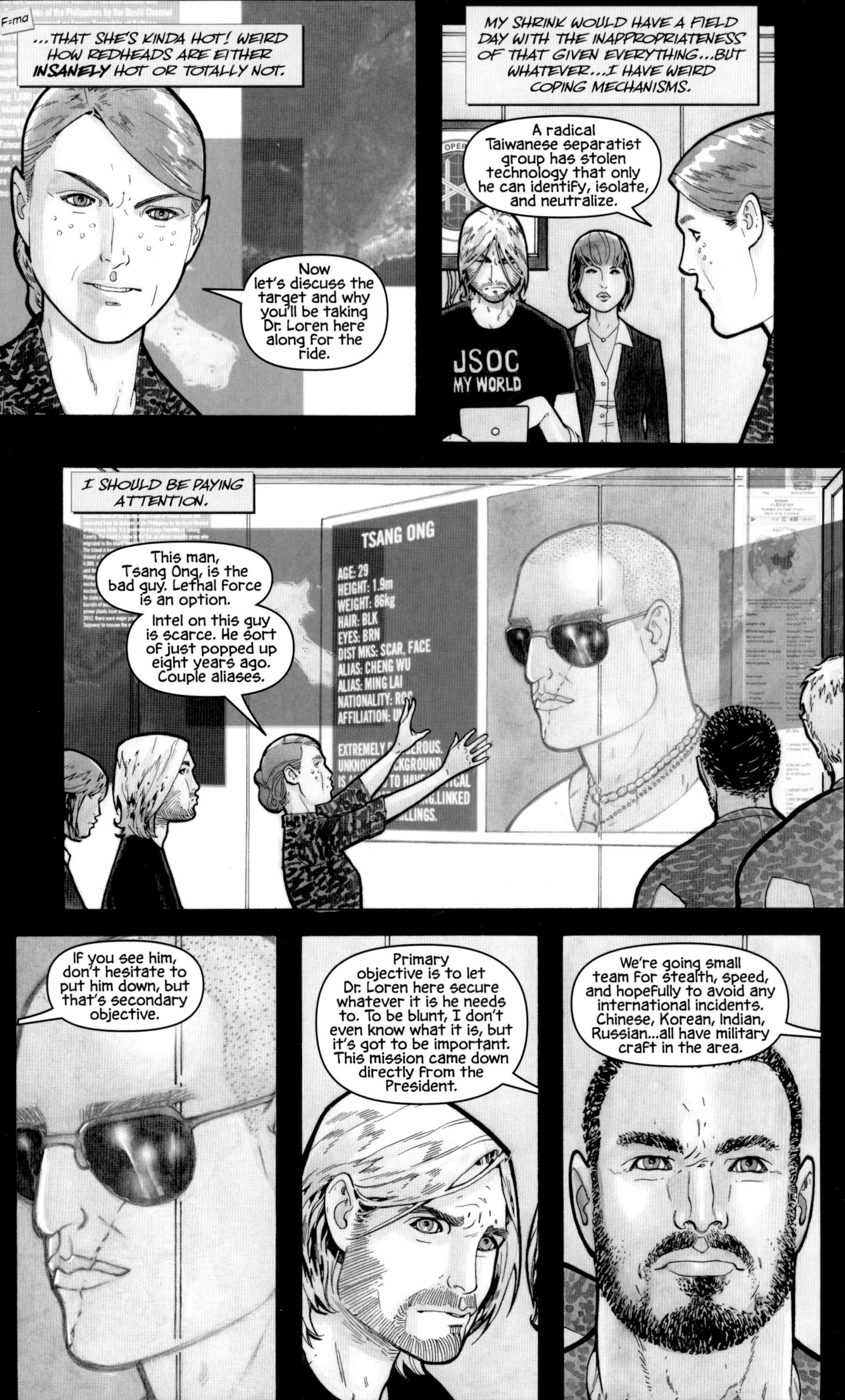
F=ma
...THAT SHE'S KINDA HOT! WEIRD HOW REDHEADS ARE EITHER INSANELY HOT OR TOTALLY NOT.
Now let's discuss the target and why you'll be taking Dr. Loren here along for the ride.
MY SHRINK WOULD HAVE A FIELD DAY WITH THE INAPPROPRIATENESS OF THAT GIVEN EVERYTHING...BUT WHATEVER...I HAVE WEIRD COPING MECHANISMS.
A radical Taiwanese separatist group has stolen technology that only he can identify, isolate, and neutralize.
JSOC
MY WORLD
I SHOULD BE PAYING ATTENTION.
TSANG ONG
AGE: 29
HEIGHT: 1.9m
WEIGHT: 86kg
HAIR: BLK
EYES: BRN
DIST MKS: SCAR, FACE
ALIAS: CHENG WU
ALIAS: MING LAI
This man, Tsang Ong, is the bad guy. Lethal force is an option.
Intel on this guy is scarce. He sort of just popped up eight years ago. Couple aliases.
If you see him, don't hesitate to put him down, but that's secondary objective.
Primary objective is to let Dr. Loren here secure whatever it is he needs to. To be blunt, I don't even know what it is, but it's got to be important. This mission came down directly from the President.
We're going small team for stealth, speed, and hopefully to avoid any international incidents. Chinese, Korean, Indian, Russian...all have military craft in the area.

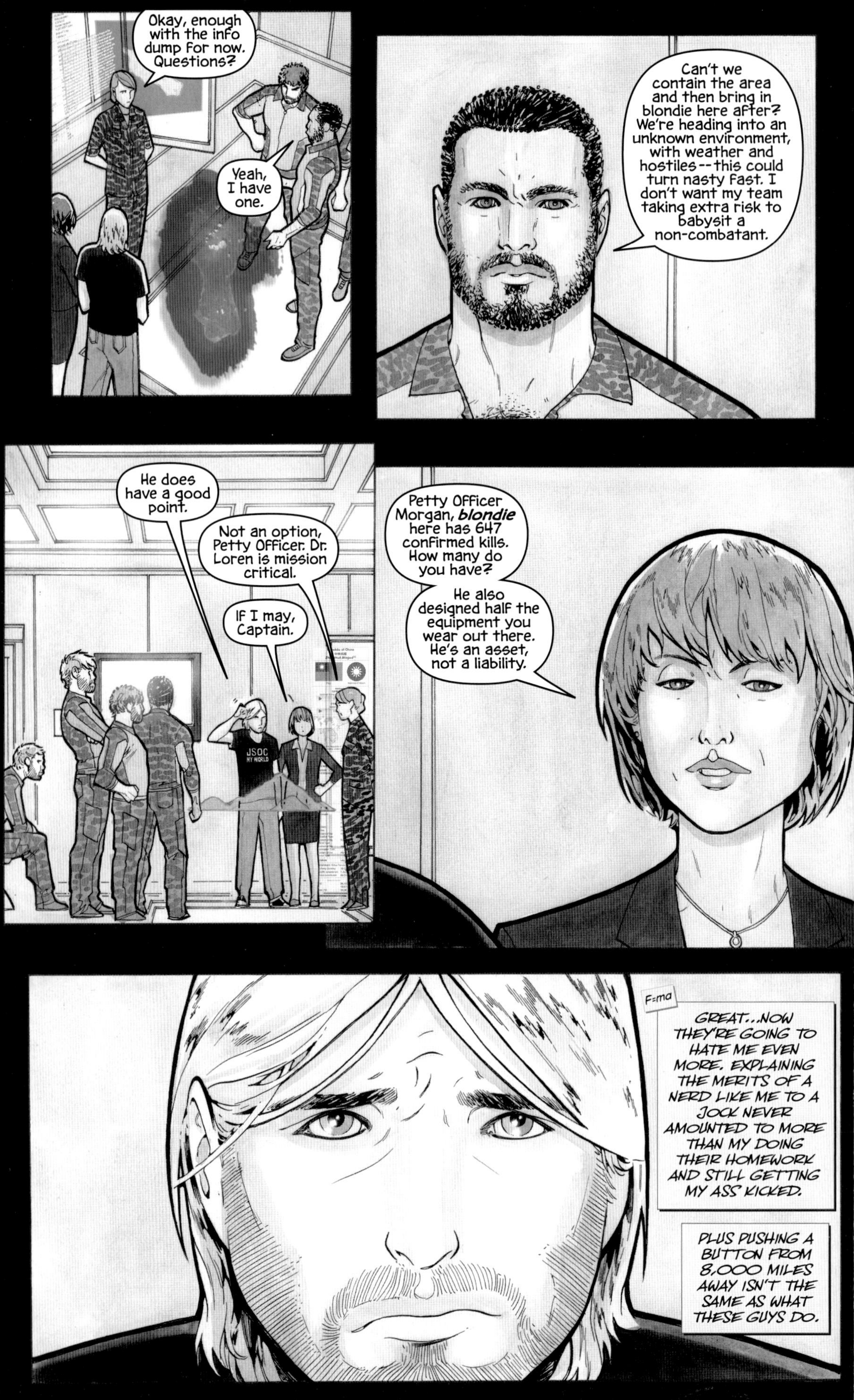

Okay, enough with the info dump for now. Questions?
Yeah, I have one.
Can't we contain the area and then bring in blondie here after? We're heading into an unknown environment, with weather and hostiles -- this could turn nasty fast. I don't want my team taking extra risk to babysit a non-combatant.
He does have a good point.
Not an option, Petty Officer. Dr. Loren is mission critical.
If I may, Captain.
JSOC MY WORLD
Petty Officer Morgan, ***blondie*** here has 647 confirmed kills. How many do you have?
He also designed half the equipment you wear out there. He's an asset, not a liability.
F=ma
GREAT...NOW THEY'RE GOING TO HATE ME EVEN MORE. EXPLAINING THE MERITS OF A NERD LIKE ME TO A JOCK NEVER AMOUNTED TO MORE THAN MY DOING THEIR HOMEWORK AND STILL GETTING MY ASS KICKED.
PLUS PUSHING A BUTTON FROM 8,000 MILES AWAY ISN'T THE SAME AS WHAT THESE GUYS DO.

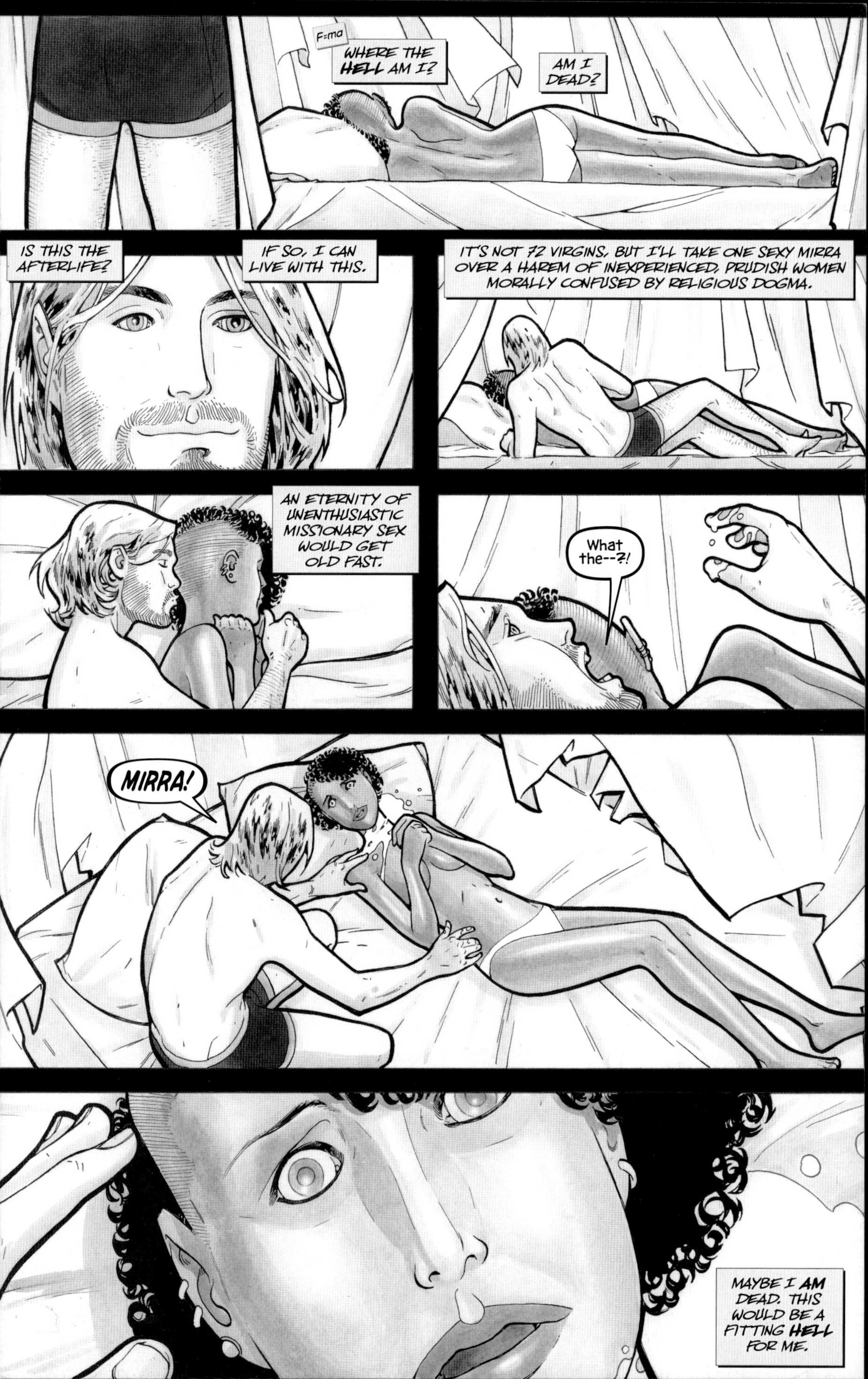
F=ma
WHERE THE HELL AM I?
AM I DEAD?
IS THIS THE AFTERLIFE?
IF SO, I CAN LIVE WITH THIS.
IT'S NOT 72 VIRGINS, BUT I'LL TAKE ONE SEXY MIRRA OVER A HAREM OF INEXPERIENCED, PRUDISH WOMEN MORALLY CONFUSED BY RELIGIOUS DOGMA.
AN ETERNITY OF UNENTHUSIASTIC MISSIONARY SEX WOULD GET OLD FAST.
What the--?!
MIRRA!
MAYBE I AM DEAD. THIS WOULD BE A FITTING HELL FOR ME.

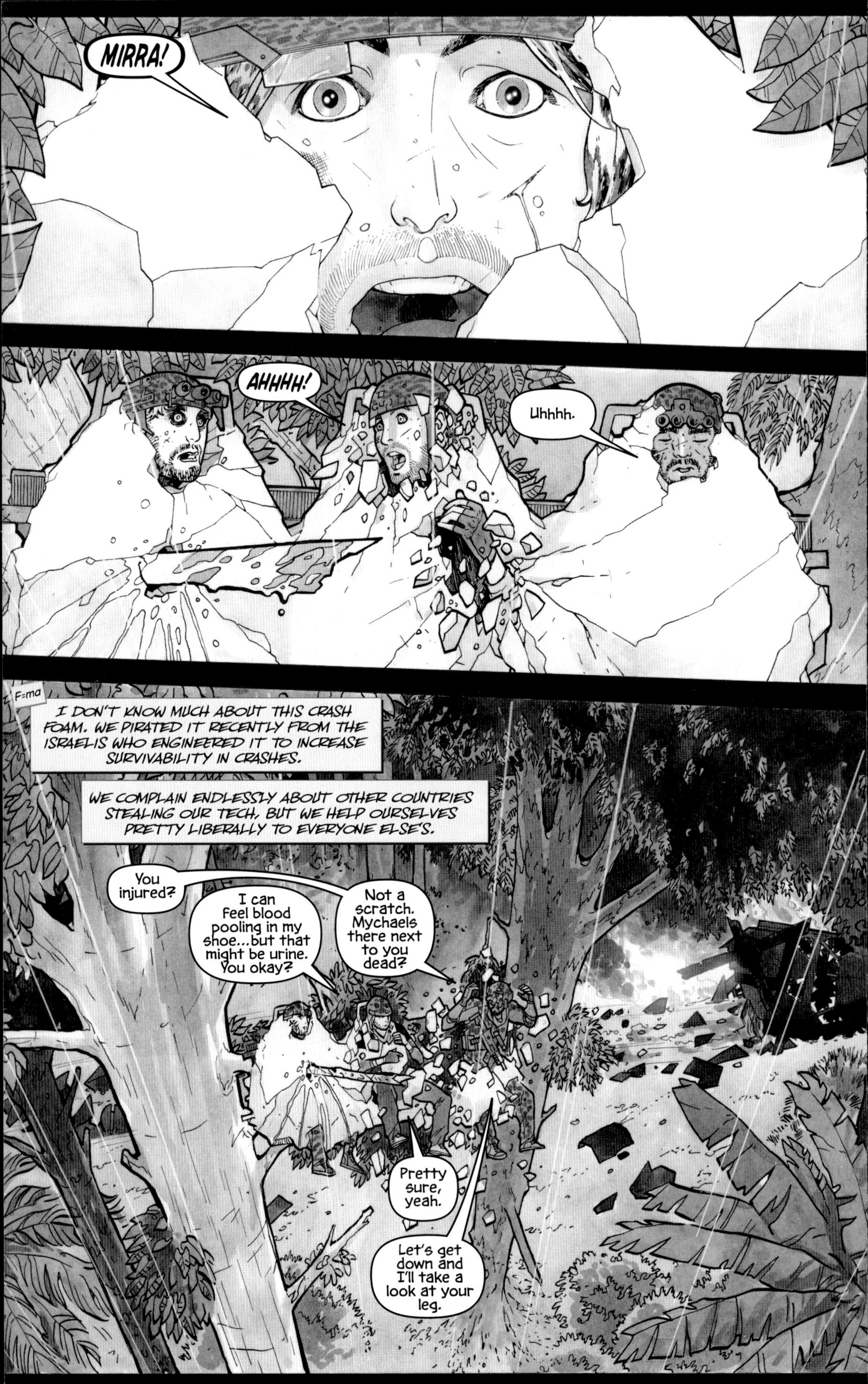
MIRRA!
AHHHH!
Uhhhh.
F=ma
I DON'T KNOW MUCH ABOUT THIS CRASH FOAM. WE PIRATED IT RECENTLY FROM THE ISRAELIS WHO ENGINEERED IT TO INCREASE SURVIVABILITY IN CRASHES.
WE COMPLAIN ENDLESSLY ABOUT OTHER COUNTRIES STEALING OUR TECH, BUT WE HELP OURSELVES PRETTY LIBERALLY TO EVERYONE ELSE'S.
You injured?
I can feel blood pooling in my shoe...but that might be urine. You okay?
Not a scratch. Mychaels there next to you dead?
Pretty sure, yeah.
Let's get down and I'll take a look at your leg.

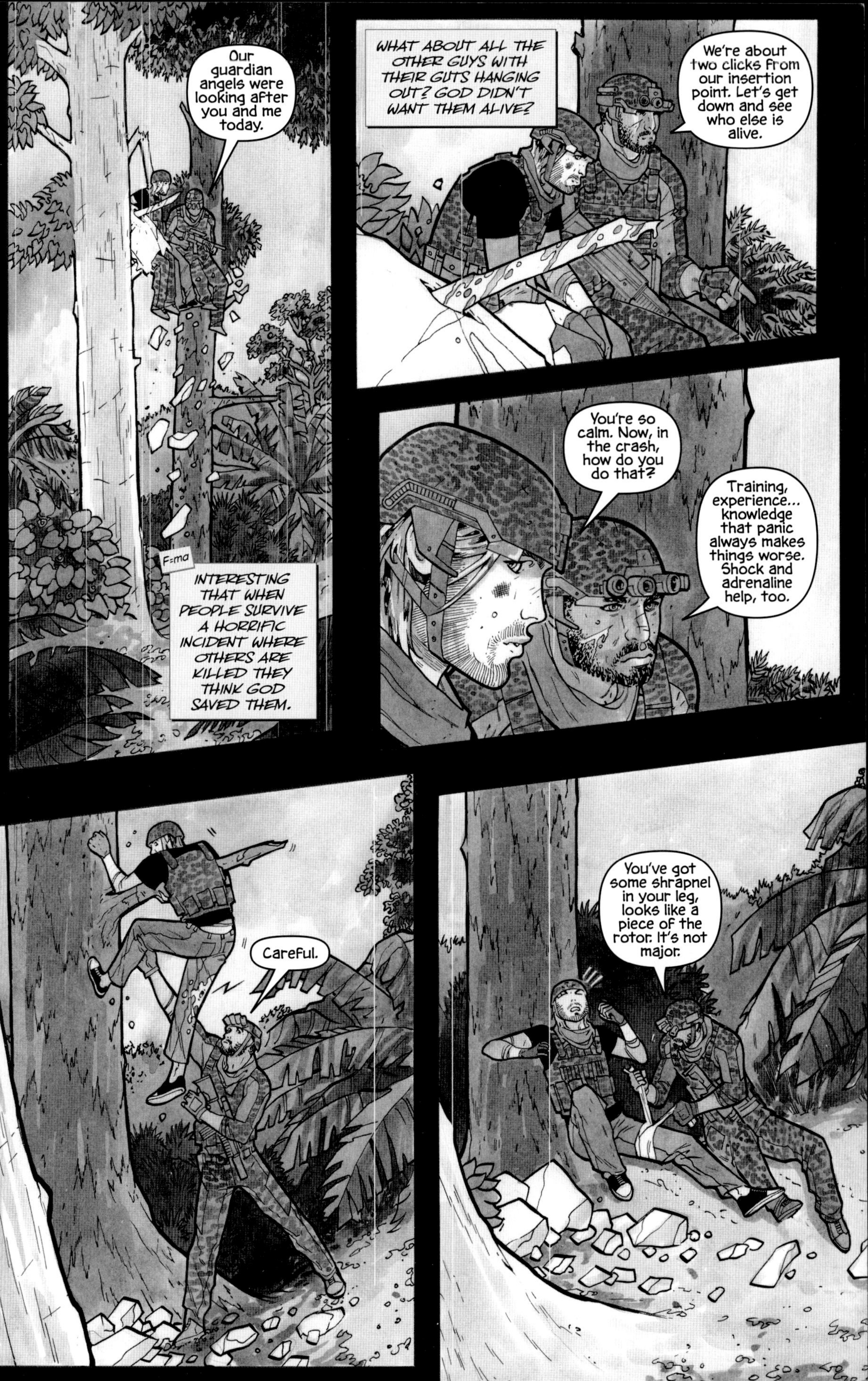
Our guardian angels were looking after you and me today.
F=ma
INTERESTING THAT WHEN PEOPLE SURVIVE A HORRIFIC INCIDENT WHERE OTHERS ARE KILLED THEY THINK GOD SAVED THEM.
WHAT ABOUT ALL THE OTHER GUYS WITH THEIR GUTS HANGING OUT? GOD DIDN'T WANT THEM ALIVE?
We're about two clicks from our insertion point. Let's get down and see who else is alive.
You're so calm. Now, in the crash, how do you do that?
Training, experience... knowledge that panic always makes things worse. Shock and adrenaline help, too.
Careful.
You've got some shrapnel in your leg, looks like a piece of the rotor. It's not major.

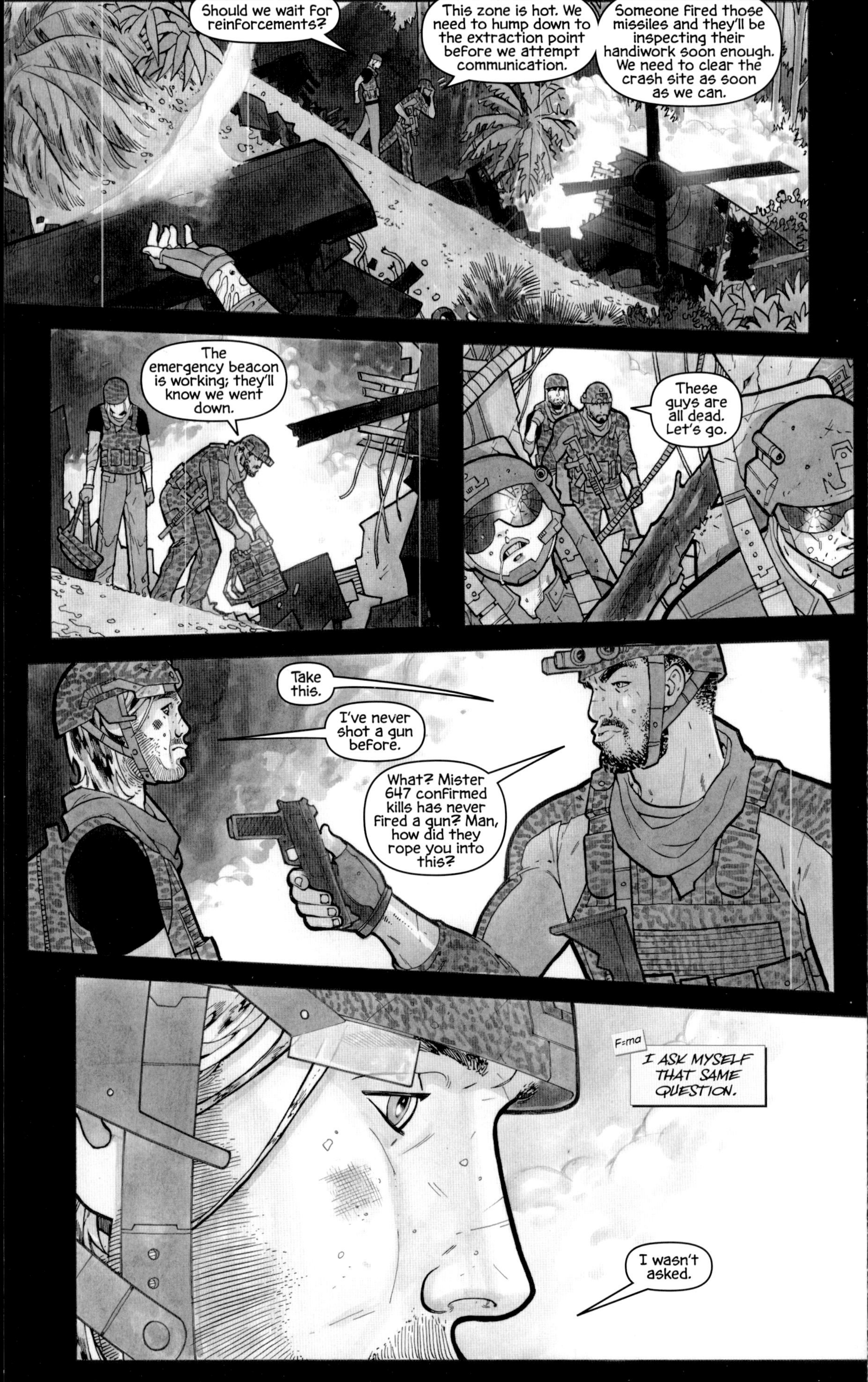
Should we wait for reinforcements?
This zone is hot. We need to hump down to the extraction point before we attempt communication.
Someone fired those missiles and they'll be inspecting their handiwork soon enough. We need to clear the crash site as soon as we can.
The emergency beacon is working; they'll know we went down.
These guys are all dead. Let's go.
Take this.
I've never shot a gun before.
What? Mister 647 confirmed kills has never fired a gun? Man, how did they rope you into this?
F=ma
I ASK MYSELF THAT SAME QUESTION.
I wasn't asked.

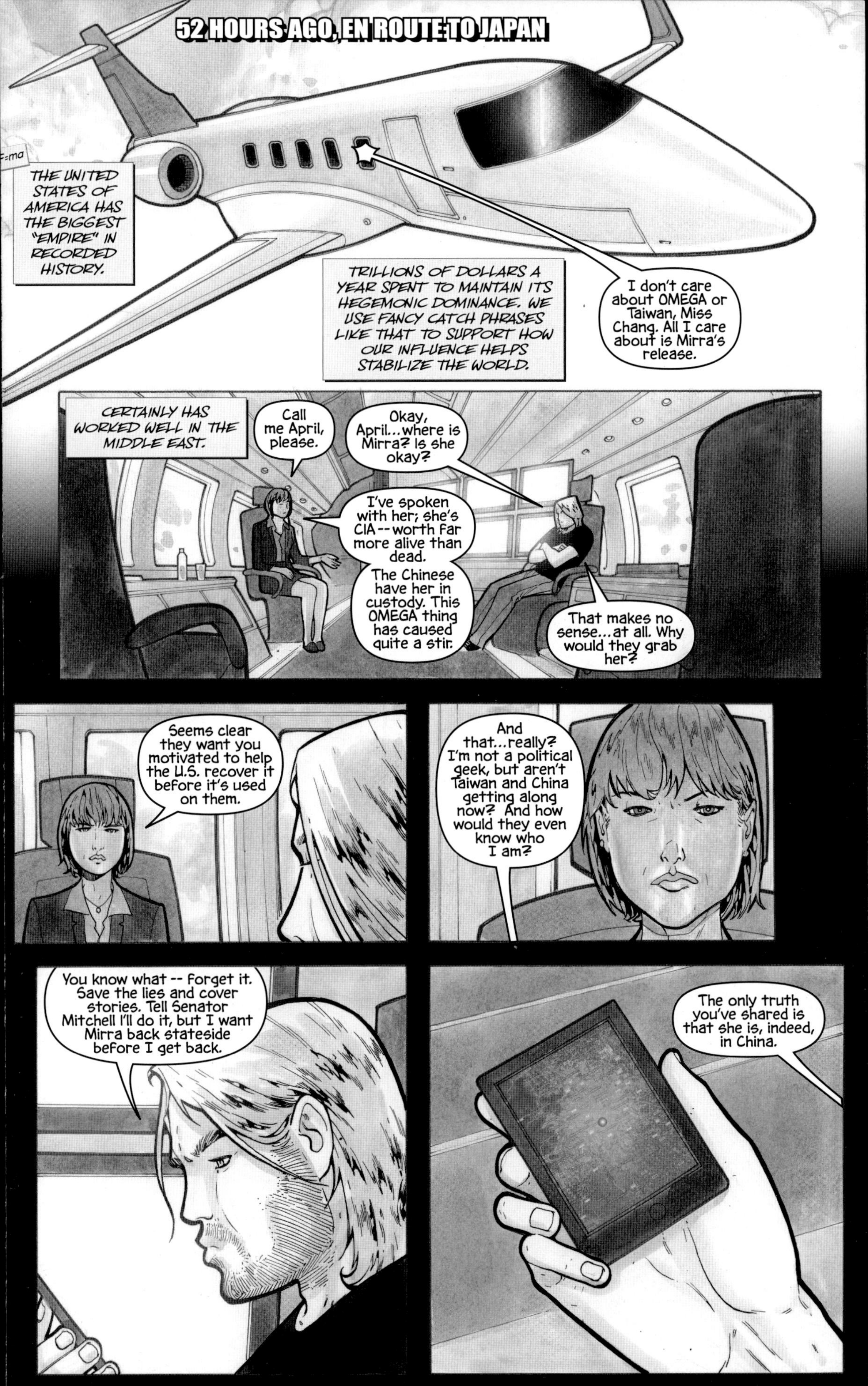
52 HOURS AGO, EN ROUTE TO JAPAN
THE UNITED STATES OF AMERICA HAS THE BIGGEST "EMPIRE" IN RECORDED HISTORY.
TRILLIONS OF DOLLARS A YEAR SPENT TO MAINTAIN ITS HEGEMONIC DOMINANCE. WE USE FANCY CATCH PHRASES LIKE THAT TO SUPPORT HOW OUR INFLUENCE HELPS STABILIZE THE WORLD.
I don't care about OMEGA or Taiwan, Miss Chang. All I care about is Mirra's release.
CERTAINLY HAS WORKED WELL IN THE MIDDLE EAST.
Call me April, please.
Okay, April...where is Mirra? Is she okay?
I've spoken with her; she's CIA--worth far more alive than dead.
The Chinese have her in custody. This OMEGA thing has caused quite a stir.
That makes no sense...at all. Why would they grab her?
Seems clear they want you motivated to help the U.S. recover it before it's used on them.
And that...really? I'm not a political geek, but aren't Taiwan and China getting along now? And how would they even know who I am?
You know what -- forget it. Save the lies and cover stories. Tell Senator Mitchell I'll do it, but I want Mirra back stateside before I get back.
The only truth you've shared is that she is, indeed, in China.

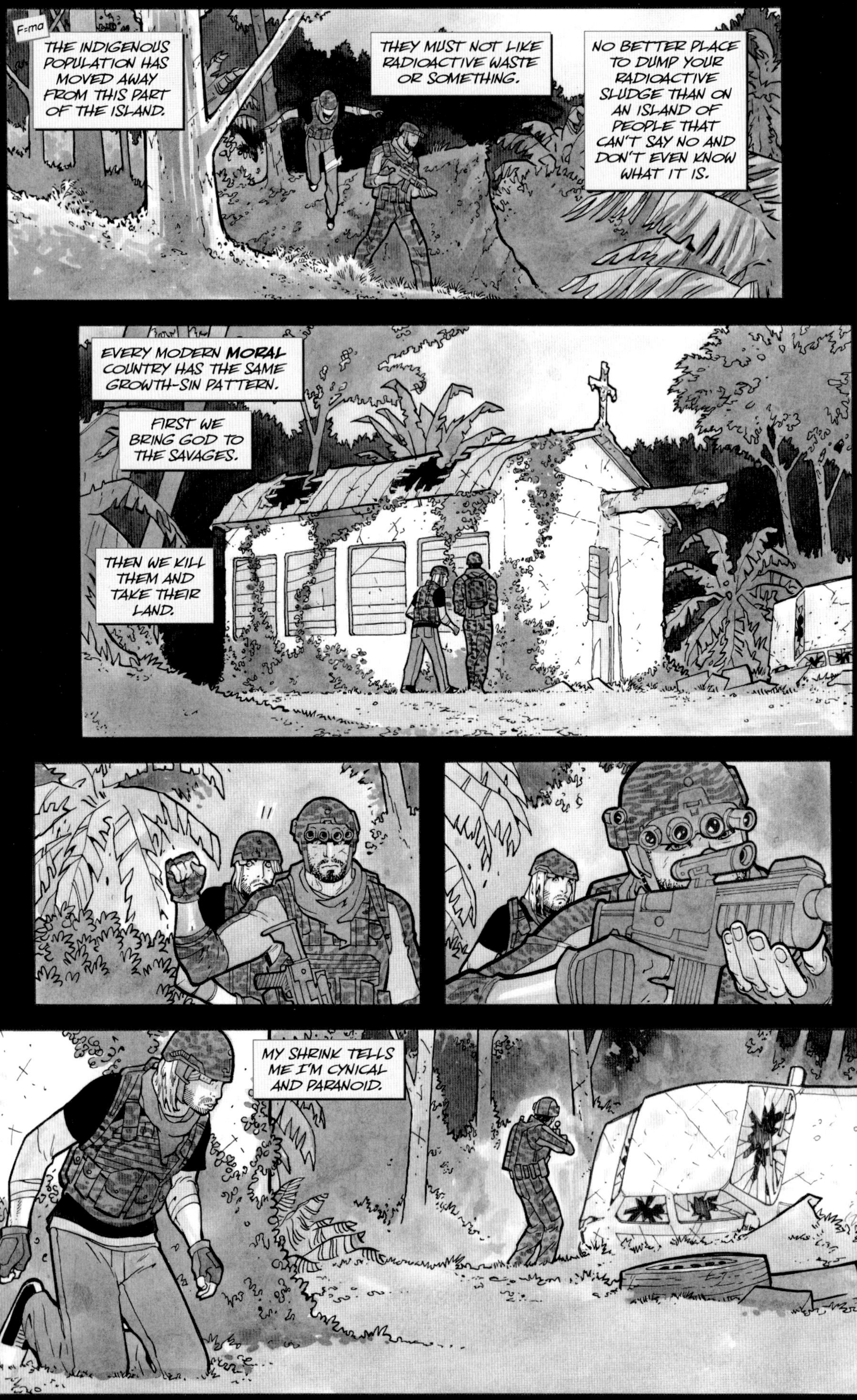
F=ma
THE INDIGENOUS POPULATION HAS MOVED AWAY FROM THIS PART OF THE ISLAND.
THEY MUST NOT LIKE RADIOACTIVE WASTE OR SOMETHING.
NO BETTER PLACE TO DUMP YOUR RADIOACTIVE SLUDGE THAN ON AN ISLAND OF PEOPLE THAT CAN'T SAY NO AND DON'T EVEN KNOW WHAT IT IS.
EVERY MODERN MORAL COUNTRY HAS THE SAME GROWTH-SIN PATTERN.
FIRST WE BRING GOD TO THE SAVAGES.
THEN WE KILL THEM AND TAKE THEIR LAND.
MY SHRINK TELLS ME I'M CYNICAL AND PARANOID.

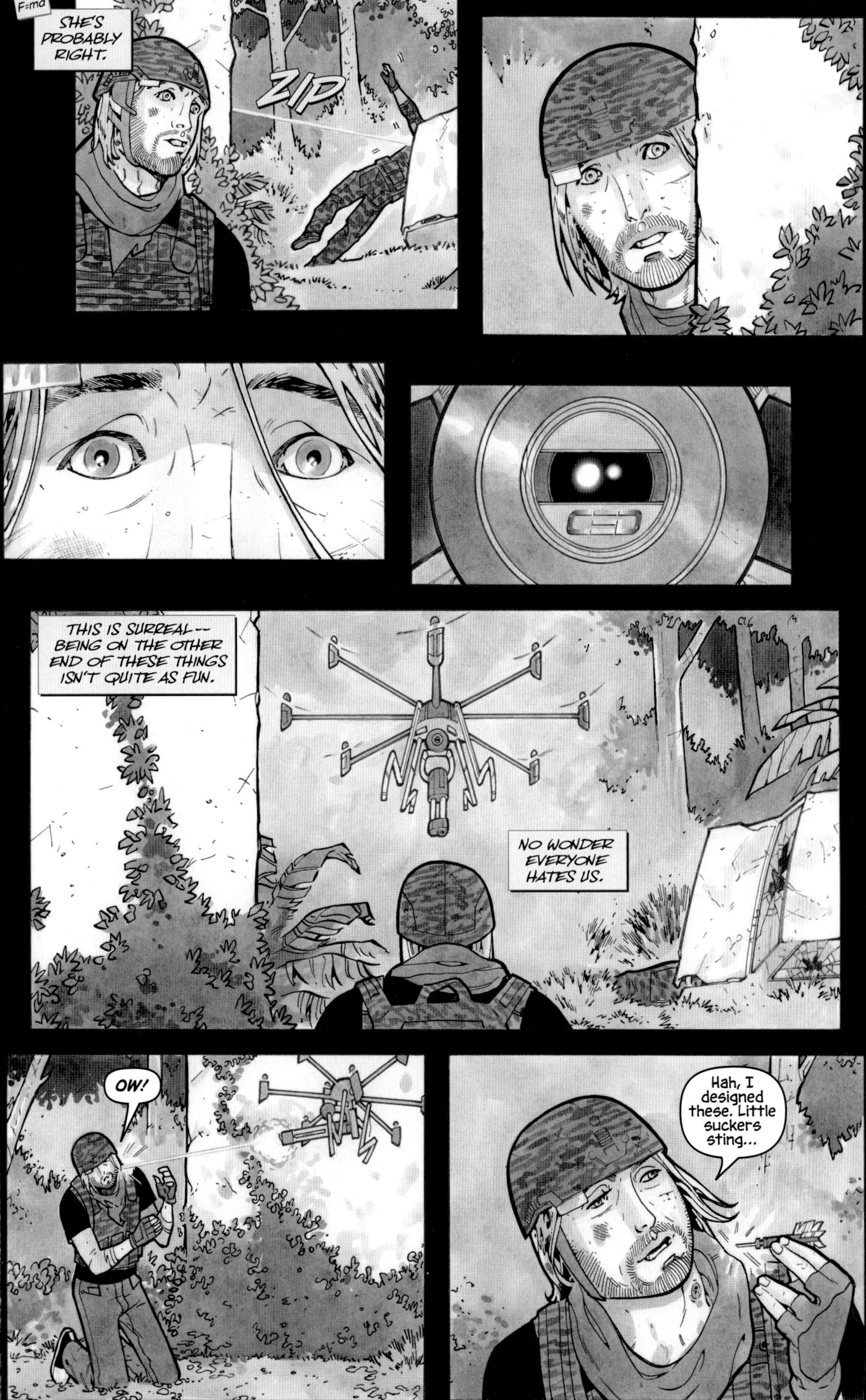
F=ma
SHE'S PROBABLY RIGHT.
ZIP
THIS IS SURREAL-- BEING ON THE OTHER END OF THESE THINGS ISN'T QUITE AS FUN.
NO WONDER EVERYONE HATES US.
OW!
Hah, I designed these. Little suckers sting...

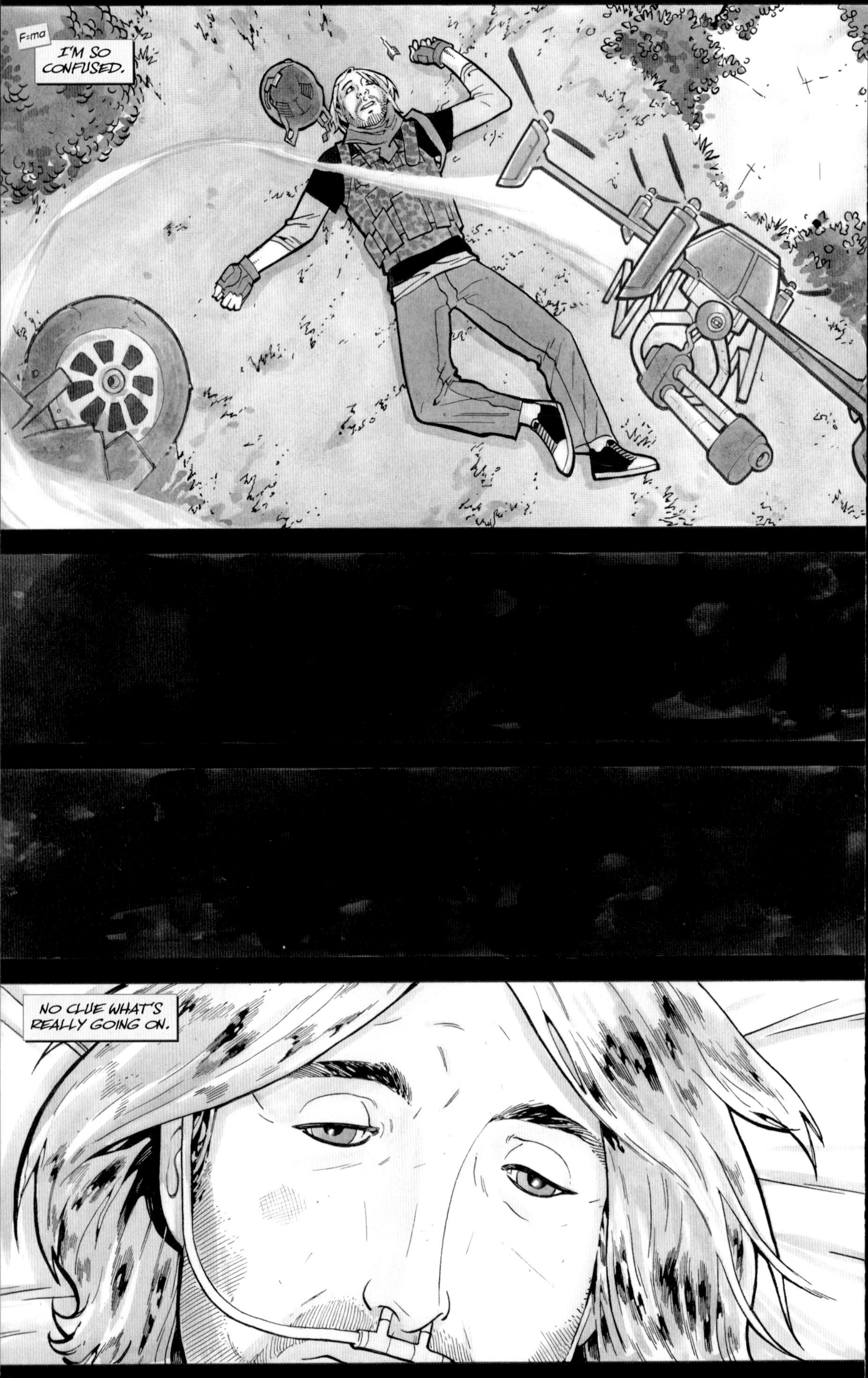
F=ma
I'M SO CONFUSED.
NO CLUE WHAT'S REALLY GOING ON.

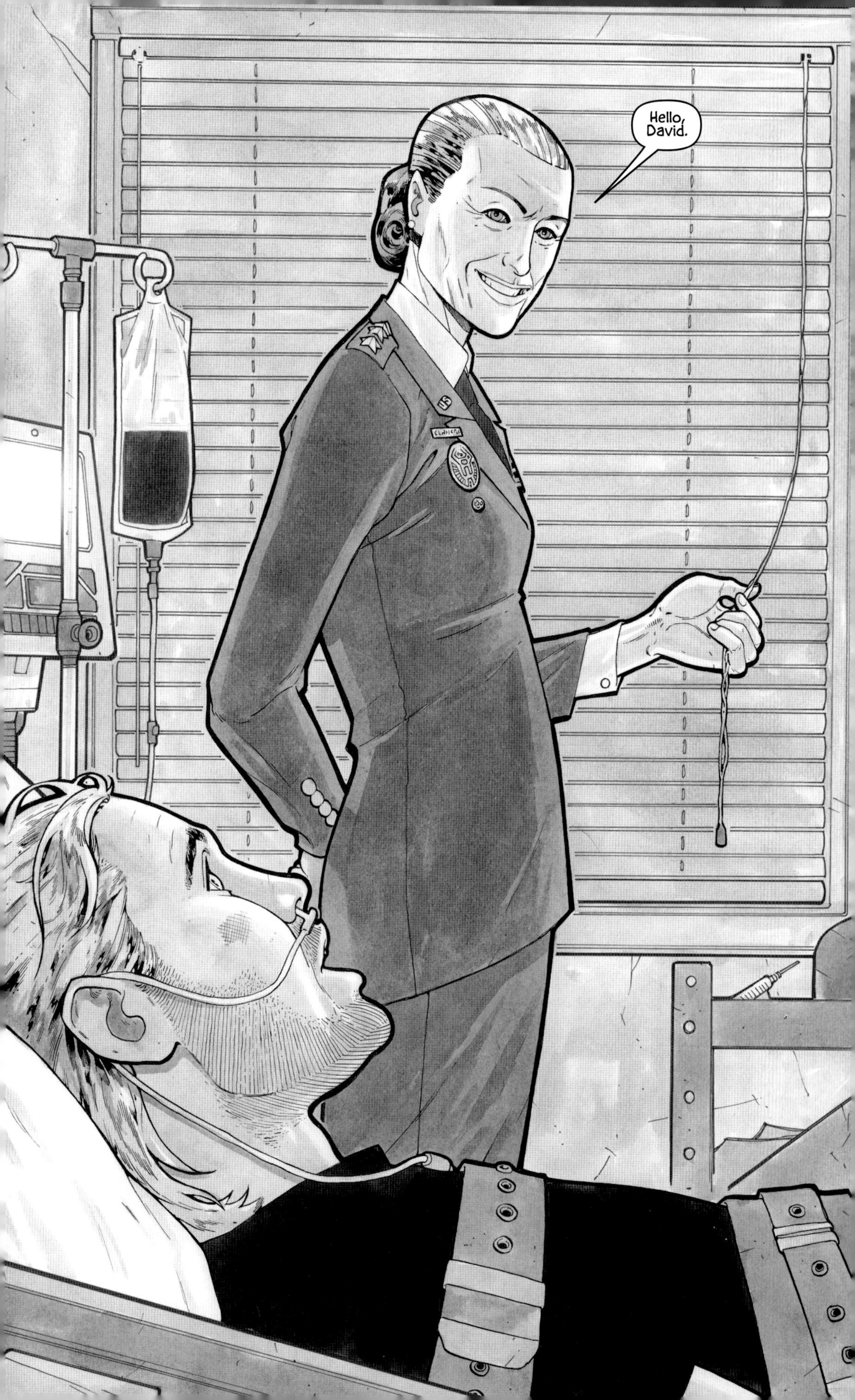
Hello, David.

CHAPTER TWO

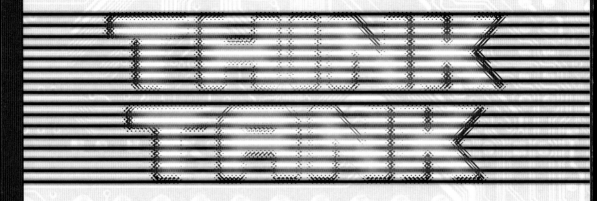

$$\oint \vec{E} \cdot d\vec{A} = \frac{1}{\varepsilon_0} q_{in} \qquad \oint \vec{B} \cdot d\vec{A} = 0 \qquad \oint \vec{E} \cdot d\vec{x} = -\frac{d}{dt} \int \vec{B} \cdot d\vec{a}$$

$$\oint \vec{B} \cdot d\vec{\ell} = \mu_0 I_{in} \qquad \vec{F} = q(\vec{v} \times \vec{B} + \vec{E}) \qquad i = \frac{dq}{dt}$$

oint charge $\quad E = \frac{1}{4\pi\varepsilon_0} \frac{q}{r^2} \qquad V = \frac{1}{4\pi\varepsilon_0} \frac{q}{r} \qquad p = qd$

$$V_f - V_i = -\int_i^f \vec{E} \cdot d\vec{s} \qquad E_x = -\frac{\partial V}{\partial x} \qquad \vec{\tau} = \vec{p} \times \vec{E}$$

$$C = \frac{Q}{V} \qquad U_E = \frac{1}{2} CV^2 = \frac{1}{2} \frac{Q^2}{C} \qquad C = \varepsilon_0 \frac{A}{d}$$

$$R = \frac{V}{i} \qquad P = Vi \qquad R = \rho \frac{L}{A}$$

"PROPAGANDA DOES NOT DECEIVE PEOPLE, iT MERELY HELPS THEM TO DECEIVE THEMSELVES."

ERiC HOFFER

$$R_{eq} = R_1 + R_2 + \cdots \qquad C_{eq} = C_1 + C_2 + \cdots$$

$$\frac{1}{R_{eq}} = \frac{1}{R_1} + \frac{1}{R_2} + \cdots \qquad \frac{1}{C_{eq}} = \frac{1}{C_1} + \frac{1}{C_2} + \cdots$$

$$d\vec{B} = \frac{\mu_0}{4\pi} \frac{i \, d\vec{s} \times \hat{r}}{r^2} \qquad B = \frac{\mu_0}{2\pi} \frac{i}{r} \qquad B = \mu_0 n i \qquad \vec{\tau} = \vec{\mu} \times$$

$$\mathcal{E} = -\frac{d\Phi}{dt} \qquad \mathcal{E} = -N \frac{d\Phi}{dt} \qquad L = \frac{|\mathcal{E}|}{\left|\frac{di}{dt}\right|} = \frac{N\Phi}{i}$$

$$u_E = \frac{1}{2} \varepsilon_0 E^2 \qquad u_B = \frac{1}{2} \frac{B^2}{\mu_0} \qquad U_B = \frac{1}{2} L i^2$$

$$q = q_0 e^{-t/\tau_c} \qquad q = C\mathcal{E}(1 - e^{-t/\tau_c}) \qquad i = i_0 e^{-t/\tau_L} \qquad i = \frac{\mathcal{E}}{R}(1 - e^{-t/\tau_L})$$

$$\tau_L = \frac{L}{R} \qquad \tau_c = RC \qquad \mu = NiA \qquad \frac{1}{4\pi\varepsilon_0} = 9 \times 10^9 \qquad \frac{\mu_0}{4\pi} = 10^{-7}$$

M means 10^6 $\qquad \mu$ means 10^{-6}

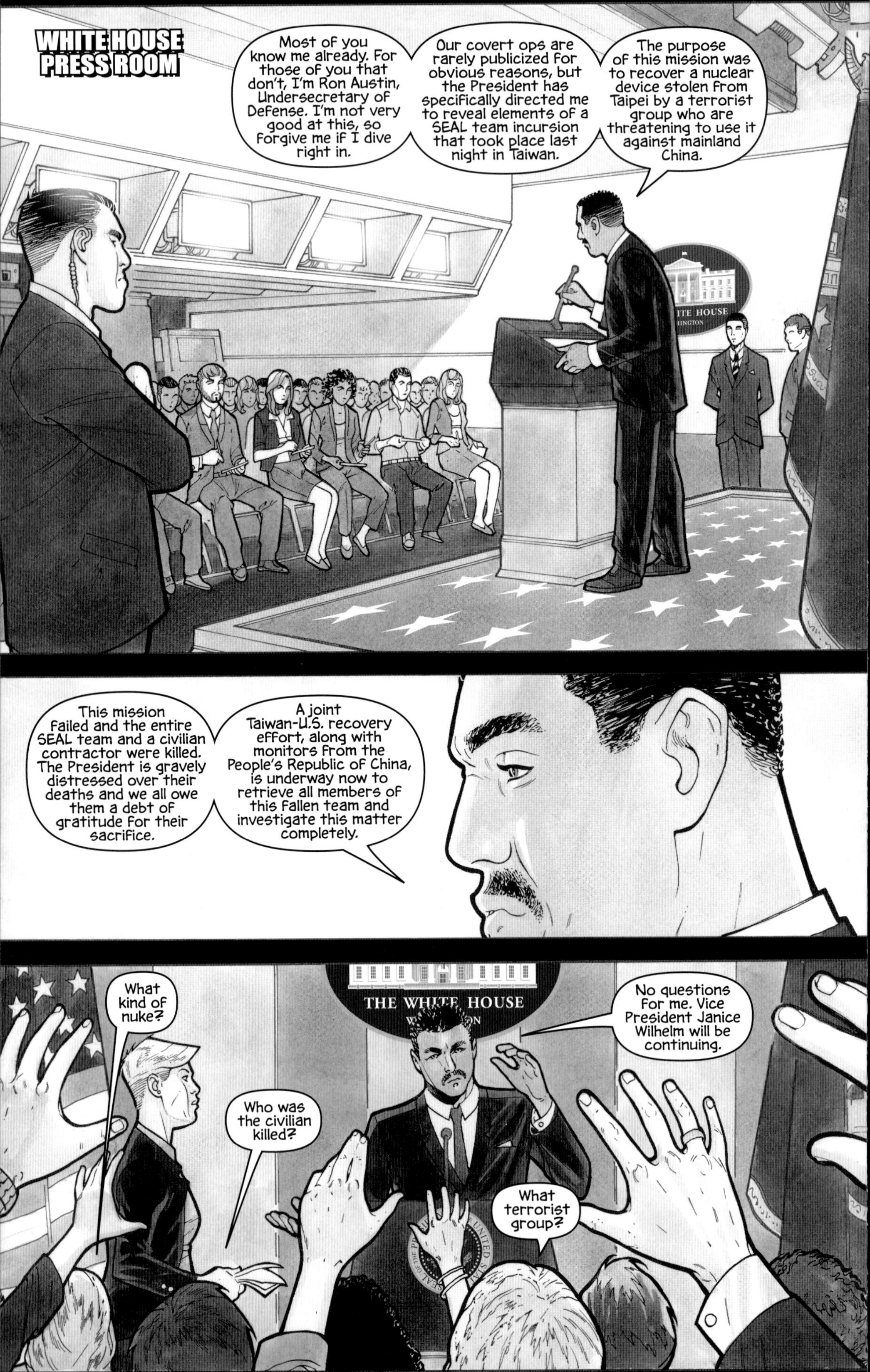
WHITE HOUSE PRESS ROOM
Most of you know me already. For those of you that don't, I'm Ron Austin, Undersecretary of Defense. I'm not very good at this, so forgive me if I dive right in.
Our covert ops are rarely publicized for obvious reasons, but the President has specifically directed me to reveal elements of a SEAL team incursion that took place last night in Taiwan.
The purpose of this mission was to recover a nuclear device stolen from Taipei by a terrorist group who are threatening to use it against mainland China.
This mission failed and the entire SEAL team and a civilian contractor were killed. The President is gravely distressed over their deaths and we all owe them a debt of gratitude for their sacrifice.
A joint Taiwan-U.S. recovery effort, along with monitors from the People's Republic of China, is underway now to retrieve all members of this fallen team and investigate this matter completely.
THE WHITE HOUSE
What kind of nuke?
Who was the civilian killed?
No questions for me. Vice President Janice Wilhelm will be continuing.
What terrorist group?

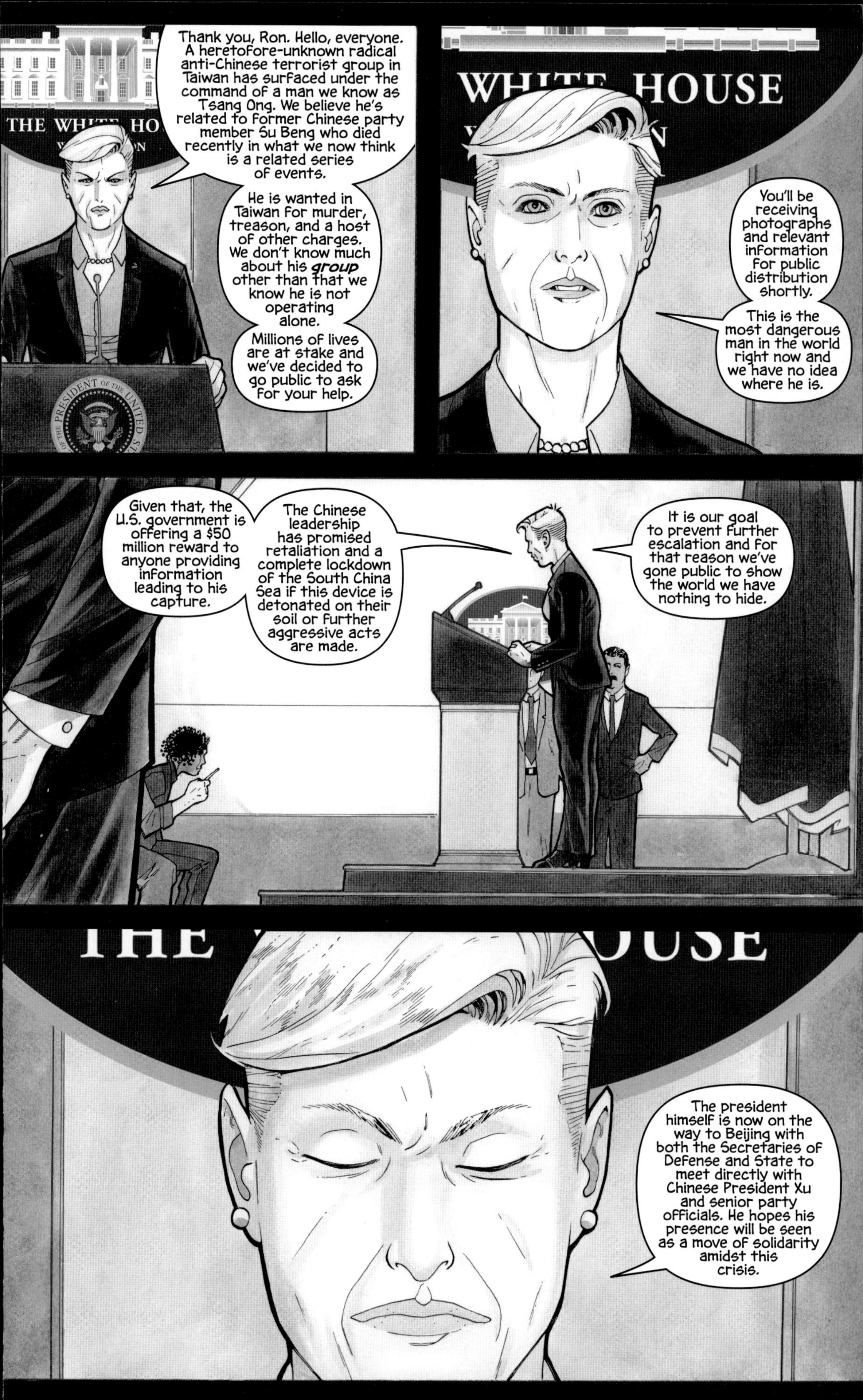
THE WHITE HO
Thank you, Ron. Hello, everyone. A heretofore-unknown radical anti-Chinese terrorist group in Taiwan has surfaced under the command of a man we know as Tsang Ong. We believe he's related to former Chinese party member Su Beng who died recently in what we now think is a related series of events.
He is wanted in Taiwan for murder, treason, and a host of other charges. We don't know much about his *group* other than that we know he is not operating alone.
Millions of lives are at stake and we've decided to go public to ask for your help.
WHITE HOUSE
You'll be receiving photographs and relevant information for public distribution shortly.
This is the most dangerous man in the world right now and we have no idea where he is.
Given that, the U.S. government is offering a $50 million reward to anyone providing information leading to his capture.
The Chinese leadership has promised retaliation and a complete lockdown of the South China Sea if this device is detonated on their soil or further aggressive acts are made.
It is our goal to prevent further escalation and for that reason we've gone public to show the world we have nothing to hide.
The president himself is now on the way to Beijing with both the Secretaries of Defense and State to meet directly with Chinese President Xu and senior party officials. He hopes his presence will be seen as a move of solidarity amidst this crisis.

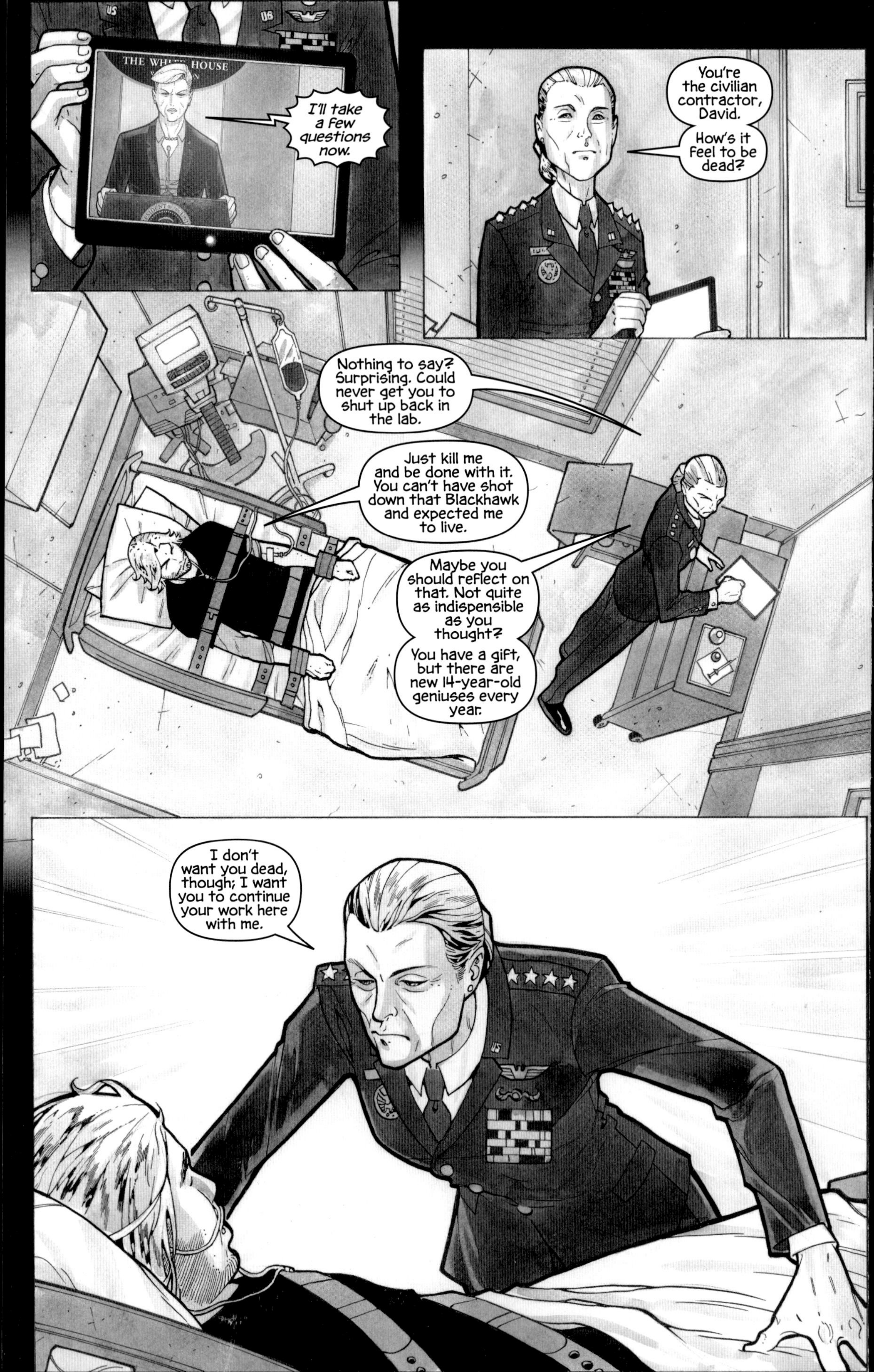
THE WHITE HOUSE
I'll take a few questions now.
You're the civilian contractor, David.
How's it feel to be dead?
Nothing to say? Surprising. Could never get you to shut up back in the lab.
Just kill me and be done with it. You can't have shot down that Blackhawk and expected me to live.
Maybe you should reflect on that. Not quite as indispensible as you thought?
You have a gift, but there are new 14-year-old geniuses every year.
I don't want you dead, though; I want you to continue your work here with me.

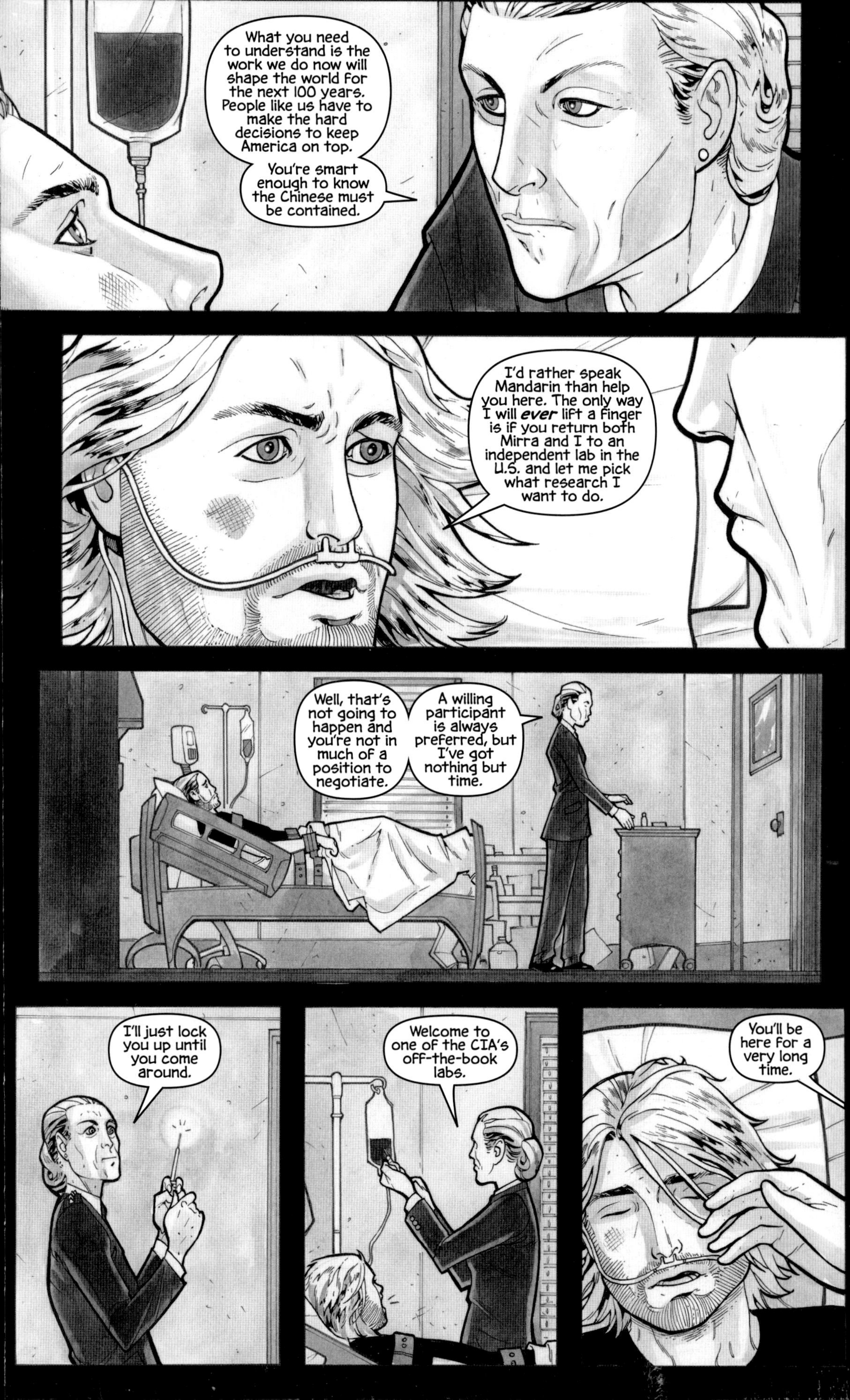
What you need to understand is the work we do now will shape the world for the next 100 years. People like us have to make the hard decisions to keep America on top.
You're smart enough to know the Chinese must be contained.
I'd rather speak Mandarin than help you here. The only way I will *ever* lift a finger is if you return both Mirra and I to an independent lab in the U.S. and let me pick what research I want to do.
Well, that's not going to happen and you're not in much of a position to negotiate.
A willing participant is always preferred, but I've got nothing but time.
I'll just lock you up until you come around.
Welcome to one of the CIA's off-the-book labs.
You'll be here for a very long time.

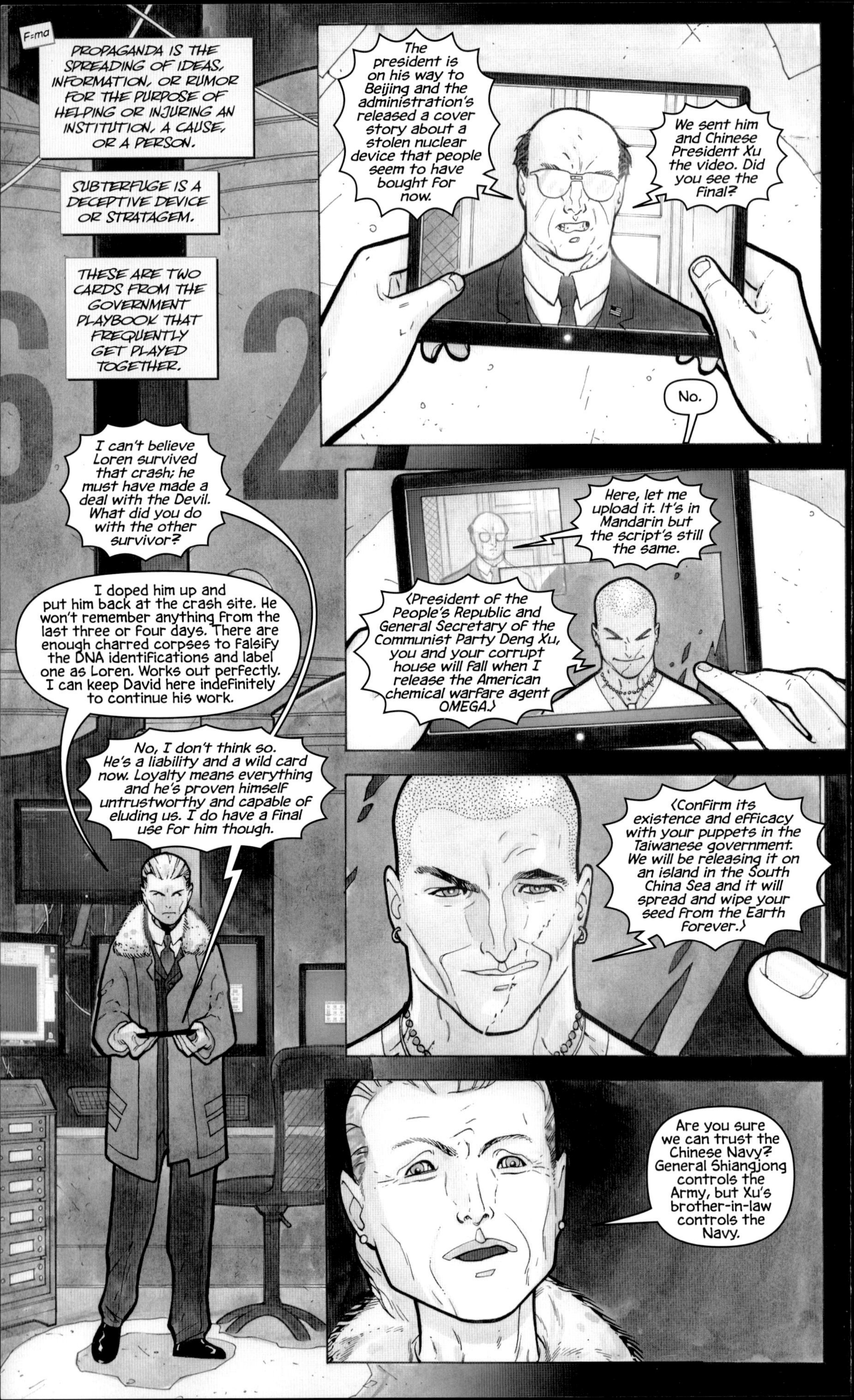
F=ma
PROPAGANDA IS THE SPREADING OF IDEAS, INFORMATION, OR RUMOR FOR THE PURPOSE OF HELPING OR INJURING AN INSTITUTION, A CAUSE, OR A PERSON.
SUBTERFUGE IS A DECEPTIVE DEVICE OR STRATAGEM.
THESE ARE TWO CARDS FROM THE GOVERNMENT PLAYBOOK THAT FREQUENTLY GET PLAYED TOGETHER.
The president is on his way to Beijing and the administration's released a cover story about a stolen nuclear device that people seem to have bought for now.
We sent him and Chinese President Xu the video. Did you see the final?
No.
Here, let me upload it. It's in Mandarin but the script's still the same.
‹President of the People's Republic and General Secretary of the Communist Party Deng Xu, you and your corrupt house will fall when I release the American chemical warfare agent OMEGA.›
‹Confirm its existence and efficacy with your puppets in the Taiwanese government. We will be releasing it on an island in the South China Sea and it will spread and wipe your seed from the Earth forever.›
Are you sure we can trust the Chinese Navy? General Shiangjong controls the Army, but Xu's brother-in-law controls the Navy.
I can't believe Loren survived that crash; he must have made a deal with the Devil. What did you do with the other survivor?
I doped him up and put him back at the crash site. He won't remember anything from the last three or four days. There are enough charred corpses to falsify the DNA identifications and label one as Loren. Works out perfectly. I can keep David here indefinitely to continue his work.
No, I don't think so. He's a liability and a wild card now. Loyalty means everything and he's proven himself untrustworthy and capable of eluding us. I do have a final use for him though.

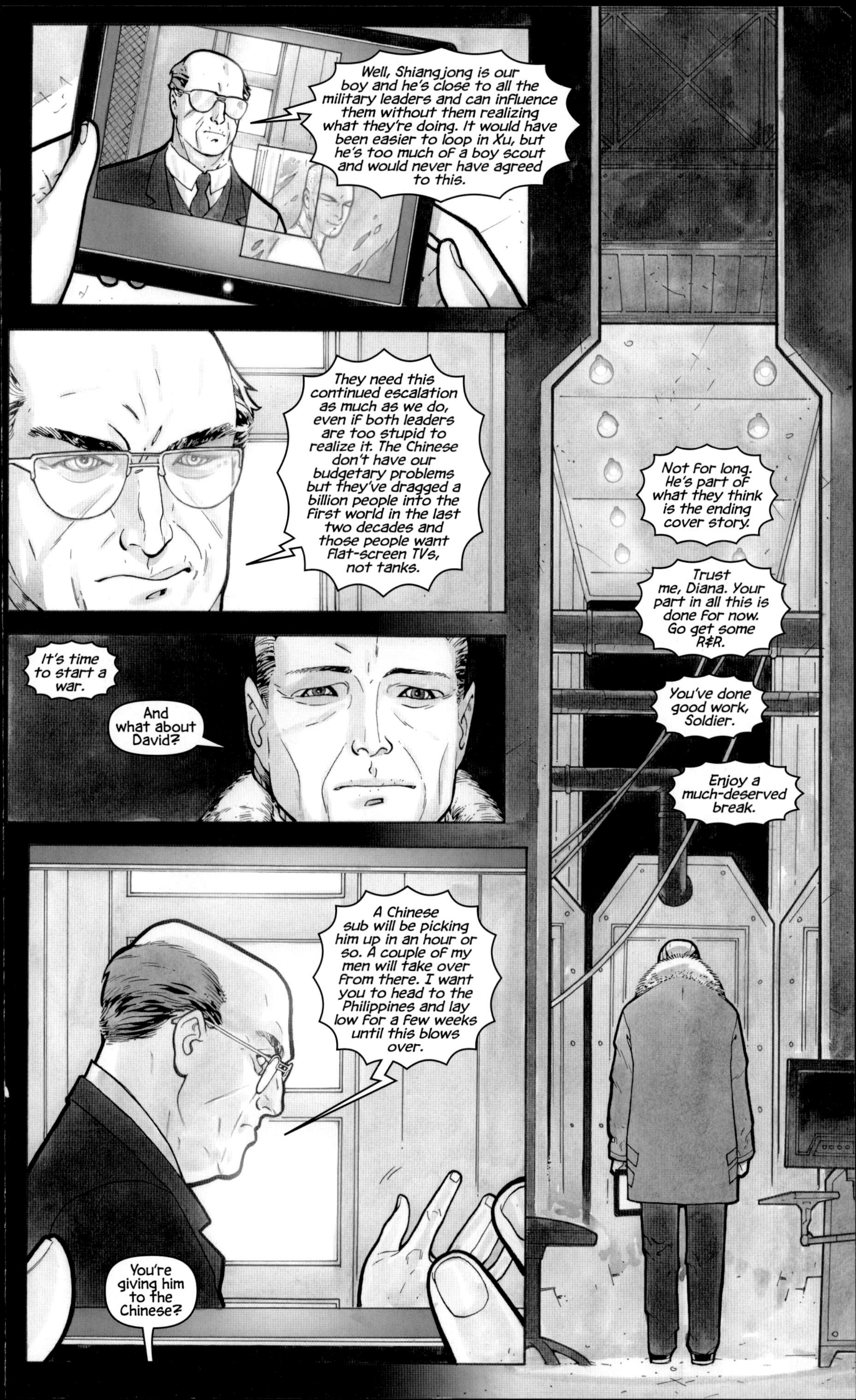

Well, Shiangjong is our boy and he's close to all the military leaders and can influence them without them realizing what they're doing. It would have been easier to loop in Xu, but he's too much of a boy scout and would never have agreed to this.
They need this continued escalation as much as we do, even if both leaders are too stupid to realize it. The Chinese don't have our budgetary problems but they've dragged a billion people into the First world in the last two decades and those people want flat-screen TVs, not tanks.
It's time to start a war.
And what about David?
A Chinese sub will be picking him up in an hour or so. A couple of my men will take over from there. I want you to head to the Philippines and lay low for a few weeks until this blows over.
You're giving him to the Chinese?
Not for long. He's part of what they think is the ending cover story.
Trust me, Diana. Your part in all this is done for now. Go get some R&R.
You've done good work, Soldier.
Enjoy a much-deserved break.

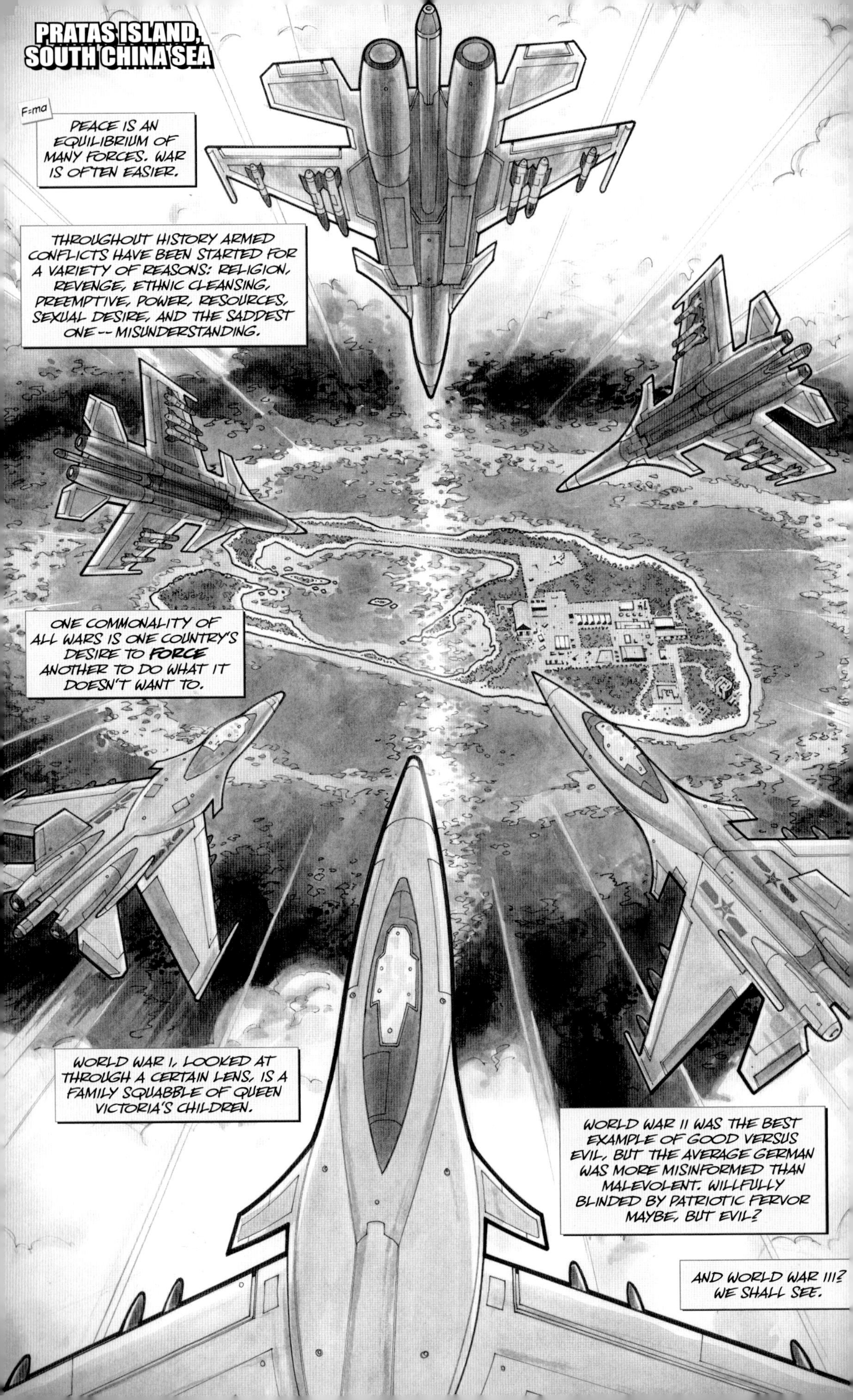
PRATAS ISLAND, SOUTH CHINA SEA
F=ma
PEACE IS AN EQUILIBRIUM OF MANY FORCES. WAR IS OFTEN EASIER.
THROUGHOUT HISTORY ARMED CONFLICTS HAVE BEEN STARTED FOR A VARIETY OF REASONS: RELIGION, REVENGE, ETHNIC CLEANSING, PREEMPTIVE, POWER, RESOURCES, SEXUAL DESIRE, AND THE SADDEST ONE -- MISUNDERSTANDING.
ONE COMMONALITY OF ALL WARS IS ONE COUNTRY'S DESIRE TO FORCE ANOTHER TO DO WHAT IT DOESN'T WANT TO.
WORLD WAR I, LOOKED AT THROUGH A CERTAIN LENS, IS A FAMILY SQUABBLE OF QUEEN VICTORIA'S CHILDREN.
WORLD WAR II WAS THE BEST EXAMPLE OF GOOD VERSUS EVIL, BUT THE AVERAGE GERMAN WAS MORE MISINFORMED THAN MALEVOLENT. WILLFULLY BLINDED BY PATRIOTIC FERVOR MAYBE, BUT EVIL?
AND WORLD WAR III? WE SHALL SEE.

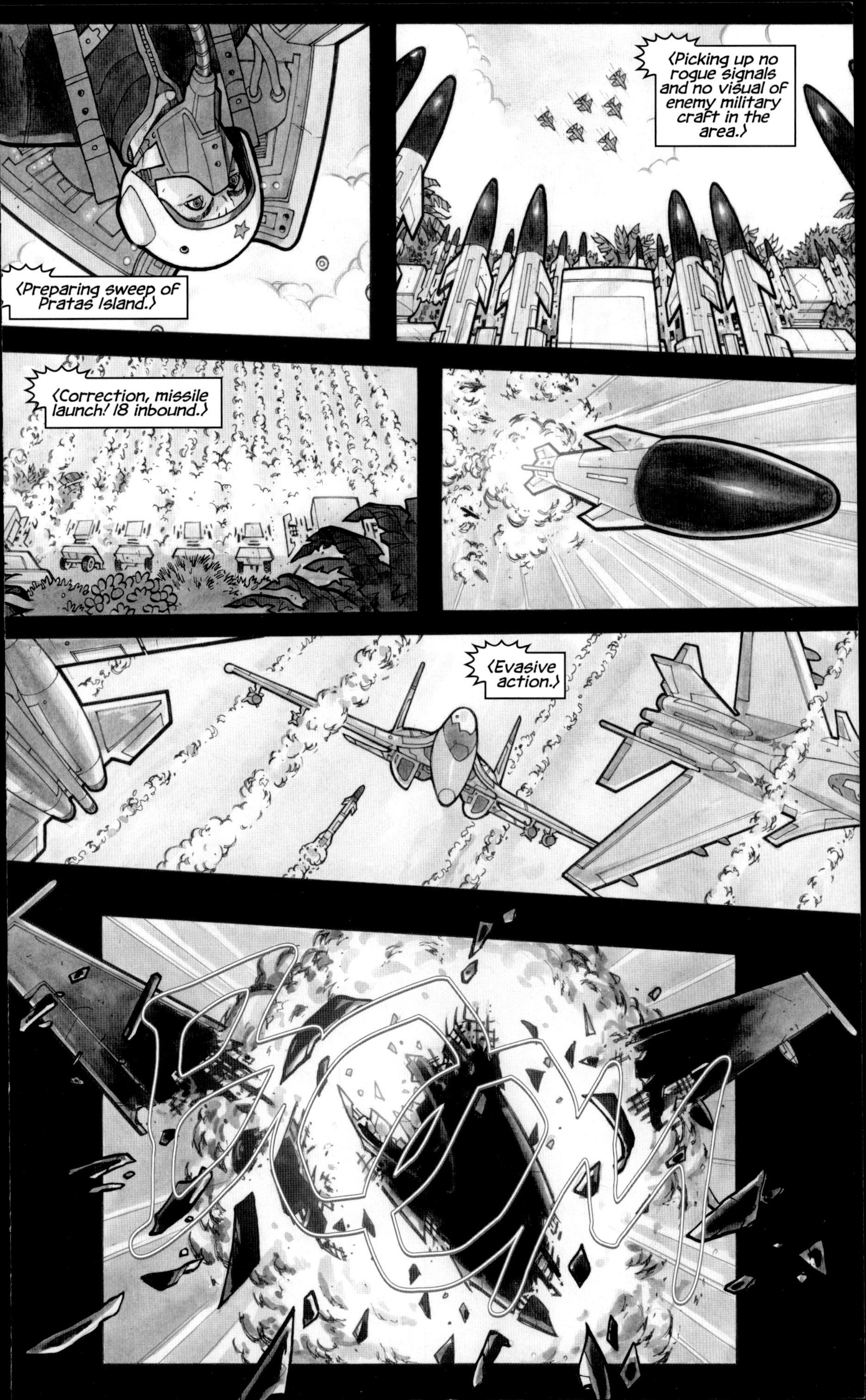
‹Preparing sweep of Pratas Island.›
‹Picking up no rogue signals and no visual of enemy military craft in the area.›
‹Correction, missile launch! 18 inbound.›
‹Evasive action.›
BOOM

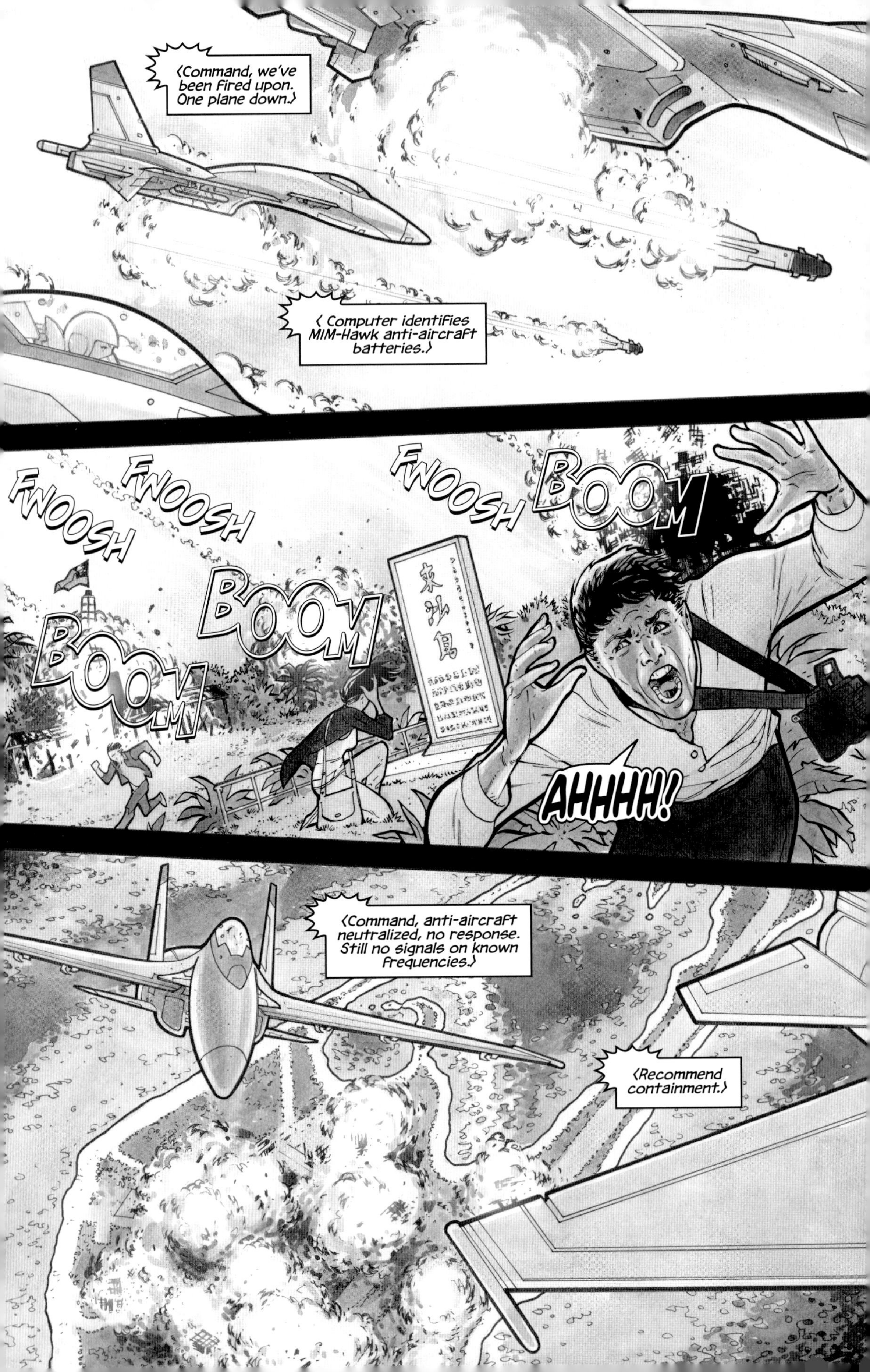

‹Command, we've been fired upon. One plane down.›
‹ Computer identifies MIM-Hawk anti-aircraft batteries.›
FWOOSH
FWOOSH
FWOOSH
BOOM
BOOM
BOOM
AHHHH!
‹Command, anti-aircraft neutralized, no response. Still no signals on known frequencies.›
‹Recommend containment.›

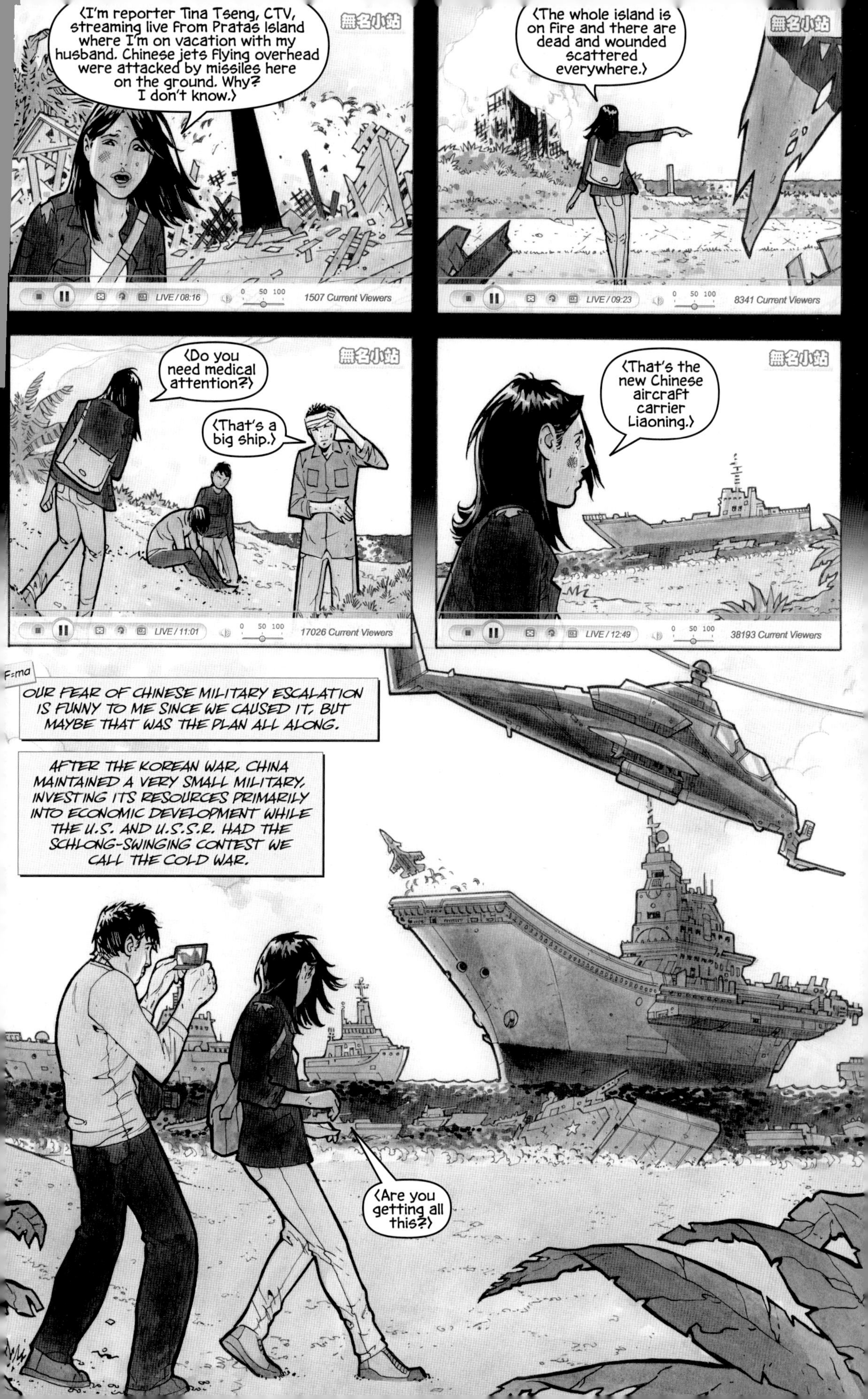
無名小站
⟨I'm reporter Tina Tseng, CTV, streaming live from Pratas Island where I'm on vacation with my husband. Chinese jets flying overhead were attacked by missiles here on the ground. Why? I don't know.⟩
LIVE / 08:16
0 50 100
1507 Current Viewers
無名小站
⟨The whole island is on fire and there are dead and wounded scattered everywhere.⟩
LIVE / 09:23
0 50 100
8341 Current Viewers
無名小站
⟨Do you need medical attention?⟩
⟨That's a big ship.⟩
LIVE / 11:01
0 50 100
17026 Current Viewers
無名小站
⟨That's the new Chinese aircraft carrier Liaoning.⟩
LIVE / 12:49
0 50 100
38193 Current Viewers
F=ma
OUR FEAR OF CHINESE MILITARY ESCALATION IS FUNNY TO ME SINCE WE CAUSED IT, BUT MAYBE THAT WAS THE PLAN ALL ALONG.
AFTER THE KOREAN WAR, CHINA MAINTAINED A VERY SMALL MILITARY, INVESTING ITS RESOURCES PRIMARILY INTO ECONOMIC DEVELOPMENT WHILE THE U.S. AND U.S.S.R. HAD THE SCHLONG-SWINGING CONTEST WE CALL THE COLD WAR.
⟨Are you getting all this?⟩

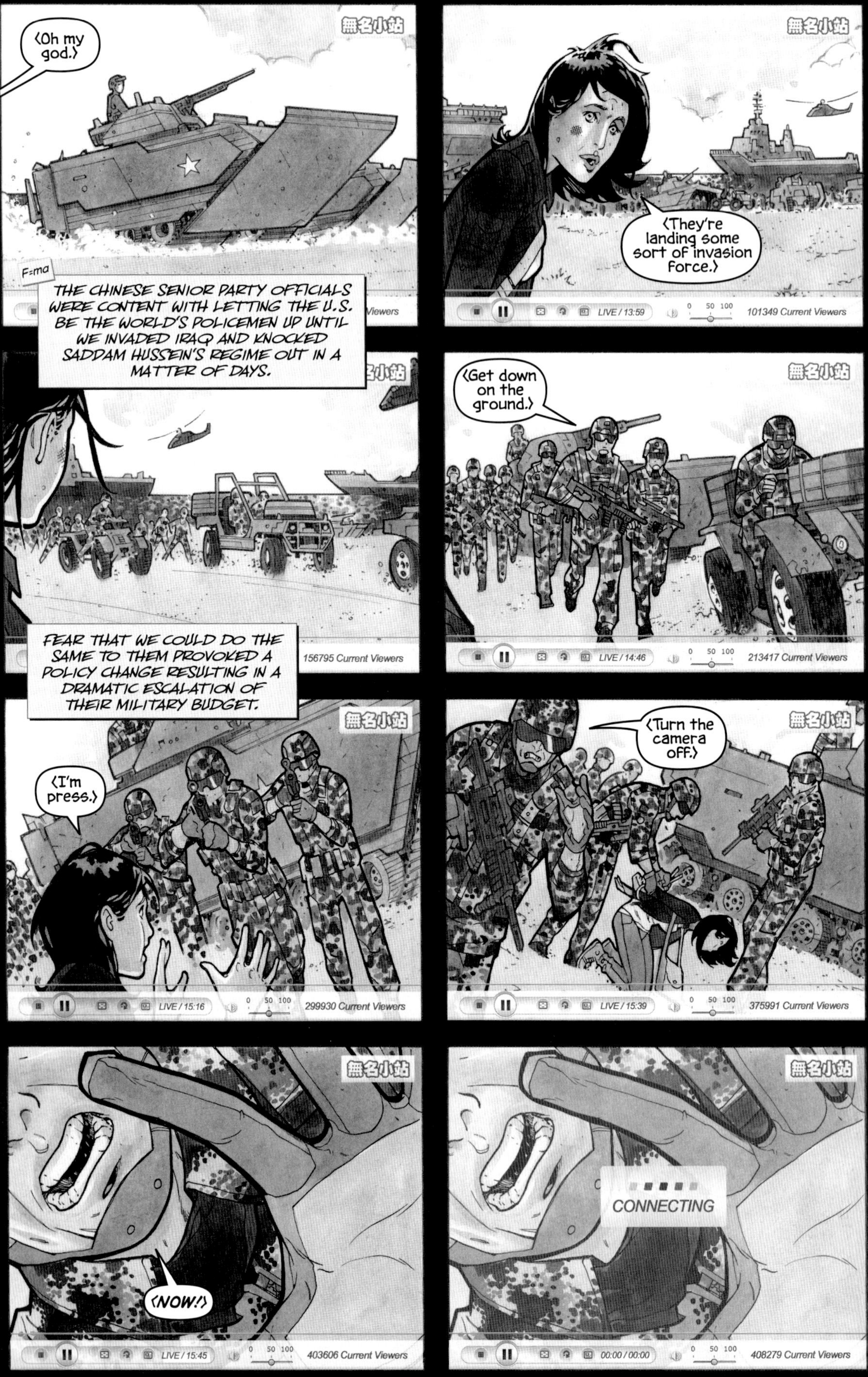
無名小站
〈Oh my god.〉
F=ma
THE CHINESE SENIOR PARTY OFFICIALS WERE CONTENT WITH LETTING THE U.S. BE THE WORLD'S POLICEMEN UP UNTIL WE INVADED IRAQ AND KNOCKED SADDAM HUSSEIN'S REGIME OUT IN A MATTER OF DAYS.
Viewers
無名小站
〈They're landing some sort of invasion force.〉
LIVE / 13:59
0 50 100
101349 Current Viewers
無名小站
156795 Current Viewers
FEAR THAT WE COULD DO THE SAME TO THEM PROVOKED A POLICY CHANGE RESULTING IN A DRAMATIC ESCALATION OF THEIR MILITARY BUDGET.
無名小站
〈Get down on the ground.〉
LIVE / 14:46
0 50 100
213417 Current Viewers
無名小站
〈I'm press.〉
LIVE / 15:16
0 50 100
299930 Current Viewers
無名小站
〈Turn the camera off.〉
LIVE / 15:39
0 50 100
375991 Current Viewers
無名小站
〈NOW!〉
LIVE / 15:45
0 50 100
403606 Current Viewers
無名小站
CONNECTING
00:00 / 00:00
0 50 100
408279 Current Viewers

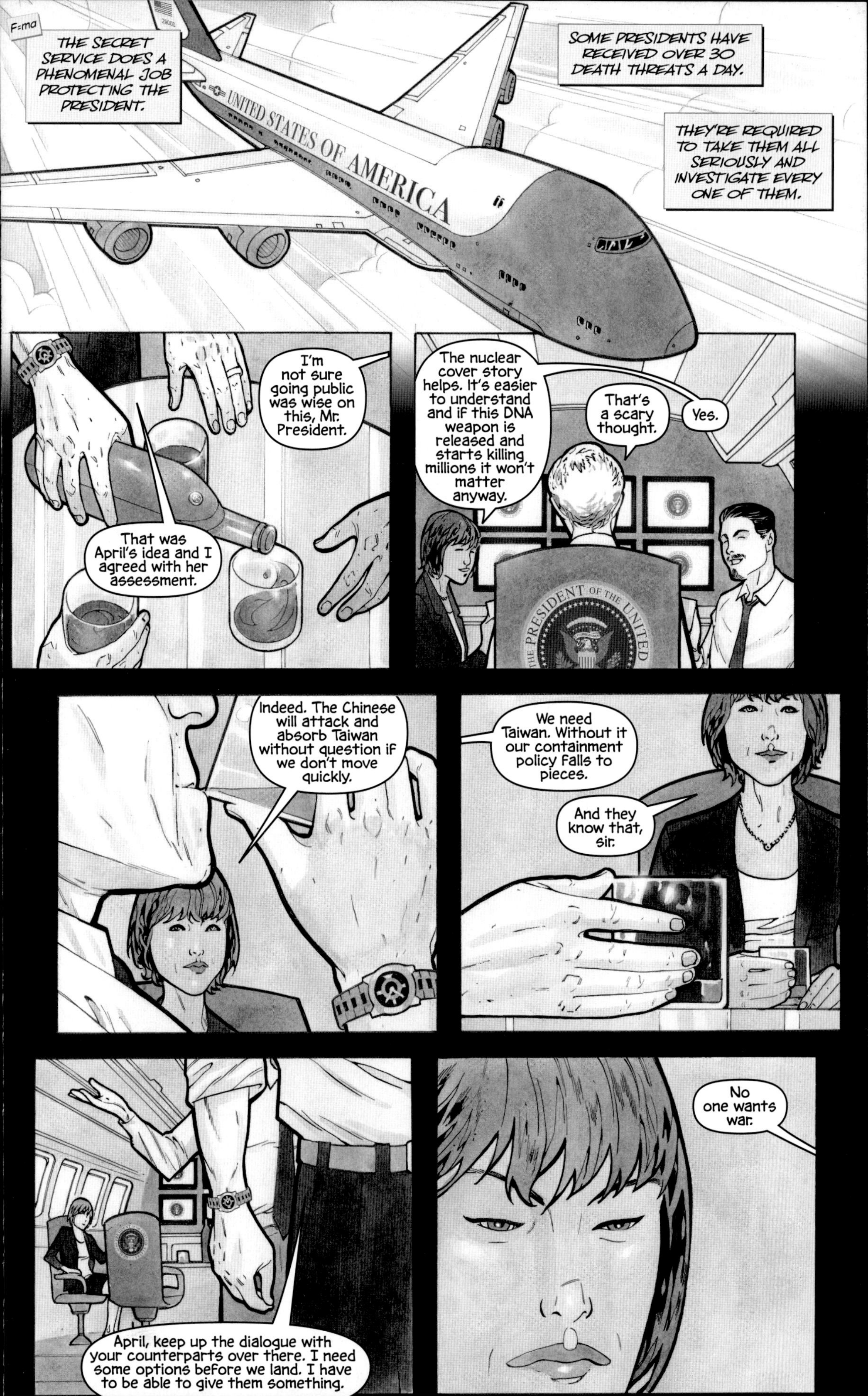
F=ma
THE SECRET SERVICE DOES A PHENOMENAL JOB PROTECTING THE PRESIDENT.
SOME PRESIDENTS HAVE RECEIVED OVER 30 DEATH THREATS A DAY.
THEY'RE REQUIRED TO TAKE THEM ALL SERIOUSLY AND INVESTIGATE EVERY ONE OF THEM.
UNITED STATES OF AMERICA
I'm not sure going public was wise on this, Mr. President.
That was April's idea and I agreed with her assessment.
The nuclear cover story helps. It's easier to understand and if this DNA weapon is released and starts killing millions it won't matter anyway.
That's a scary thought.
Yes.
THE PRESIDENT OF THE UNITED
Indeed. The Chinese will attack and absorb Taiwan without question if we don't move quickly.
We need Taiwan. Without it our containment policy falls to pieces.
And they know that, sir.
April, keep up the dialogue with your counterparts over there. I need some options before we land. I have to be able to give them something.
No one wants war.

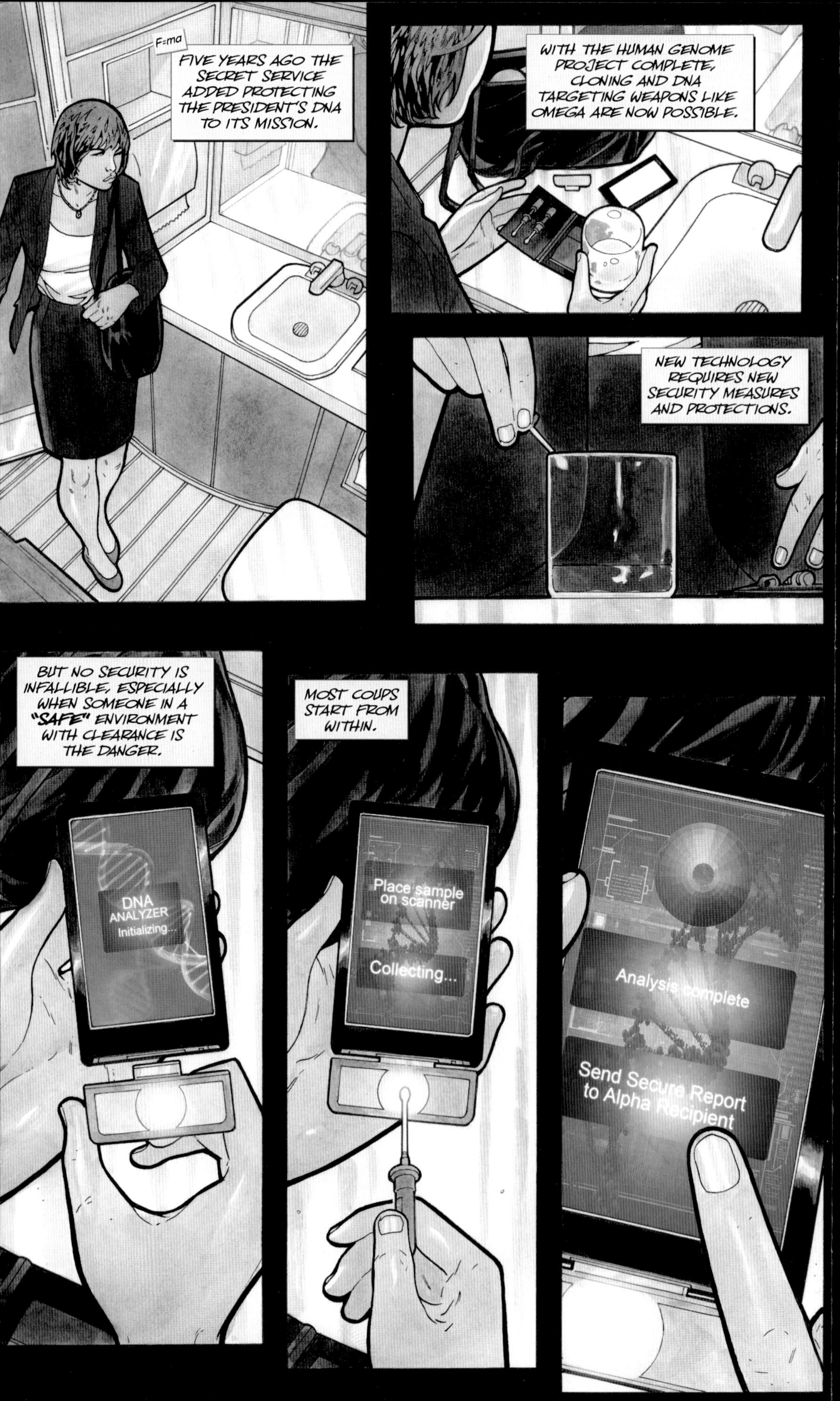

F=ma
FIVE YEARS AGO THE SECRET SERVICE ADDED PROTECTING THE PRESIDENT'S DNA TO ITS MISSION.
WITH THE HUMAN GENOME PROJECT COMPLETE, CLONING AND DNA TARGETING WEAPONS LIKE OMEGA ARE NOW POSSIBLE.
NEW TECHNOLOGY REQUIRES NEW SECURITY MEASURES AND PROTECTIONS.
BUT NO SECURITY IS INFALLIBLE, ESPECIALLY WHEN SOMEONE IN A "SAFE" ENVIRONMENT WITH CLEARANCE IS THE DANGER.
DNA ANALYZER Initializing...
MOST COUPS START FROM WITHIN.
Place sample on scanner
Collecting...
Analysis complete
Send Secure Report to Alpha Recipient

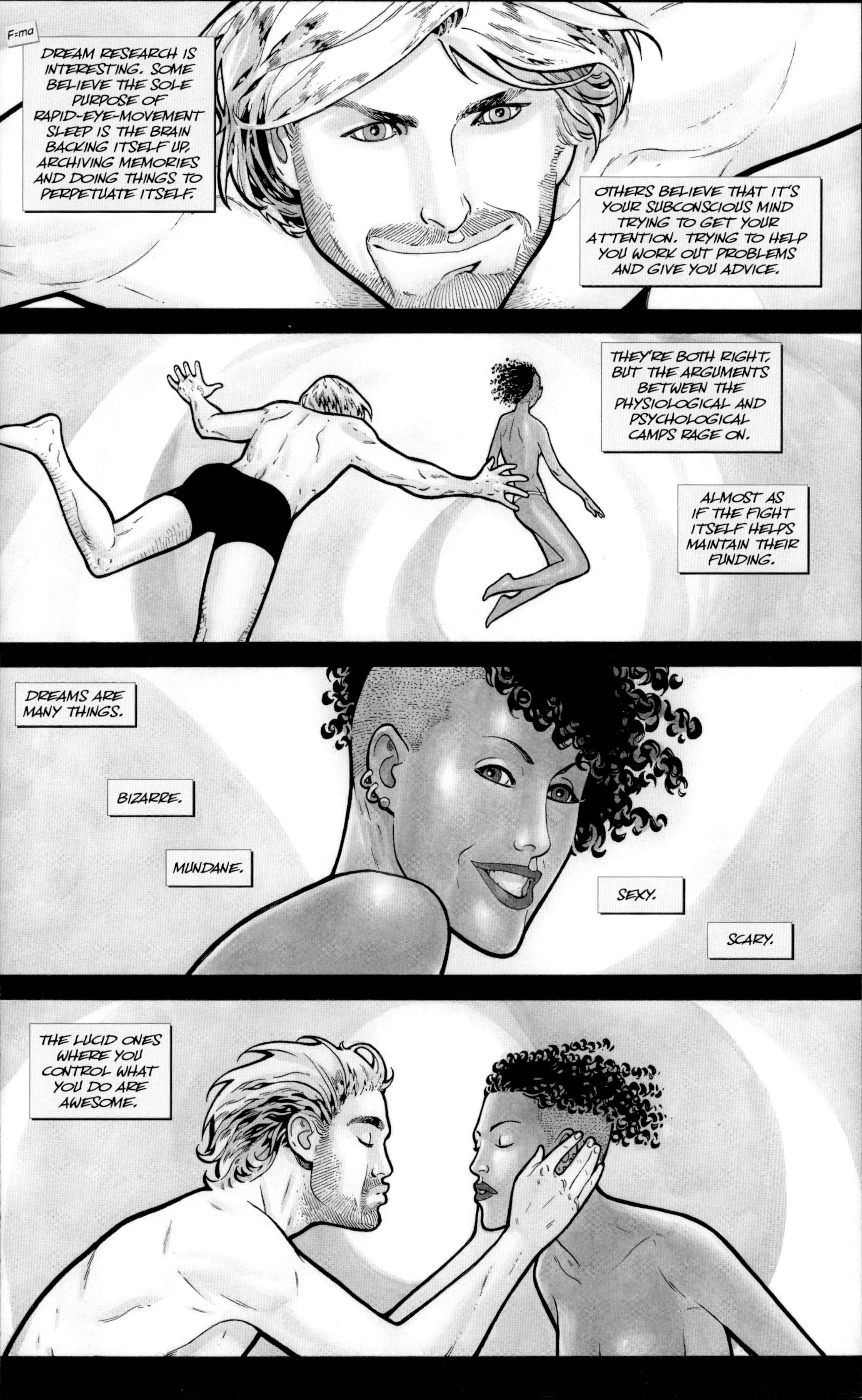
F=ma
DREAM RESEARCH IS INTERESTING. SOME BELIEVE THE SOLE PURPOSE OF RAPID-EYE-MOVEMENT SLEEP IS THE BRAIN BACKING ITSELF UP, ARCHIVING MEMORIES AND DOING THINGS TO PERPETUATE ITSELF.
OTHERS BELIEVE THAT IT'S YOUR SUBCONSCIOUS MIND TRYING TO GET YOUR ATTENTION. TRYING TO HELP YOU WORK OUT PROBLEMS AND GIVE YOU ADVICE.
THEY'RE BOTH RIGHT, BUT THE ARGUMENTS BETWEEN THE PHYSIOLOGICAL AND PSYCHOLOGICAL CAMPS RAGE ON.
ALMOST AS IF THE FIGHT ITSELF HELPS MAINTAIN THEIR FUNDING.
DREAMS ARE MANY THINGS.
BIZARRE.
MUNDANE.
SEXY.
SCARY.
THE LUCID ONES WHERE YOU CONTROL WHAT YOU DO ARE AWESOME.

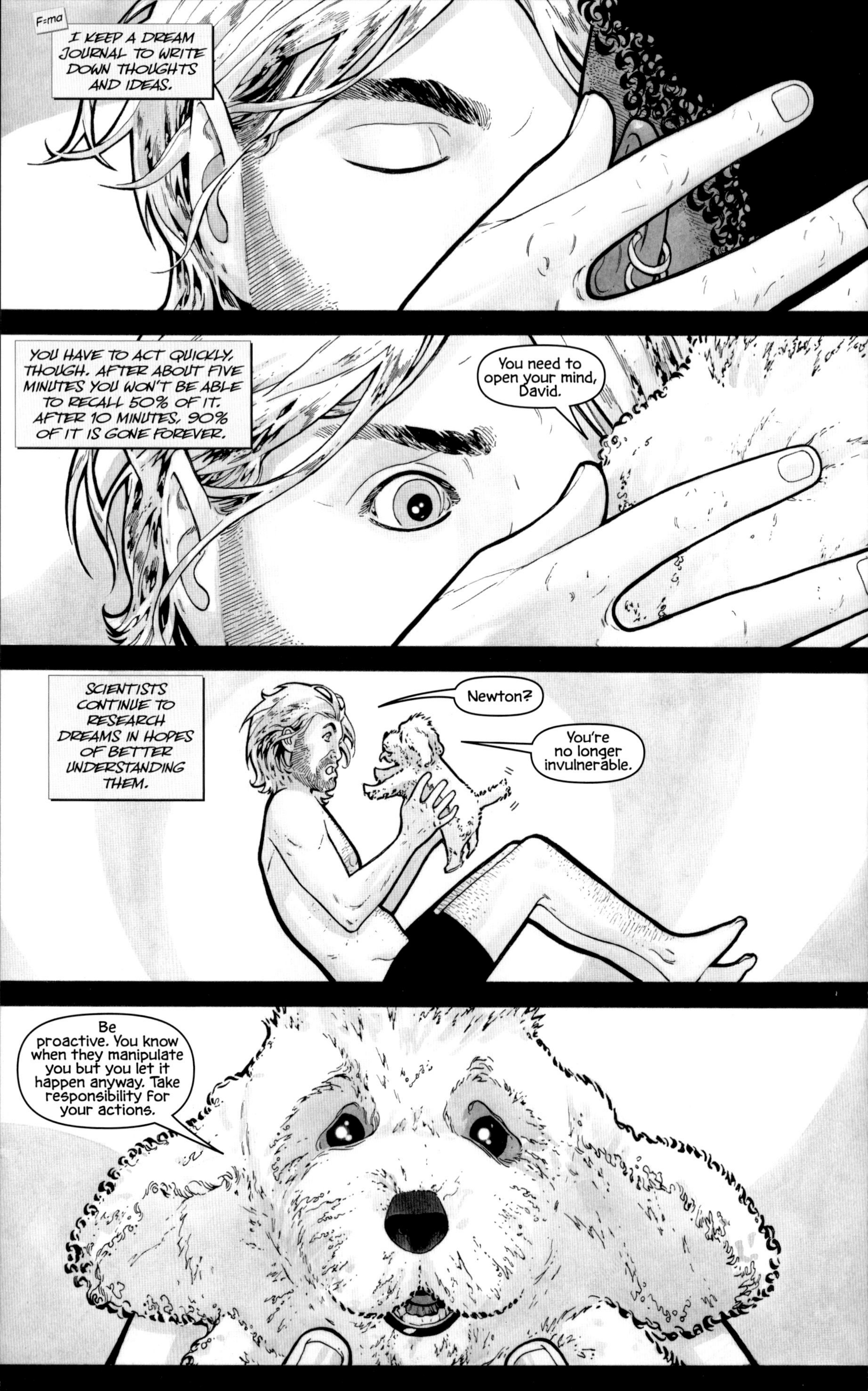
F=ma
I KEEP A DREAM JOURNAL TO WRITE DOWN THOUGHTS AND IDEAS.
YOU HAVE TO ACT QUICKLY, THOUGH. AFTER ABOUT FIVE MINUTES YOU WON'T BE ABLE TO RECALL 50% OF IT. AFTER 10 MINUTES, 90% OF IT IS GONE FOREVER.
You need to open your mind, David.
SCIENTISTS CONTINUE TO RESEARCH DREAMS IN HOPES OF BETTER UNDERSTANDING THEM.
Newton?
You're no longer invulnerable.
Be proactive. You know when they manipulate you but you let it happen anyway. Take responsibility for your actions.

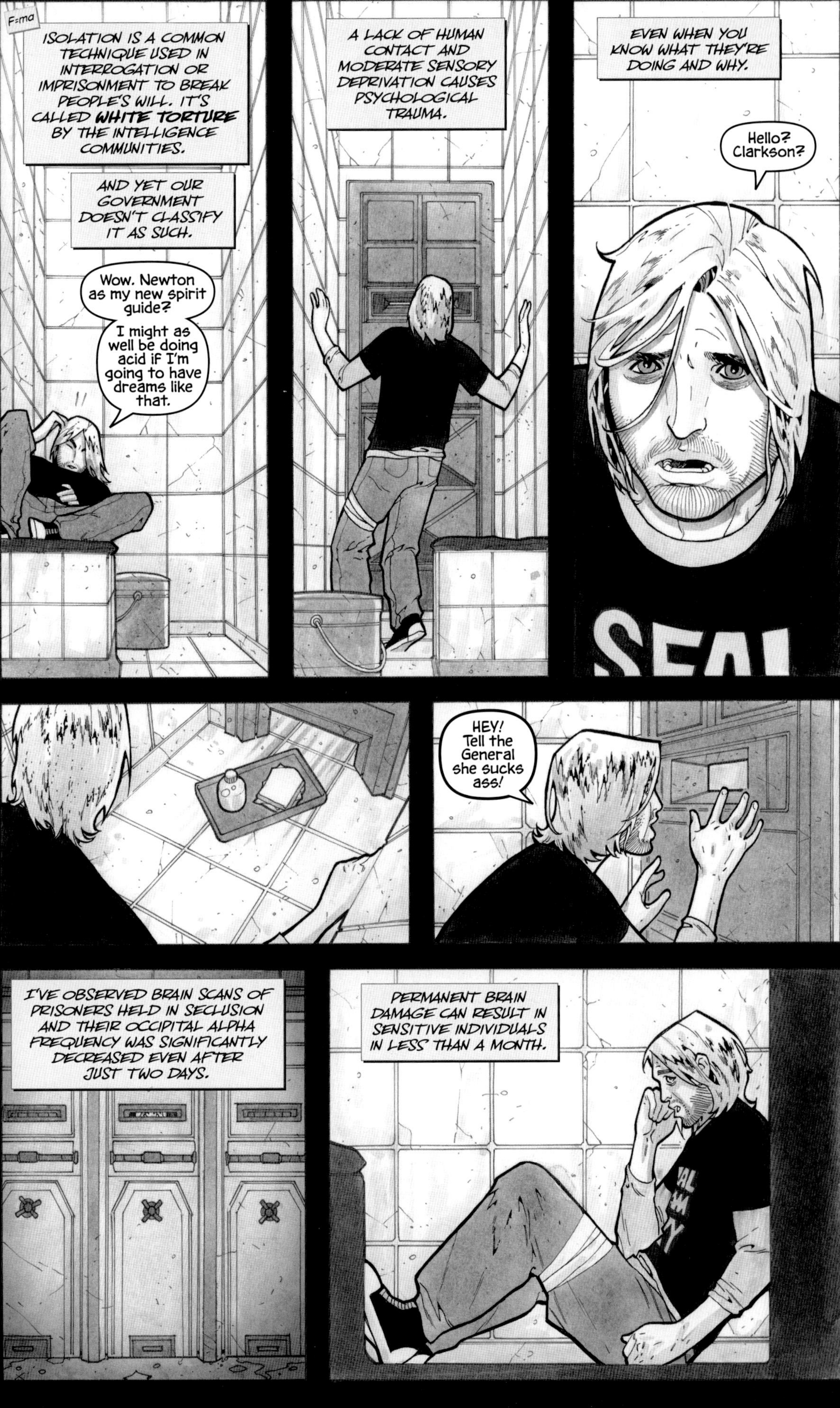
F=ma
ISOLATION IS A COMMON TECHNIQUE USED IN INTERROGATION OR IMPRISONMENT TO BREAK PEOPLE'S WILL. IT'S CALLED WHITE TORTURE BY THE INTELLIGENCE COMMUNITIES.
AND YET OUR GOVERNMENT DOESN'T CLASSIFY IT AS SUCH.
Wow. Newton as my new spirit guide?
I might as well be doing acid if I'm going to have dreams like that.
A LACK OF HUMAN CONTACT AND MODERATE SENSORY DEPRIVATION CAUSES PSYCHOLOGICAL TRAUMA.
EVEN WHEN YOU KNOW WHAT THEY'RE DOING AND WHY.
Hello? Clarkson?
HEY! Tell the General she sucks ass!
I'VE OBSERVED BRAIN SCANS OF PRISONERS HELD IN SECLUSION AND THEIR OCCIPITAL ALPHA FREQUENCY WAS SIGNIFICANTLY DECREASED EVEN AFTER JUST TWO DAYS.
PERMANENT BRAIN DAMAGE CAN RESULT IN SENSITIVE INDIVIDUALS IN LESS THAN A MONTH.

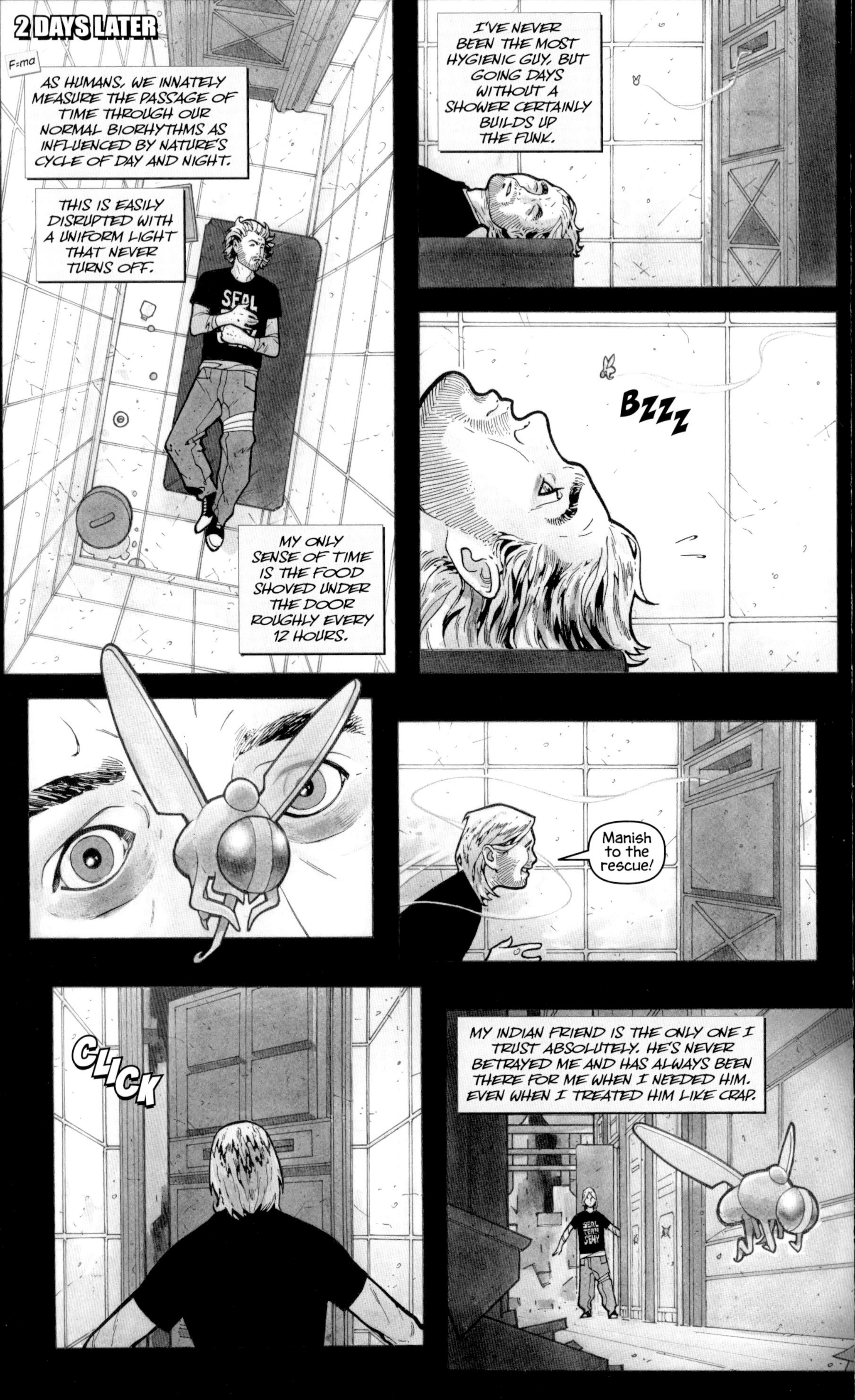
2 DAYS LATER
F=ma
AS HUMANS, WE INNATELY MEASURE THE PASSAGE OF TIME THROUGH OUR NORMAL BIORHYTHMS AS INFLUENCED BY NATURE'S CYCLE OF DAY AND NIGHT.
THIS IS EASILY DISRUPTED WITH A UNIFORM LIGHT THAT NEVER TURNS OFF.
MY ONLY SENSE OF TIME IS THE FOOD SHOVED UNDER THE DOOR ROUGHLY EVERY 12 HOURS.
I'VE NEVER BEEN THE MOST HYGIENIC GUY, BUT GOING DAYS WITHOUT A SHOWER CERTAINLY BUILDS UP THE FUNK.
BZZZ
Manish to the rescue!
CLICK
MY INDIAN FRIEND IS THE ONLY ONE I TRUST ABSOLUTELY. HE'S NEVER BETRAYED ME AND HAS ALWAYS BEEN THERE FOR ME WHEN I NEEDED HIM. EVEN WHEN I TREATED HIM LIKE CRAP.

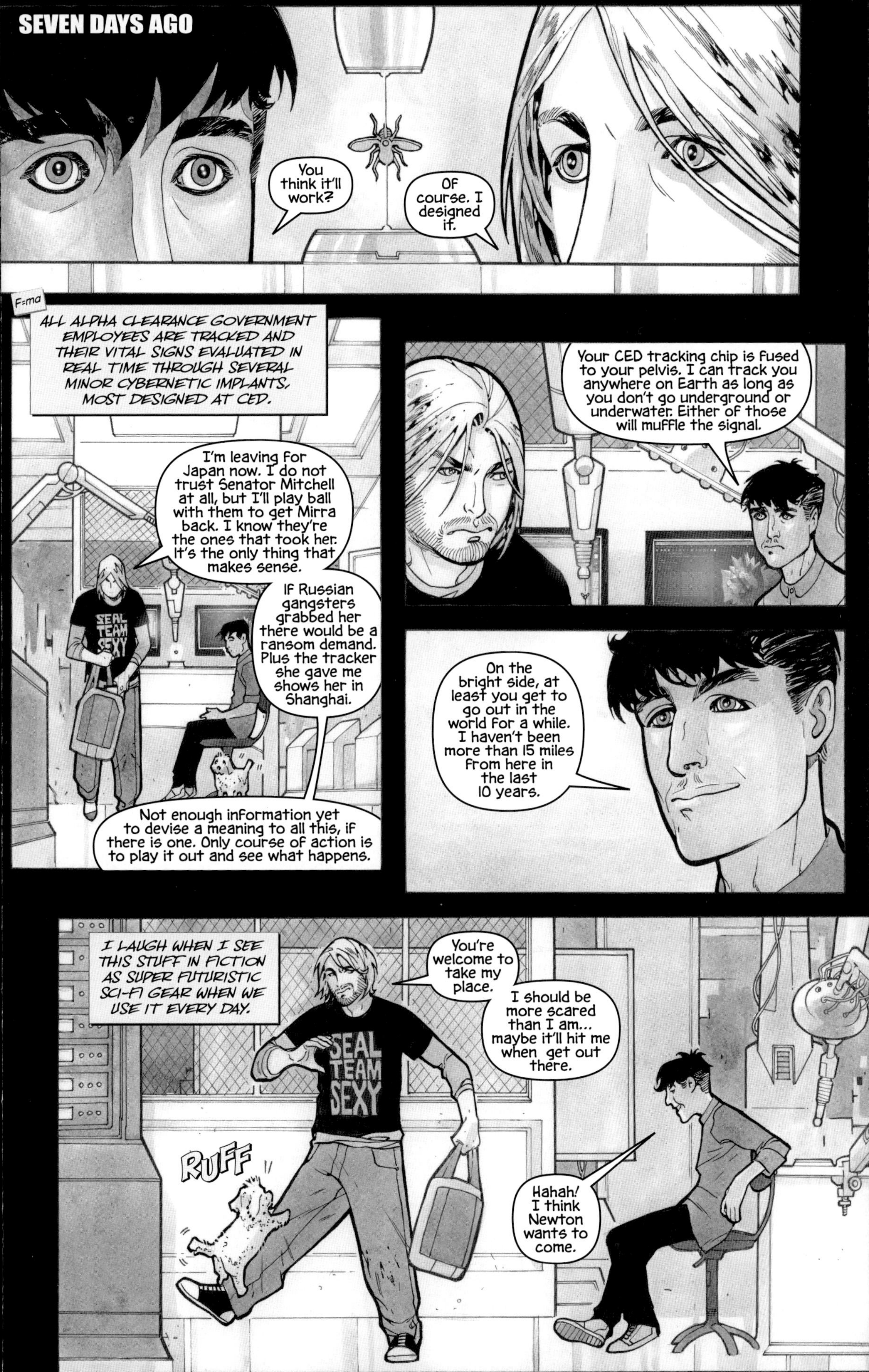

SEVEN DAYS AGO
You think it'll work?
Of course. I designed it.
F=ma
ALL ALPHA CLEARANCE GOVERNMENT EMPLOYEES ARE TRACKED AND THEIR VITAL SIGNS EVALUATED IN REAL TIME THROUGH SEVERAL MINOR CYBERNETIC IMPLANTS, MOST DESIGNED AT CED.
I'm leaving for Japan now. I do not trust Senator Mitchell at all, but I'll play ball with them to get Mirra back. I know they're the ones that took her. It's the only thing that makes sense.
If Russian gangsters grabbed her there would be a ransom demand. Plus the tracker she gave me shows her in Shanghai.
Not enough information yet to devise a meaning to all this, if there is one. Only course of action is to play it out and see what happens.
SEAL TEAM SEXY
Your CED tracking chip is fused to your pelvis. I can track you anywhere on Earth as long as you don't go underground or underwater. Either of those will muffle the signal.
On the bright side, at least you get to go out in the world for a while. I haven't been more than 15 miles from here in the last 10 years.
I LAUGH WHEN I SEE THIS STUFF IN FICTION AS SUPER FUTURISTIC SCI-FI GEAR WHEN WE USE IT EVERY DAY.
You're welcome to take my place.
I should be more scared than I am... maybe it'll hit me when get out there.
SEAL TEAM SEXY
RUFF
Hahah! I think Newton wants to come.

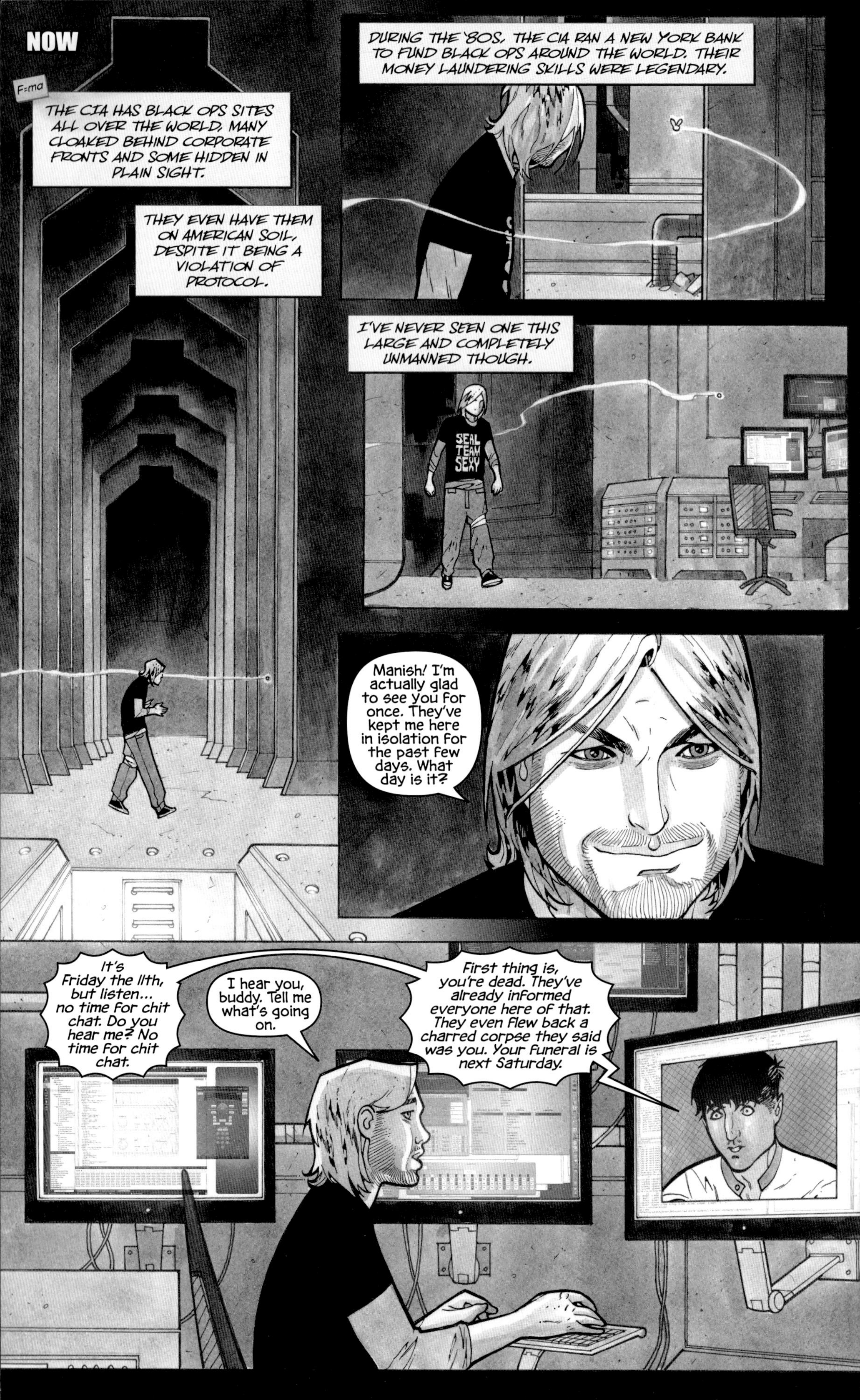
NOW
F=ma
THE CIA HAS BLACK OPS SITES ALL OVER THE WORLD, MANY CLOAKED BEHIND CORPORATE FRONTS AND SOME HIDDEN IN PLAIN SIGHT.
THEY EVEN HAVE THEM ON AMERICAN SOIL, DESPITE IT BEING A VIOLATION OF PROTOCOL.
DURING THE '80S, THE CIA RAN A NEW YORK BANK TO FUND BLACK OPS AROUND THE WORLD. THEIR MONEY LAUNDERING SKILLS WERE LEGENDARY.
I'VE NEVER SEEN ONE THIS LARGE AND COMPLETELY UNMANNED THOUGH.
SEAL TEAM SEXY
Manish! I'm actually glad to see you for once. They've kept me here in isolation for the past few days. What day is it?
It's Friday the 11th, but listen... no time for chit chat. Do you hear me? No time for chit chat.
I hear you, buddy. Tell me what's going on.
First thing is, you're dead. They've already informed everyone here of that. They even flew back a charred corpse they said was you. Your funeral is next Saturday.

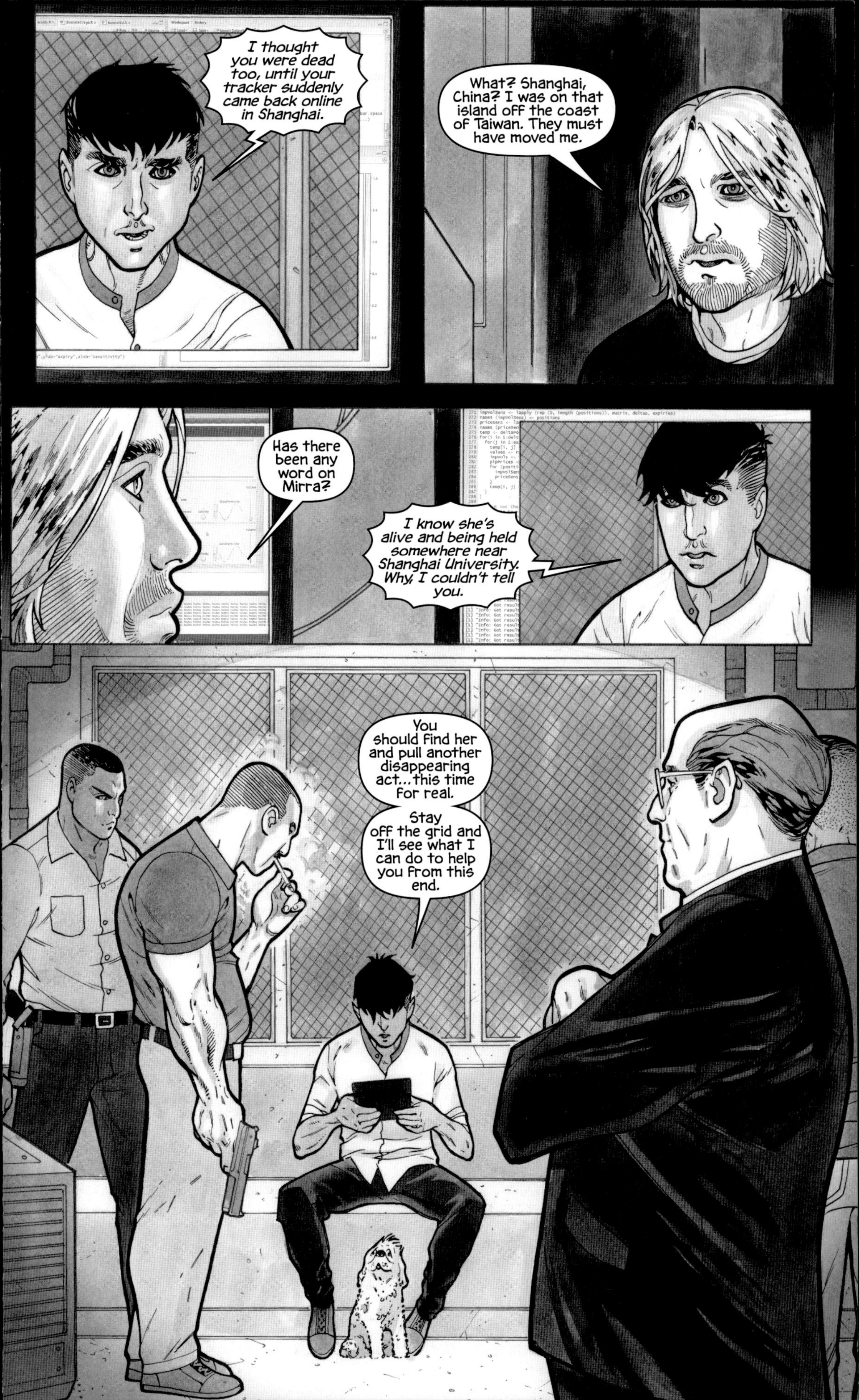
I thought you were dead too, until your tracker suddenly came back online in Shanghai.
What? Shanghai, China? I was on that island off the coast of Taiwan. They must have moved me.
Has there been any word on Mirra?
I know she's alive and being held somewhere near Shanghai University. Why, I couldn't tell you.
You should find her and pull another disappearing act...this time for real.
Stay off the grid and I'll see what I can do to help you from this end.

CHAPTER THREE

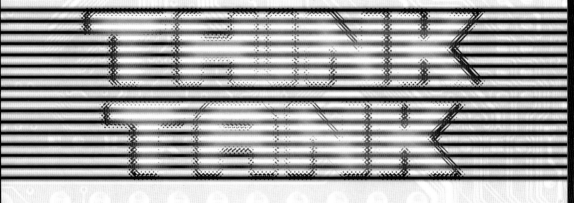

$$\oint \vec{E} \cdot d\vec{A} = \frac{1}{\varepsilon_0} q_{in} \qquad \oint \vec{B} \cdot d\vec{A} = 0 \qquad \oint \vec{E} \cdot d\vec{x} = -\frac{d}{dt}$$

$$\oint \vec{B} \cdot d\vec{l} = \mu_0 I_{in} \qquad \vec{F} = q(\vec{v} \times \vec{B} + \vec{E}) \qquad i = \frac{dq}{dt}$$

oint charge $\quad E = \frac{1}{4\pi\varepsilon_0} \frac{q}{r^2} \qquad V = \frac{1}{4\pi\varepsilon_0} \frac{q}{r} \qquad p = qd$

$$V_f - V_i = -\int_i^f \vec{E} \cdot d\vec{s} \qquad E_x = -\frac{\partial V}{\partial x} \qquad \vec{\tau} = \vec{p} \times \vec{E}$$

$C = \qquad \qquad \varepsilon_0 \frac{A}{d}$

$$R = \qquad \qquad P =$$

R_{eq}

R_{eq}

$$dB = \frac{\mu_0}{4\pi} \frac{}{r^2} \qquad B = \frac{}{2\pi} \frac{}{r}$$

"IF YOU TELL A LIE BIG ENOUGH AND
KEEP REPEATING IT, PEOPLE WILL
EVENTUALLY COME TO BELIEVE IT. THE
LIE CAN BE MAINTAINED ONLY FOR SUCH
TIME AS THE STATE CAN SHIELD THE
PEOPLE FROM THE POLITICAL, ECONOMIC
AND/OR MILITARY CONSEQUENCES OF THE
LIE. IT THUS BECOMES VITALLY IMPORTANT
FOR THE STATE TO USE ALL OF ITS
POWERS TO REPRESS DISSENT, FOR THE
TRUTH IS THE MORTAL ENEMY OF THE
LIE, AND THUS BY EXTENSION, THE TRUTH
IS THE GREATEST ENEMY OF THE STATE."

—JOSEPH GOEBBELS

$$\mathcal{E} = -\frac{d\Phi}{dt} \qquad \mathcal{E} = -N\frac{d\Phi}{dt} \qquad L = \frac{|\varepsilon|}{\left|\frac{di}{dt}\right|} = \frac{N\Phi}{i}$$

$$u_E = \frac{1}{2}\varepsilon_0 E^2 \qquad u_B = \frac{1}{2}\frac{B^2}{\mu_0} \qquad U_B = \frac{1}{2}Li^2$$

$$= q_0 e^{-t/\tau_c} \qquad q = C\mathcal{E}(1-e^{-t/\tau_c}) \qquad i = i_0 e^{-t/\tau_L} \qquad i = \frac{\mathcal{E}}{R}(1-e^{-t/\tau_L})$$

$$= \frac{L}{R} \qquad \tau_c = RC \qquad \mu = NiA \qquad \frac{1}{4\pi\varepsilon_0} = 9\times10^9 \qquad \frac{\mu_0}{4\pi} = 10^{-7}$$

M means 10^6 $\qquad \mu$ means 10^{-6}

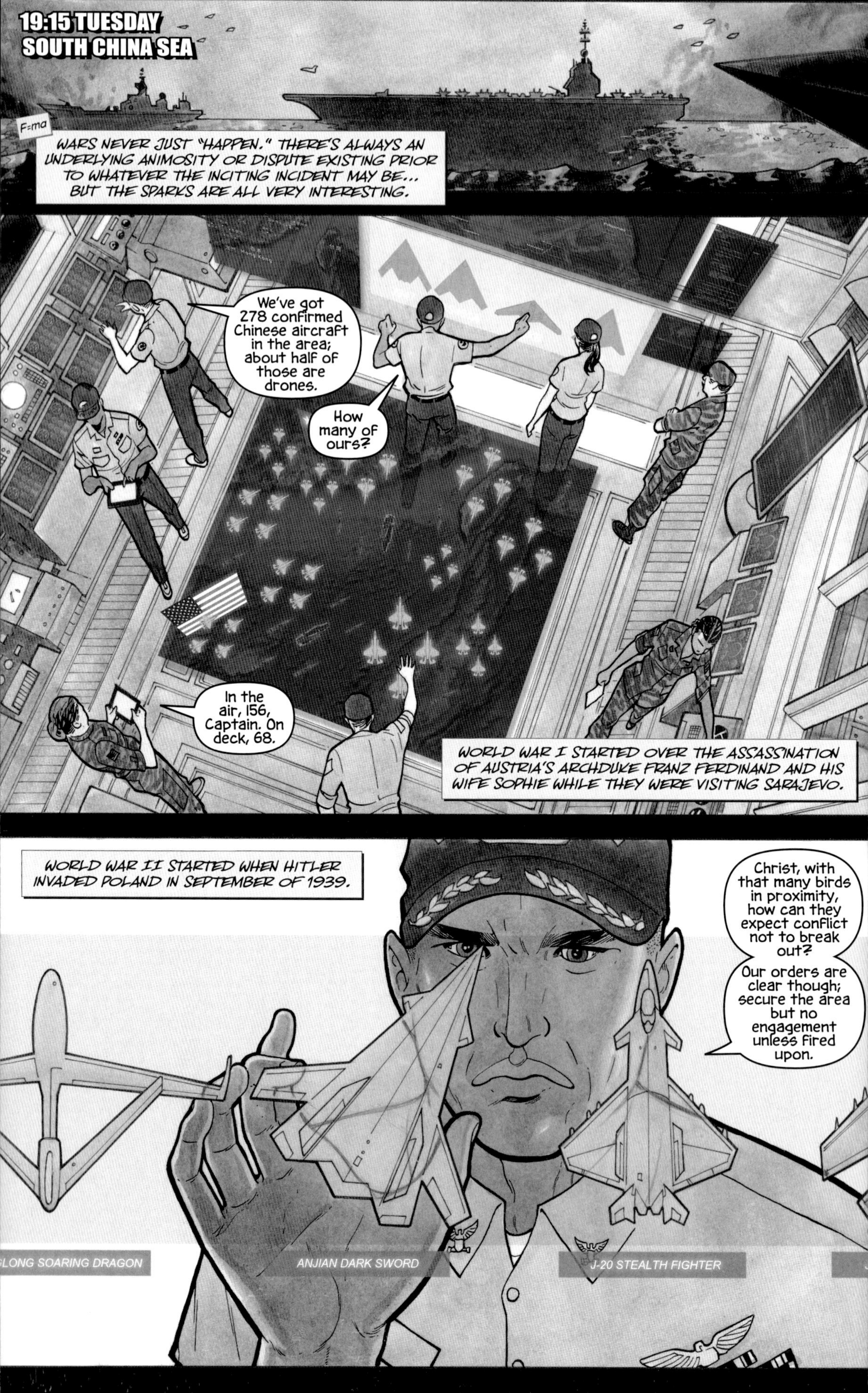
19:15 TUESDAY
SOUTH CHINA SEA
F=ma
WARS NEVER JUST "HAPPEN." THERE'S ALWAYS AN UNDERLYING ANIMOSITY OR DISPUTE EXISTING PRIOR TO WHATEVER THE INCITING INCIDENT MAY BE... BUT THE SPARKS ARE ALL VERY INTERESTING.
We've got 278 confirmed Chinese aircraft in the area; about half of those are drones.
How many of ours?
In the air, 156, Captain. On deck, 68.
WORLD WAR I STARTED OVER THE ASSASSINATION OF AUSTRIA'S ARCHDUKE FRANZ FERDINAND AND HIS WIFE SOPHIE WHILE THEY WERE VISITING SARAJEVO.
WORLD WAR II STARTED WHEN HITLER INVADED POLAND IN SEPTEMBER OF 1939.
Christ, with that many birds in proximity, how can they expect conflict not to break out?
Our orders are clear though; secure the area but no engagement unless fired upon.
LONG SOARING DRAGON
ANJIAN DARK SWORD
J-20 STEALTH FIGHTER

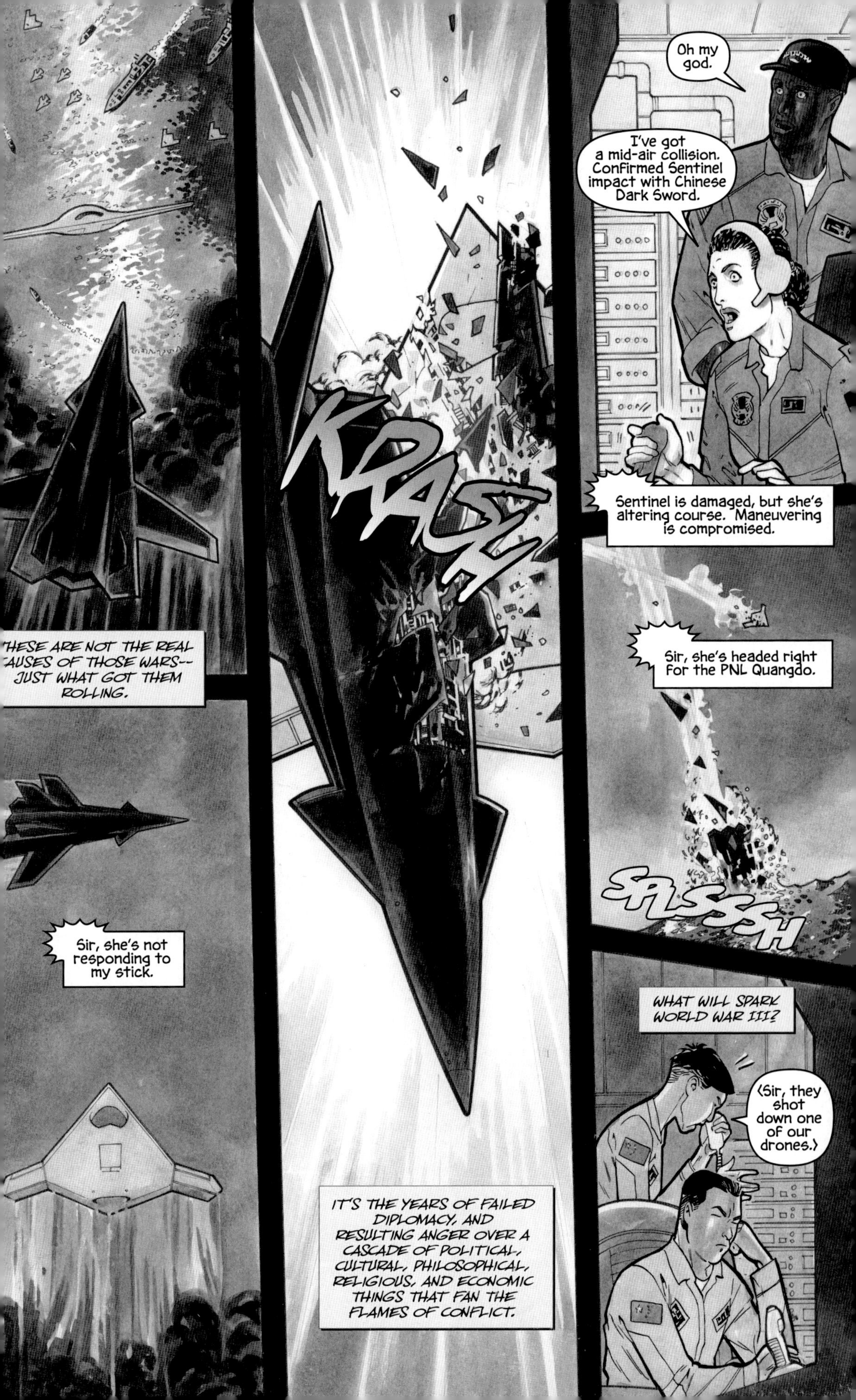
THESE ARE NOT THE REAL CAUSES OF THOSE WARS-- JUST WHAT GOT THEM ROLLING.
Sir, she's not responding to my stick.
KRASH
IT'S THE YEARS OF FAILED DIPLOMACY, AND RESULTING ANGER OVER A CASCADE OF POLITICAL, CULTURAL, PHILOSOPHICAL, RELIGIOUS, AND ECONOMIC THINGS THAT FAN THE FLAMES OF CONFLICT.
Oh my god.
I've got a mid-air collision. Confirmed Sentinel impact with Chinese Dark Sword.
Sentinel is damaged, but she's altering course. Maneuvering is compromised.
Sir, she's headed right for the PNL Quangdo.
SPLSSSH
WHAT WILL SPARK WORLD WAR III?
‹Sir, they shot down one of our drones.›

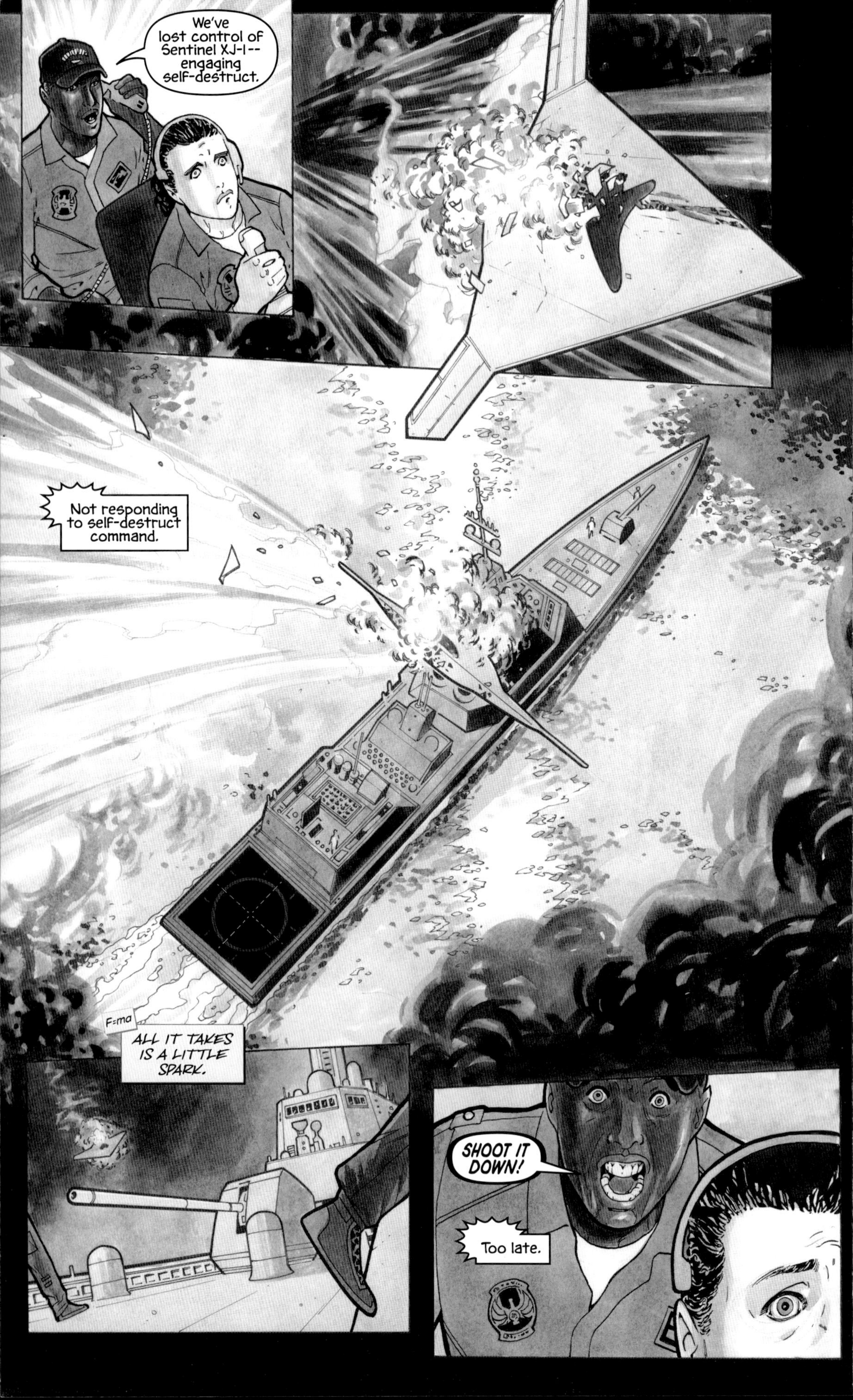
We've lost control of Sentinel XJ-1-- engaging self-destruct.
Not responding to self-destruct command.
F=ma
ALL IT TAKES IS A LITTLE SPARK.
SHOOT IT DOWN!
Too late.

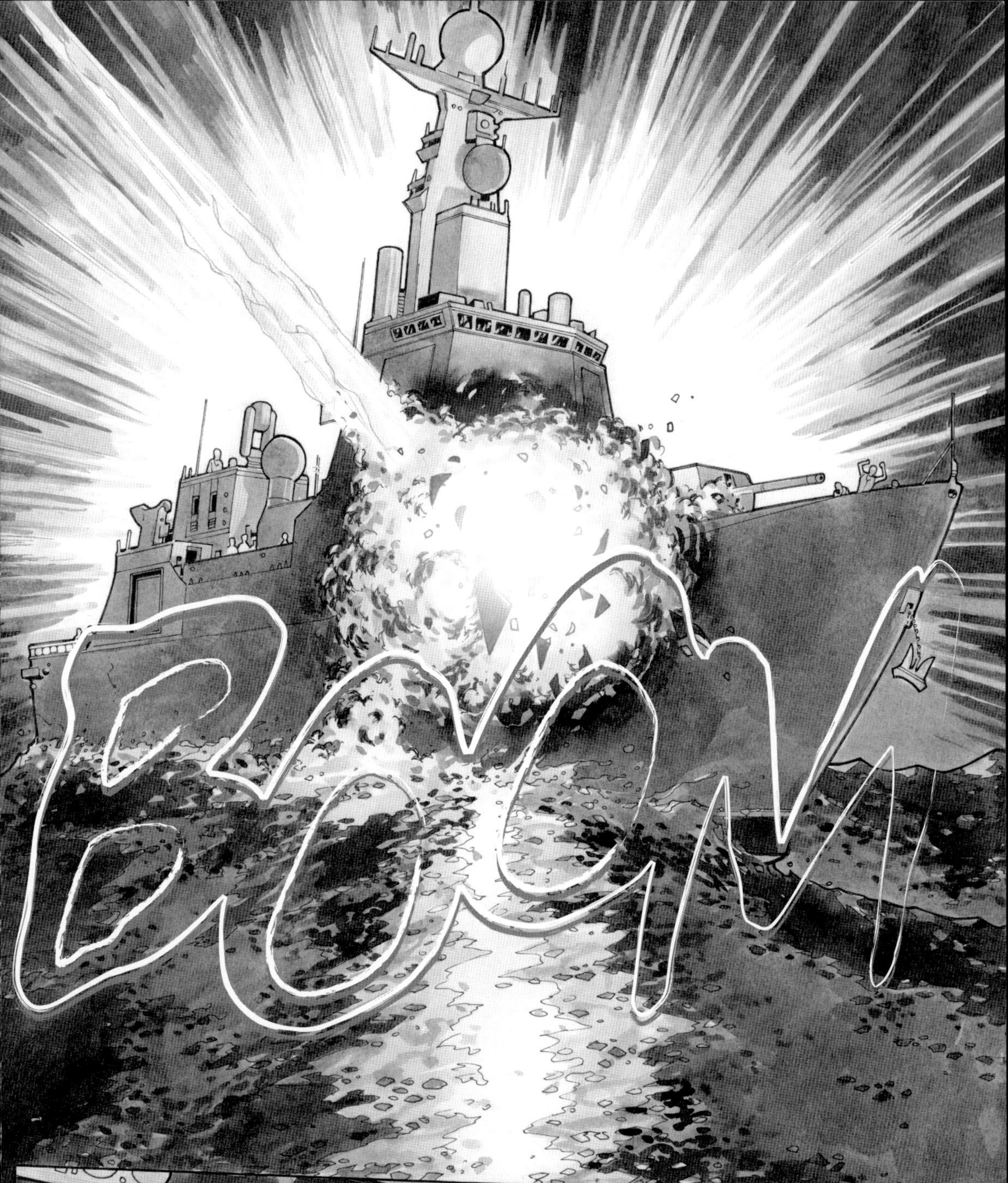
BOOM

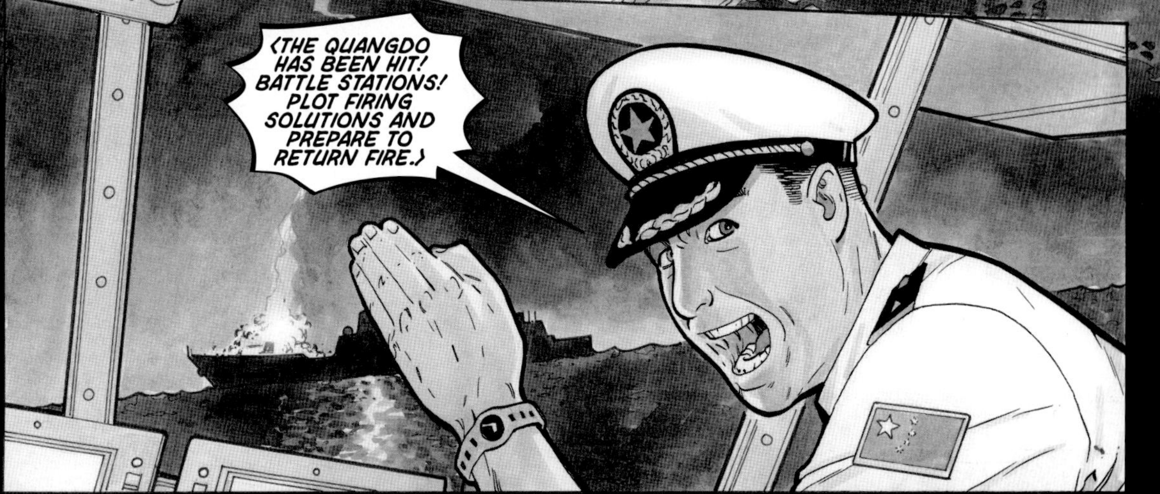
<THE QUANGDO HAS BEEN HIT! BATTLE STATIONS! PLOT FIRING SOLUTIONS AND PREPARE TO RETURN FIRE.>

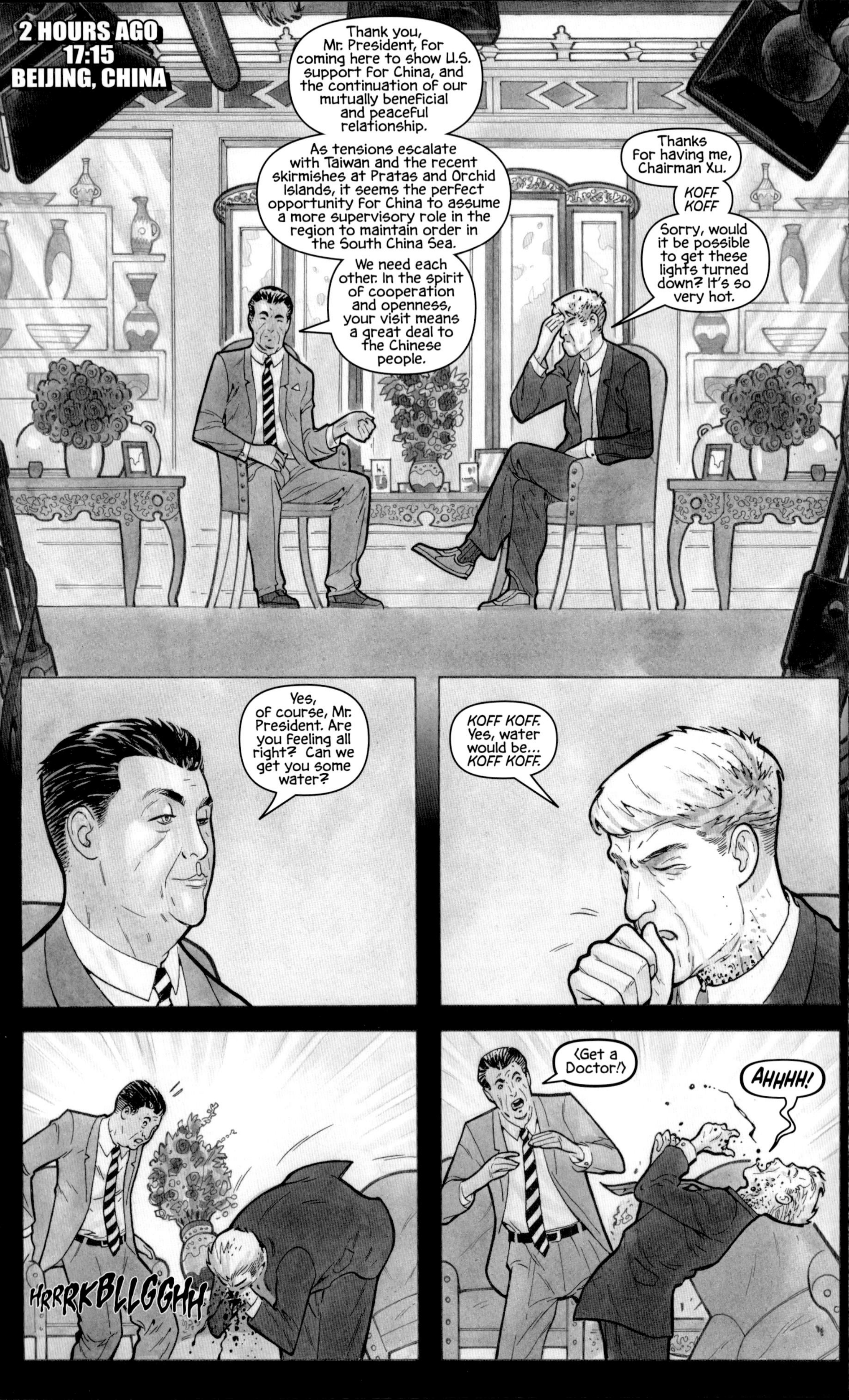
2 HOURS AGO
17:15
BEIJING, CHINA
Thank you, Mr. President, for coming here to show U.S. support for China, and the continuation of our mutually beneficial and peaceful relationship.
As tensions escalate with Taiwan and the recent skirmishes at Pratas and Orchid Islands, it seems the perfect opportunity for China to assume a more supervisory role in the region to maintain order in the South China Sea.
We need each other. In the spirit of cooperation and openness, your visit means a great deal to the Chinese people.
Thanks for having me, Chairman Xu.
KOFF KOFF
Sorry, would it be possible to get these lights turned down? It's so very hot.
Yes, of course, Mr. President. Are you feeling all right? Can we get you some water?
KOFF KOFF. Yes, water would be... KOFF KOFF.
HRRRKBLLGGHH
‹Get a Doctor!›
AHHHH!

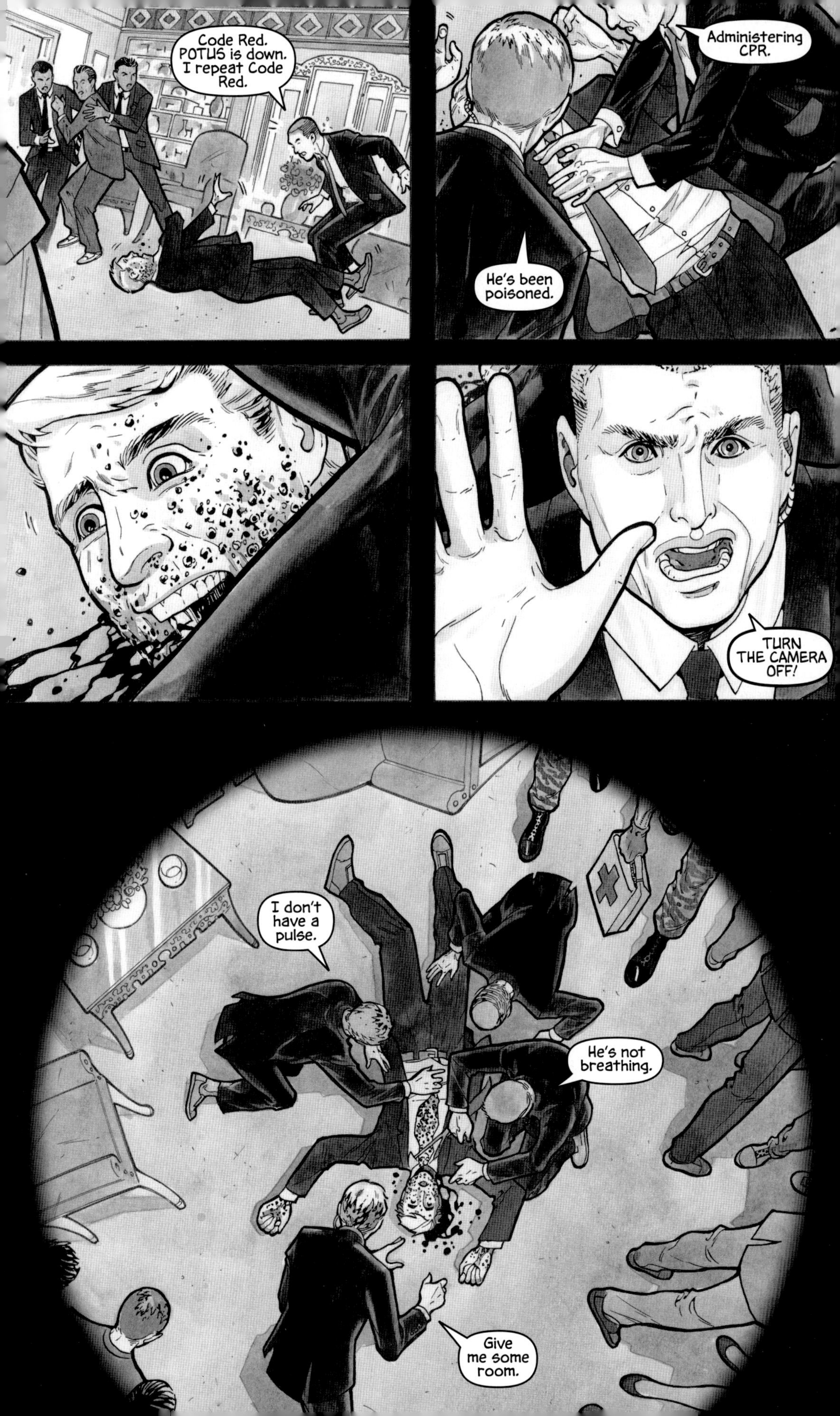
Code Red. POTUS is down. I repeat Code Red.
Administering CPR.
He's been poisoned.
TURN THE CAMERA OFF!
I don't have a pulse.
He's not breathing.
Give me some room.

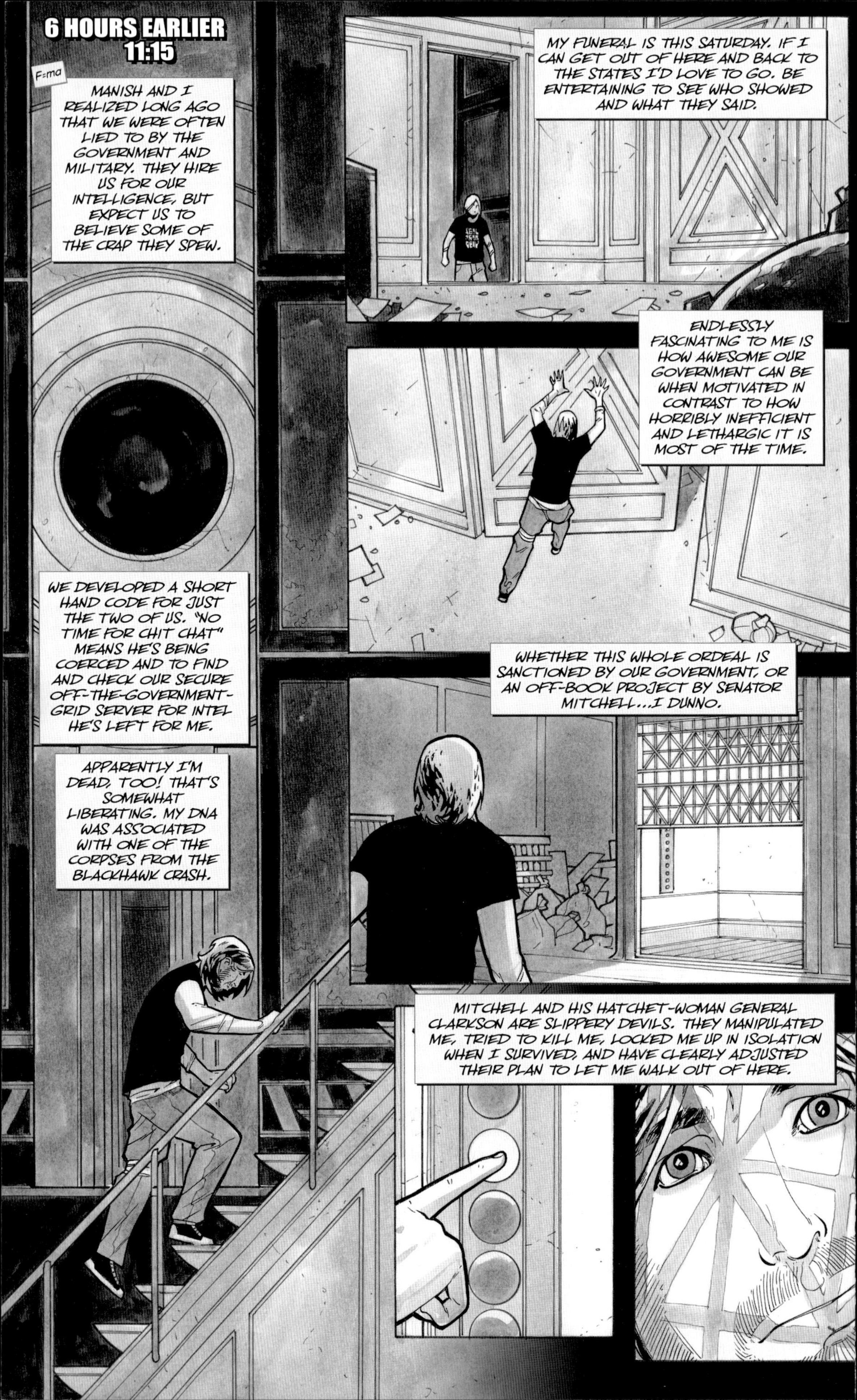

6 HOURS EARLIER
11:15
F=ma
MANISH AND I REALIZED LONG AGO THAT WE WERE OFTEN LIED TO BY THE GOVERNMENT AND MILITARY. THEY HIRE US FOR OUR INTELLIGENCE, BUT EXPECT US TO BELIEVE SOME OF THE CRAP THEY SPEW.
MY FUNERAL IS THIS SATURDAY. IF I CAN GET OUT OF HERE AND BACK TO THE STATES I'D LOVE TO GO. BE ENTERTAINING TO SEE WHO SHOWED AND WHAT THEY SAID.
ENDLESSLY FASCINATING TO ME IS HOW AWESOME OUR GOVERNMENT CAN BE WHEN MOTIVATED IN CONTRAST TO HOW HORRIBLY INEFFICIENT AND LETHARGIC IT IS MOST OF THE TIME.
WE DEVELOPED A SHORT HAND CODE FOR JUST THE TWO OF US. "NO TIME FOR CHIT CHAT" MEANS HE'S BEING COERCED AND TO FIND AND CHECK OUR SECURE OFF-THE-GOVERNMENT-GRID SERVER FOR INTEL HE'S LEFT FOR ME.
WHETHER THIS WHOLE ORDEAL IS SANCTIONED BY OUR GOVERNMENT, OR AN OFF-BOOK PROJECT BY SENATOR MITCHELL...I DUNNO.
APPARENTLY I'M DEAD, TOO! THAT'S SOMEWHAT LIBERATING. MY DNA WAS ASSOCIATED WITH ONE OF THE CORPSES FROM THE BLACKHAWK CRASH.
MITCHELL AND HIS HATCHET-WOMAN GENERAL CLARKSON ARE SLIPPERY DEVILS. THEY MANIPULATED ME, TRIED TO KILL ME, LOCKED ME UP IN ISOLATION WHEN I SURVIVED, AND HAVE CLEARLY ADJUSTED THEIR PLAN TO LET ME WALK OUT OF HERE.

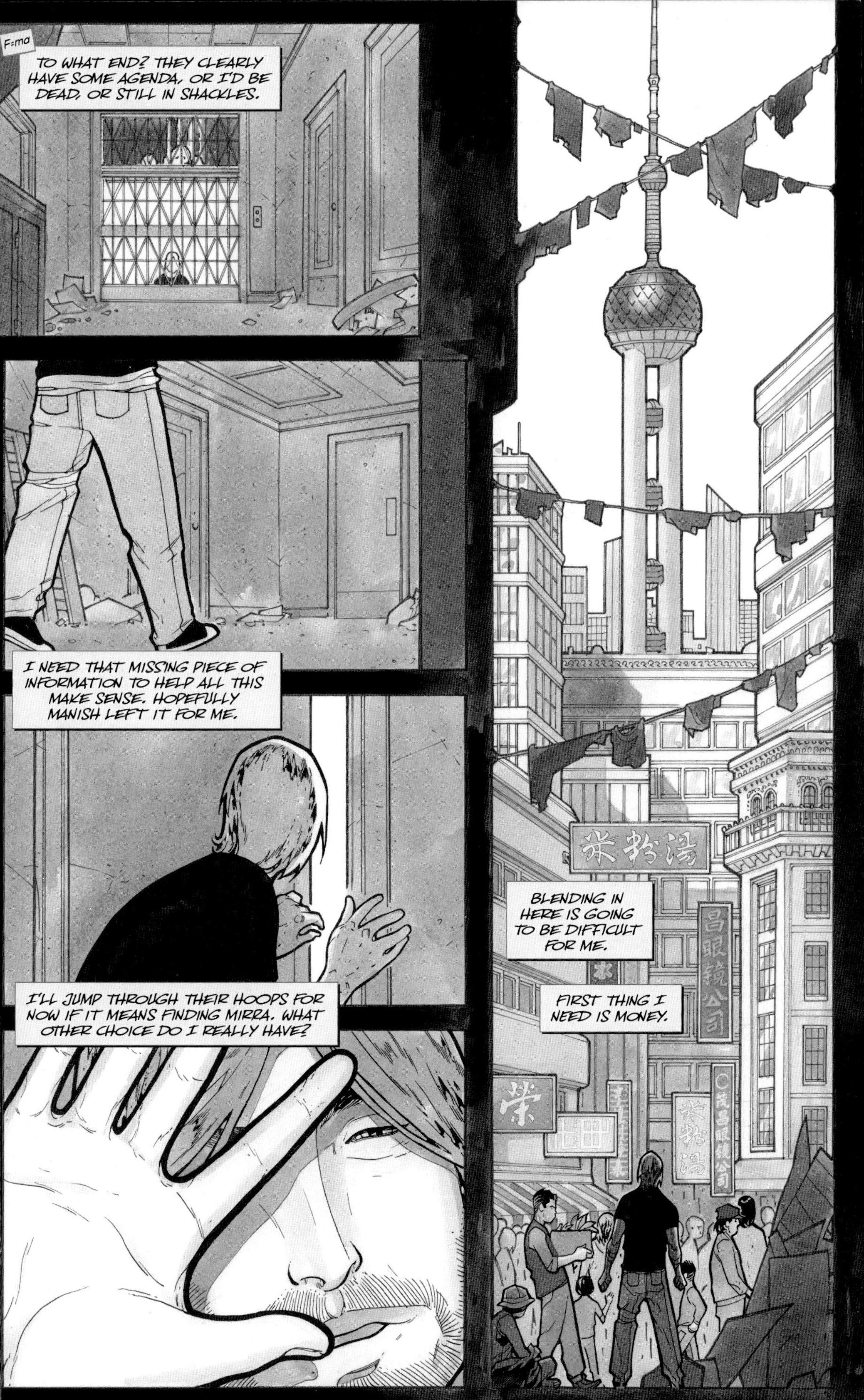
F=ma
TO WHAT END? THEY CLEARLY HAVE SOME AGENDA, OR I'D BE DEAD, OR STILL IN SHACKLES.
I NEED THAT MISSING PIECE OF INFORMATION TO HELP ALL THIS MAKE SENSE. HOPEFULLY MANISH LEFT IT FOR ME.
I'LL JUMP THROUGH THEIR HOOPS FOR NOW IF IT MEANS FINDING MIRRA. WHAT OTHER CHOICE DO I REALLY HAVE?
BLENDING IN HERE IS GOING TO BE DIFFICULT FOR ME.
FIRST THING I NEED IS MONEY.

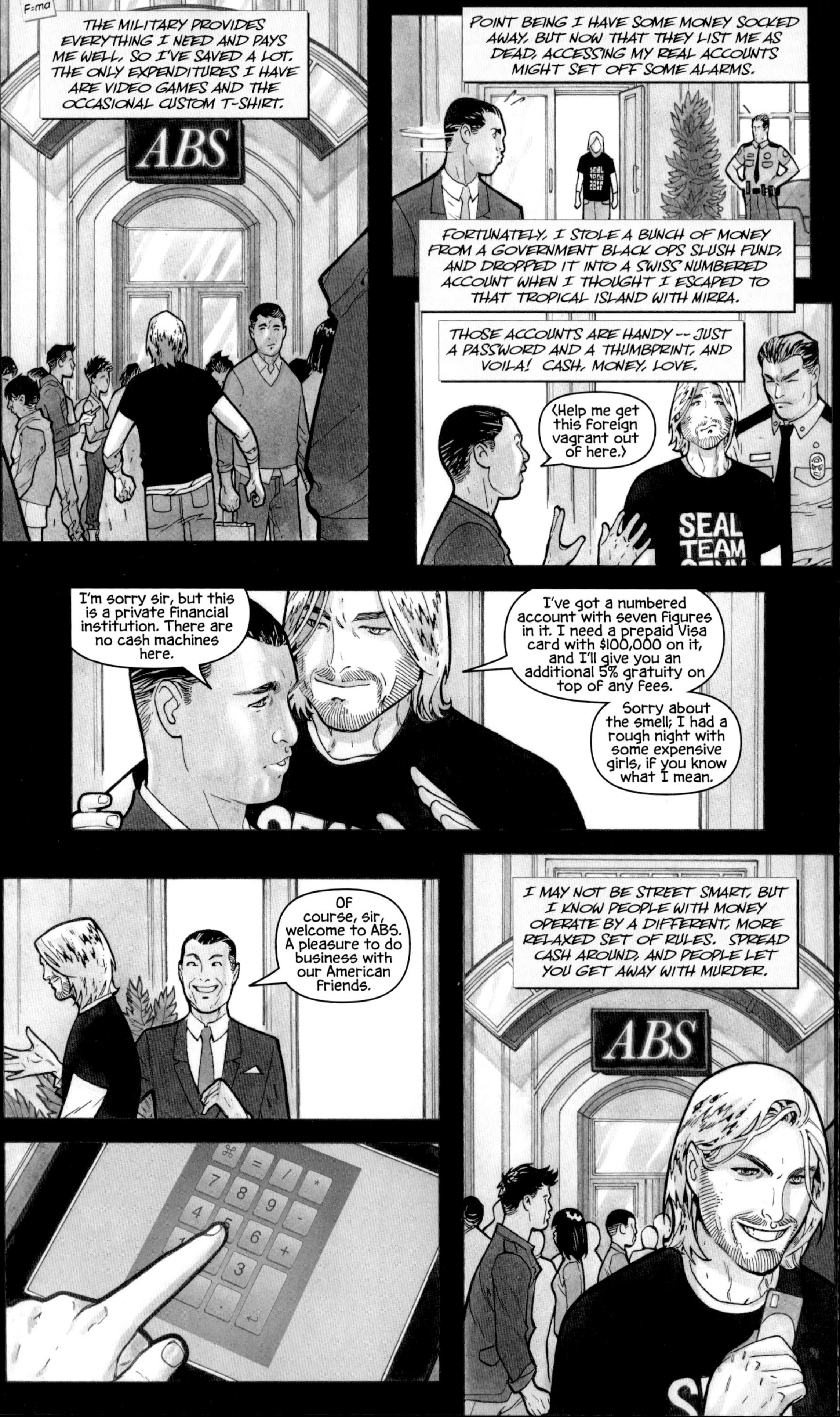
F=ma
THE MILITARY PROVIDES EVERYTHING I NEED AND PAYS ME WELL, SO I'VE SAVED A LOT. THE ONLY EXPENDITURES I HAVE ARE VIDEO GAMES AND THE OCCASIONAL CUSTOM T-SHIRT.
ABS
POINT BEING I HAVE SOME MONEY SOCKED AWAY, BUT NOW THAT THEY LIST ME AS DEAD, ACCESSING MY REAL ACCOUNTS MIGHT SET OFF SOME ALARMS.
FORTUNATELY, I STOLE A BUNCH OF MONEY FROM A GOVERNMENT BLACK OPS SLUSH FUND, AND DROPPED IT INTO A SWISS NUMBERED ACCOUNT WHEN I THOUGHT I ESCAPED TO THAT TROPICAL ISLAND WITH MIRRA.
THOSE ACCOUNTS ARE HANDY -- JUST A PASSWORD AND A THUMBPRINT, AND VOILA! CASH, MONEY, LOVE.
⟨Help me get this foreign vagrant out of here.⟩
SEAL TEAM
I'm sorry sir, but this is a private financial institution. There are no cash machines here.
I've got a numbered account with seven figures in it. I need a prepaid Visa card with $100,000 on it, and I'll give you an additional 5% gratuity on top of any fees.
Sorry about the smell; I had a rough night with some expensive girls, if you know what I mean.
Of course, sir, welcome to ABS. A pleasure to do business with our American friends.
I MAY NOT BE STREET SMART, BUT I KNOW PEOPLE WITH MONEY OPERATE BY A DIFFERENT, MORE RELAXED SET OF RULES. SPREAD CASH AROUND, AND PEOPLE LET YOU GET AWAY WITH MURDER.
ABS

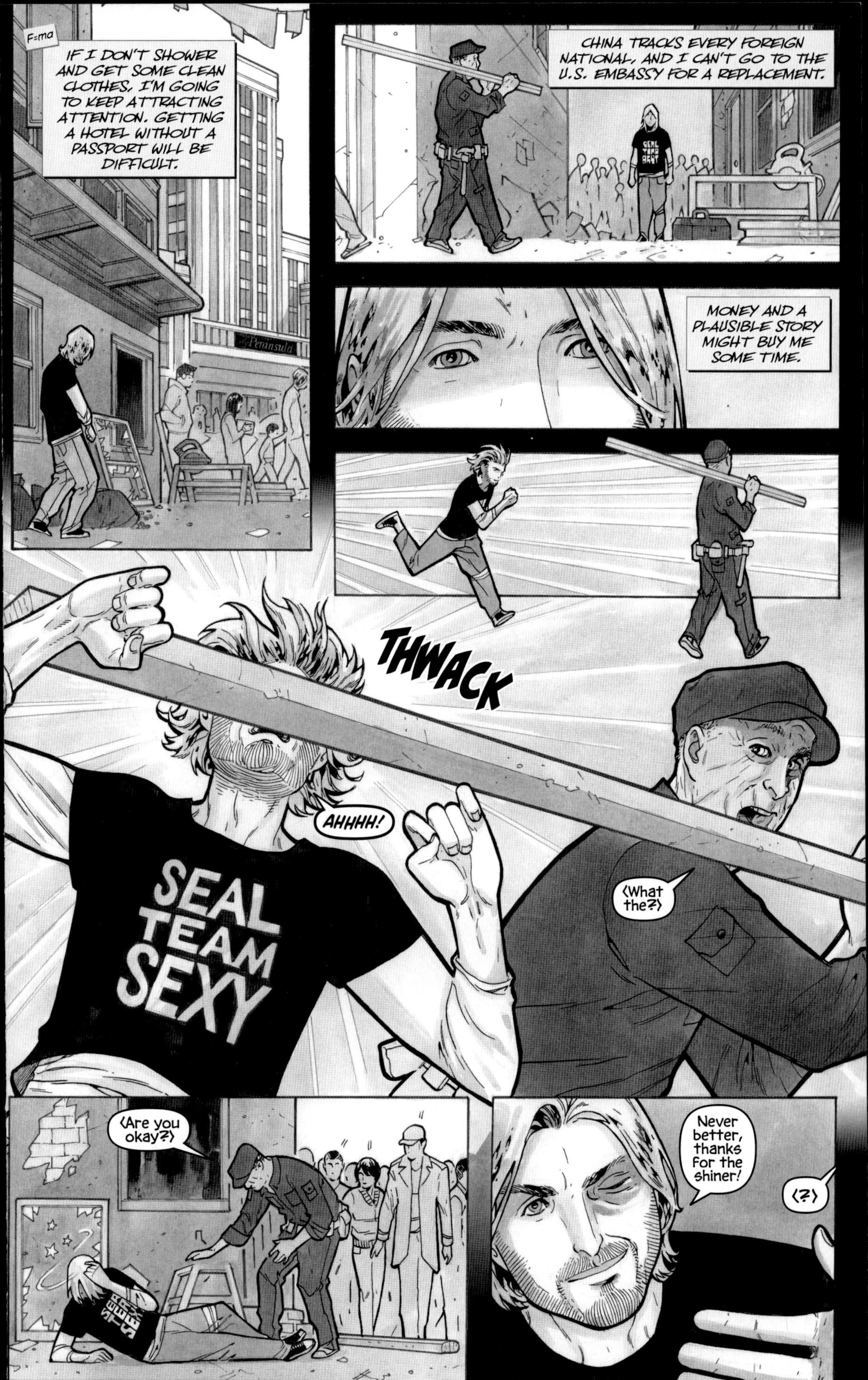
F=ma
IF I DON'T SHOWER AND GET SOME CLEAN CLOTHES, I'M GOING TO KEEP ATTRACTING ATTENTION. GETTING A HOTEL WITHOUT A PASSPORT WILL BE DIFFICULT.
Peninsula
CHINA TRACKS EVERY FOREIGN NATIONAL, AND I CAN'T GO TO THE U.S. EMBASSY FOR A REPLACEMENT.
MONEY AND A PLAUSIBLE STORY MIGHT BUY ME SOME TIME.
THWACK
AHHHH!
SEAL TEAM SEXY
⟨What the?⟩
⟨Are you okay?⟩
Never better, thanks for the shiner!
⟨?⟩

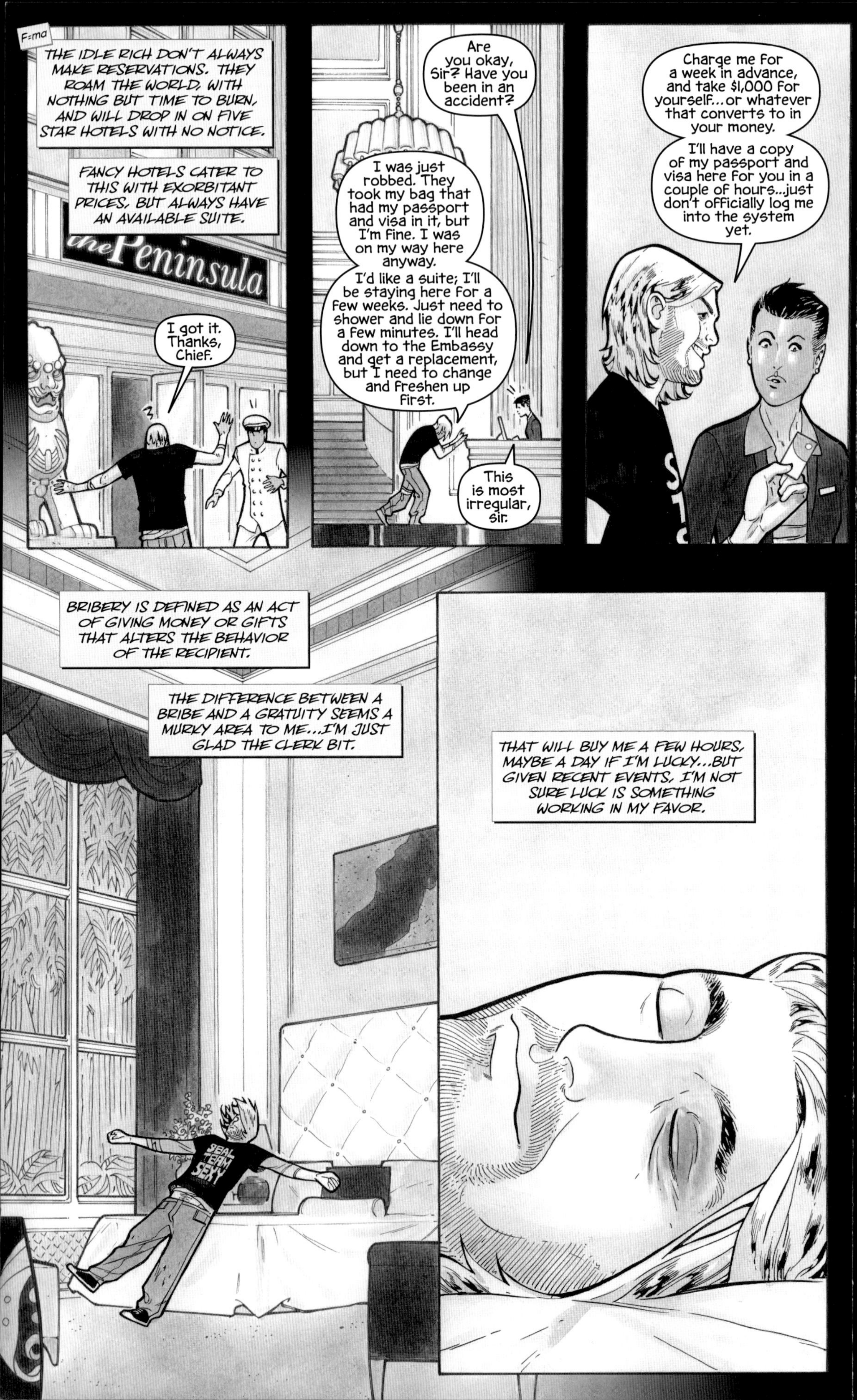
F=ma
THE IDLE RICH DON'T ALWAYS MAKE RESERVATIONS. THEY ROAM THE WORLD, WITH NOTHING BUT TIME TO BURN, AND WILL DROP IN ON FIVE STAR HOTELS WITH NO NOTICE.
FANCY HOTELS CATER TO THIS WITH EXORBITANT PRICES, BUT ALWAYS HAVE AN AVAILABLE SUITE.
the Peninsula
I got it. Thanks, Chief.
Are you okay, Sir? Have you been in an accident?
I was just robbed. They took my bag that had my passport and visa in it, but I'm fine. I was on my way here anyway.
I'd like a suite; I'll be staying here for a few weeks. Just need to shower and lie down for a few minutes. I'll head down to the Embassy and get a replacement, but I need to change and freshen up first.
This is most irregular, sir.
Charge me for a week in advance, and take $1,000 for yourself...or whatever that converts to in your money.
I'll have a copy of my passport and visa here for you in a couple of hours...just don't officially log me into the system yet.
BRIBERY IS DEFINED AS AN ACT OF GIVING MONEY OR GIFTS THAT ALTERS THE BEHAVIOR OF THE RECIPIENT.
THE DIFFERENCE BETWEEN A BRIBE AND A GRATUITY SEEMS A MURKY AREA TO ME...I'M JUST GLAD THE CLERK BIT.
SEAL TEAM SEXY
THAT WILL BUY ME A FEW HOURS, MAYBE A DAY IF I'M LUCKY...BUT GIVEN RECENT EVENTS, I'M NOT SURE LUCK IS SOMETHING WORKING IN MY FAVOR.

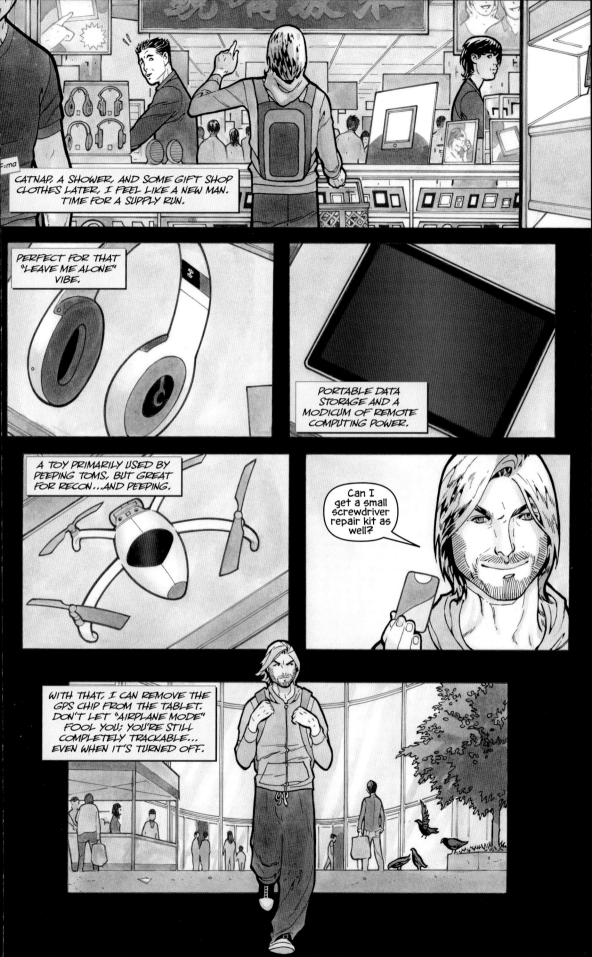

CATNAP, A SHOWER, AND SOME GIFT SHOP CLOTHES LATER, I FEEL LIKE A NEW MAN. TIME FOR A SUPPLY RUN.

PERFECT FOR THAT "LEAVE ME ALONE" VIBE.

PORTABLE DATA STORAGE AND A MODICUM OF REMOTE COMPUTING POWER.

A TOY PRIMARILY USED BY PEEPING TOMS, BUT GREAT FOR RECON...AND PEEPING.

Can I get a small screwdriver repair kit as well?

WITH THAT, I CAN REMOVE THE GPS CHIP FROM THE TABLET. DON'T LET "AIRPLANE MODE" FOOL YOU; YOU'RE STILL COMPLETELY TRACKABLE... EVEN WHEN IT'S TURNED OFF.

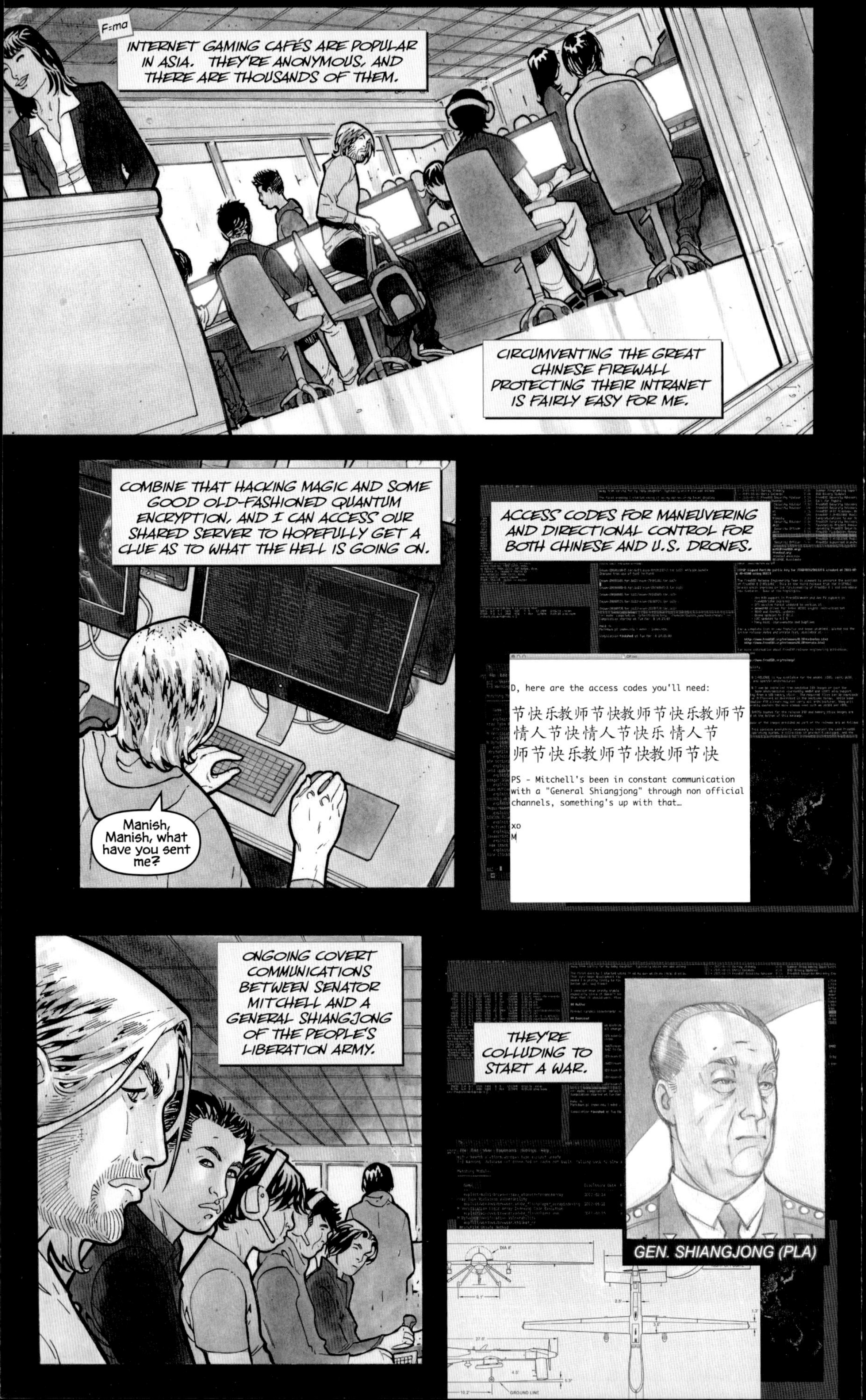
F=ma
INTERNET GAMING CAFÉS ARE POPULAR IN ASIA. THEY'RE ANONYMOUS, AND THERE ARE THOUSANDS OF THEM.
CIRCUMVENTING THE GREAT CHINESE FIREWALL PROTECTING THEIR INTRANET IS FAIRLY EASY FOR ME.
COMBINE THAT HACKING MAGIC AND SOME GOOD OLD-FASHIONED QUANTUM ENCRYPTION, AND I CAN ACCESS OUR SHARED SERVER TO HOPEFULLY GET A CLUE AS TO WHAT THE HELL IS GOING ON.
Manish, Manish, what have you sent me?
ACCESS CODES FOR MANEUVERING AND DIRECTIONAL CONTROL FOR BOTH CHINESE AND U.S. DRONES.
D, here are the access codes you'll need:
节快乐教师节快教师节快乐教师节
情人节快情人节快乐 情人节
师节快乐教师节快教师节快
PS - Mitchell's been in constant communication with a "General Shiangjong" through non official channels, something's up with that…
xo
M
ONGOING COVERT COMMUNICATIONS BETWEEN SENATOR MITCHELL AND A GENERAL SHIANGJONG OF THE PEOPLE'S LIBERATION ARMY.
THEY'RE COLLUDING TO START A WAR.
GEN. SHIANGJONG (PLA)
GROUND LINE

F=ma

IF THEY WANT TO BLOW EACH OTHER UP, WHY SHOULD I CARE?

TRANSFERRING DATA...

I WANT TO FIND MIRRA AND DISAPPEAR FOR REAL THIS TIME.

Why do they have you at Shanghai University, honey?

Mirra Sway
Location:
31.3183 N, 121.2872 E
Shanghai University

Wonder if I know anyone over there?

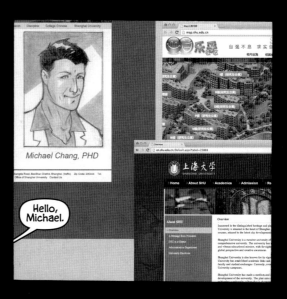

Michael Chang, PHD

Hello, Michael.

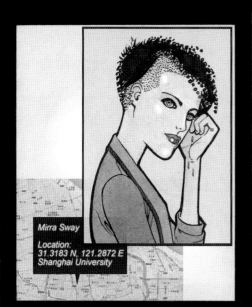

Mirra Sway

Location:
31.3183 N, 121.2872 E
Shanghai University

DR. MICHAEL CHANG USED TO CHEAT OFF OF ME IN ORGANIC CHEMISTRY BACK AT CAL TECH. HE'LL DEFINITELY SEE ME, BUT CALLING AHEAD WOULD BE A MISTAKE. TIME TO DROP BY AN OLD FRIEND UNANNOUNCED.

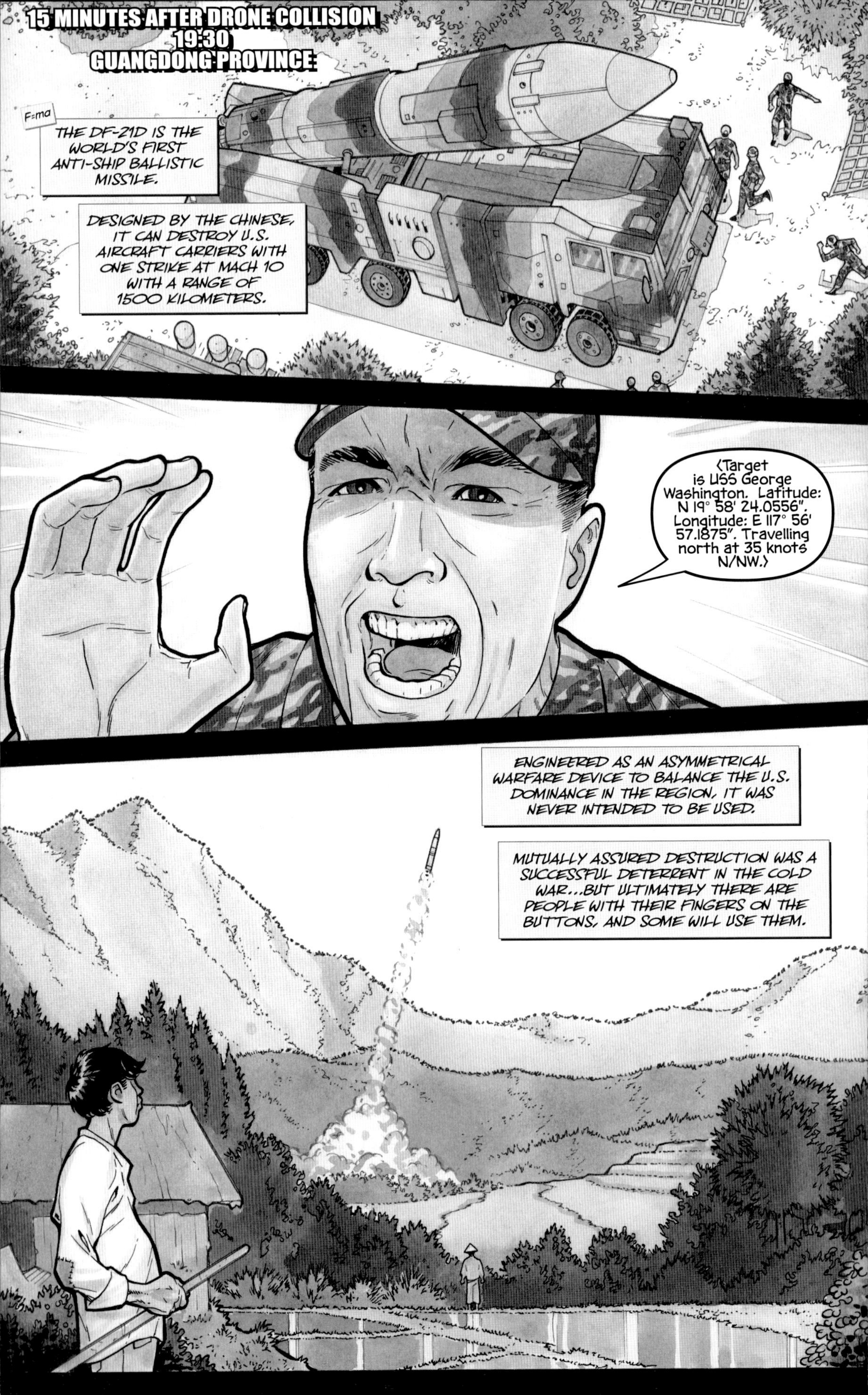
15 MINUTES AFTER DRONE COLLISION
19:30
GUANGDONG PROVINCE:
F=ma
THE DF-21D IS THE WORLD'S FIRST ANTI-SHIP BALLISTIC MISSILE.
DESIGNED BY THE CHINESE, IT CAN DESTROY U.S. AIRCRAFT CARRIERS WITH ONE STRIKE AT MACH 10 WITH A RANGE OF 1500 KILOMETERS.
⟨Target is USS George Washington. Latitude: N 19° 58' 24.0556". Longitude: E 117° 56' 57.1875". Travelling north at 35 knots N/NW.⟩
ENGINEERED AS AN ASYMMETRICAL WARFARE DEVICE TO BALANCE THE U.S. DOMINANCE IN THE REGION, IT WAS NEVER INTENDED TO BE USED.
MUTUALLY ASSURED DESTRUCTION WAS A SUCCESSFUL DETERRENT IN THE COLD WAR...BUT ULTIMATELY THERE ARE PEOPLE WITH THEIR FINGERS ON THE BUTTONS, AND SOME WILL USE THEM.

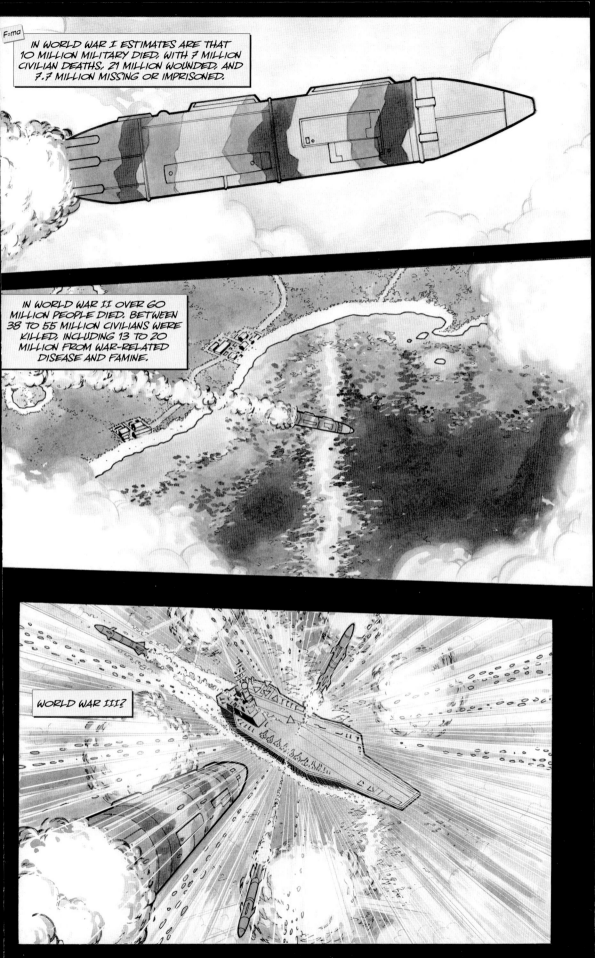

F=ma

IN WORLD WAR I ESTIMATES ARE THAT
10 MILLION MILITARY DIED, WITH 7 MILLION
CIVILIAN DEATHS, 21 MILLION WOUNDED, AND
7.7 MILLION MISSING OR IMPRISONED.

IN WORLD WAR II OVER 60
MILLION PEOPLE DIED. BETWEEN
38 TO 55 MILLION CIVILIANS WERE
KILLED, INCLUDING 13 TO 20
MILLION FROM WAR-RELATED
DISEASE AND FAMINE.

WORLD WAR III?

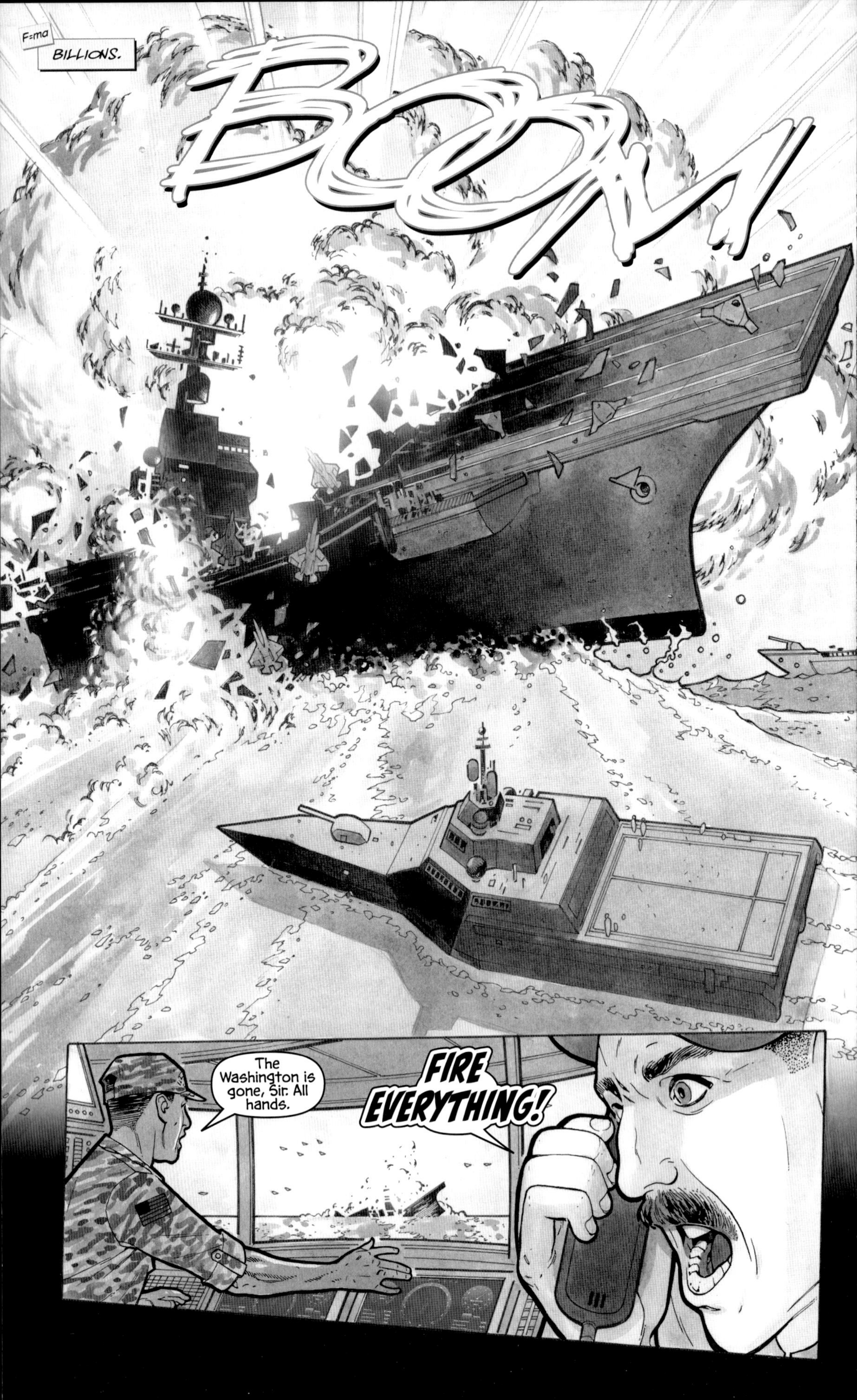
F=ma
BILLIONS.
BOOM
The Washington is gone, Sir. All hands.
FIRE EVERYTHING!

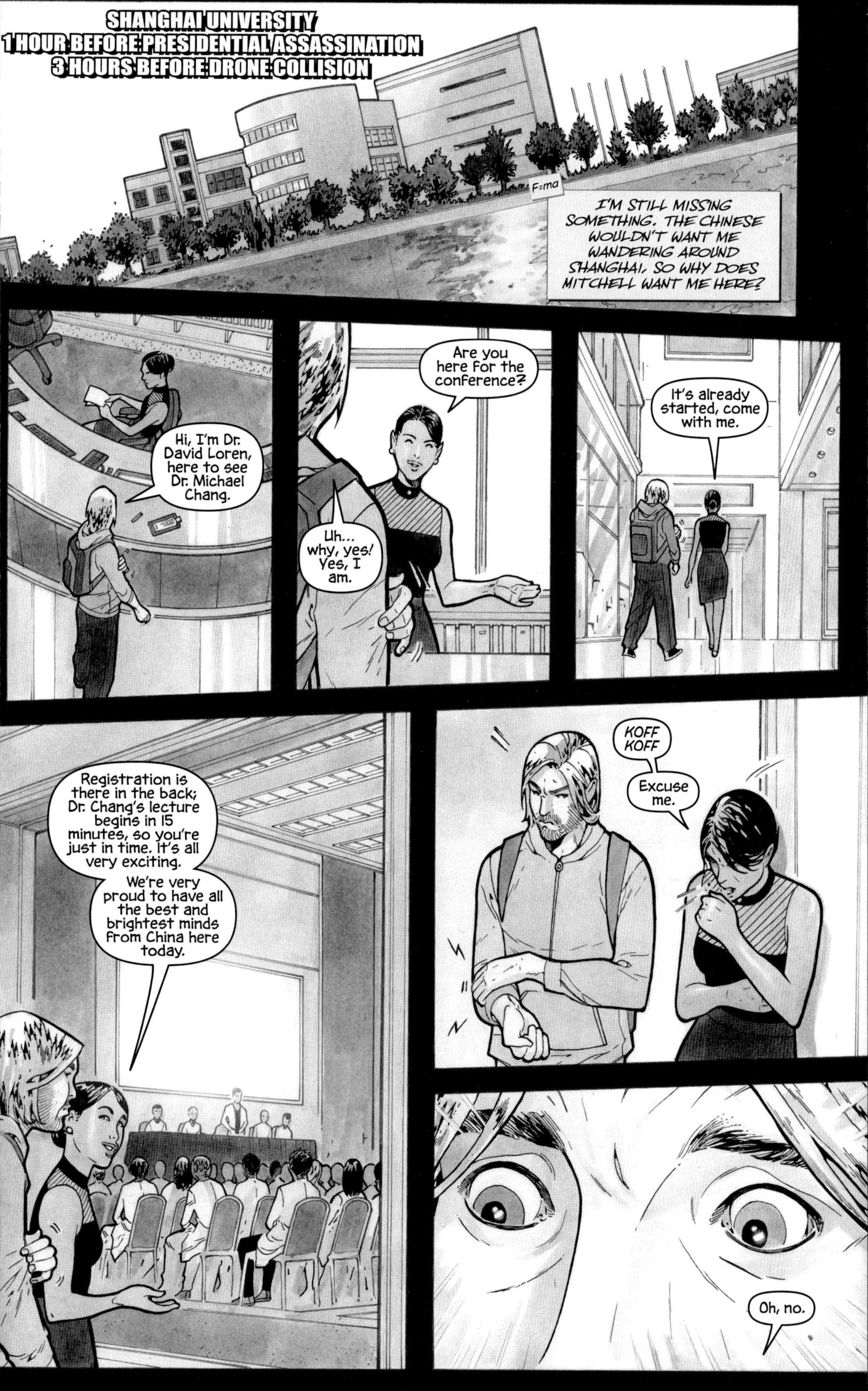
SHANGHAI UNIVERSITY
1 HOUR BEFORE PRESIDENTIAL ASSASSINATION
3 HOURS BEFORE DRONE COLLISION
F=ma
I'M STILL MISSING SOMETHING. THE CHINESE WOULDN'T WANT ME WANDERING AROUND SHANGHAI, SO WHY DOES MITCHELL WANT ME HERE?
Hi, I'm Dr. David Loren, here to see Dr. Michael Chang.
Are you here for the conference?
Uh... why, yes! Yes, I am.
It's already started, come with me.
Registration is there in the back; Dr. Chang's lecture begins in 15 minutes, so you're just in time. It's all very exciting.
We're very proud to have all the best and brightest minds from China here today.
KOFF KOFF
Excuse me.
Oh, no.

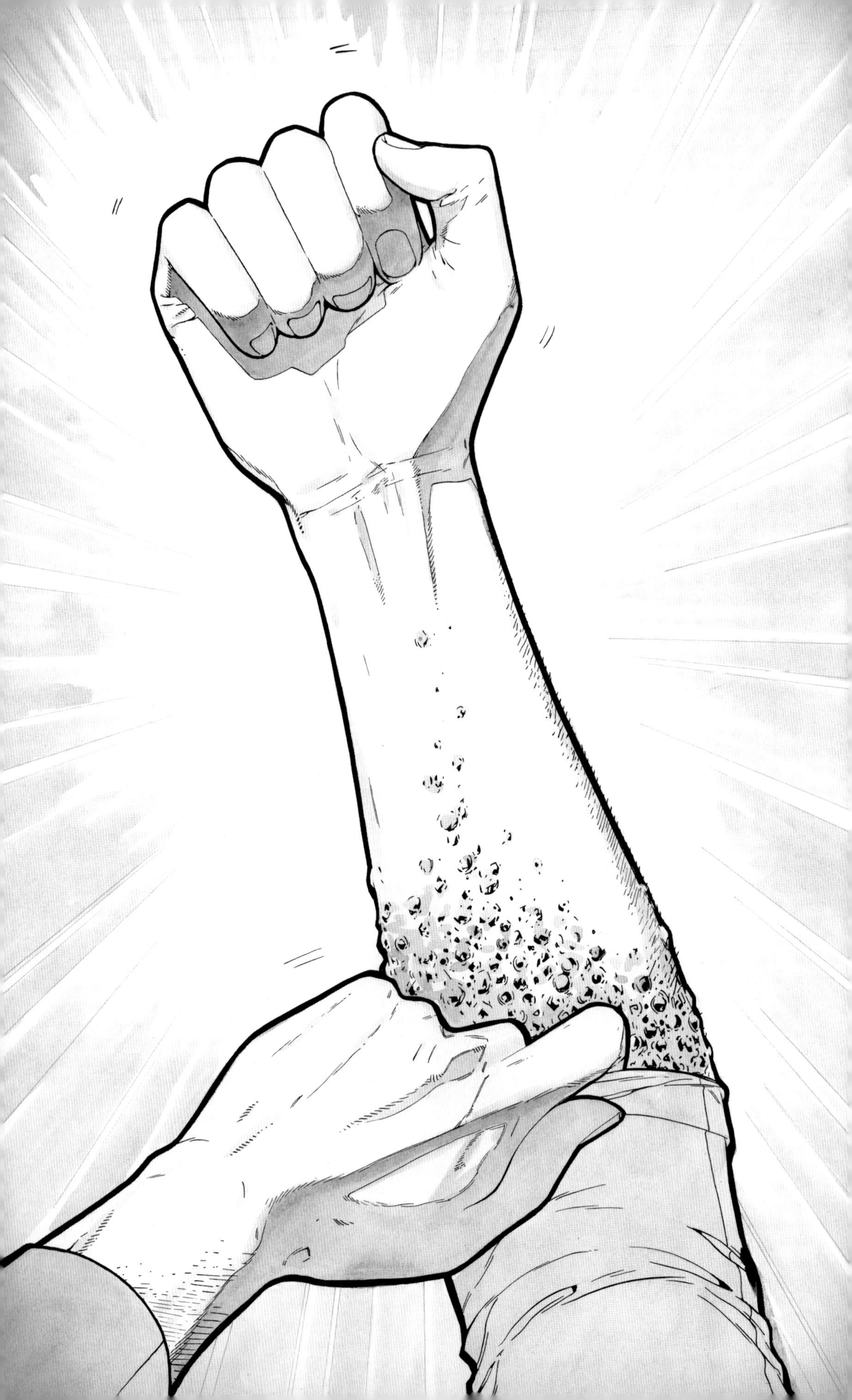

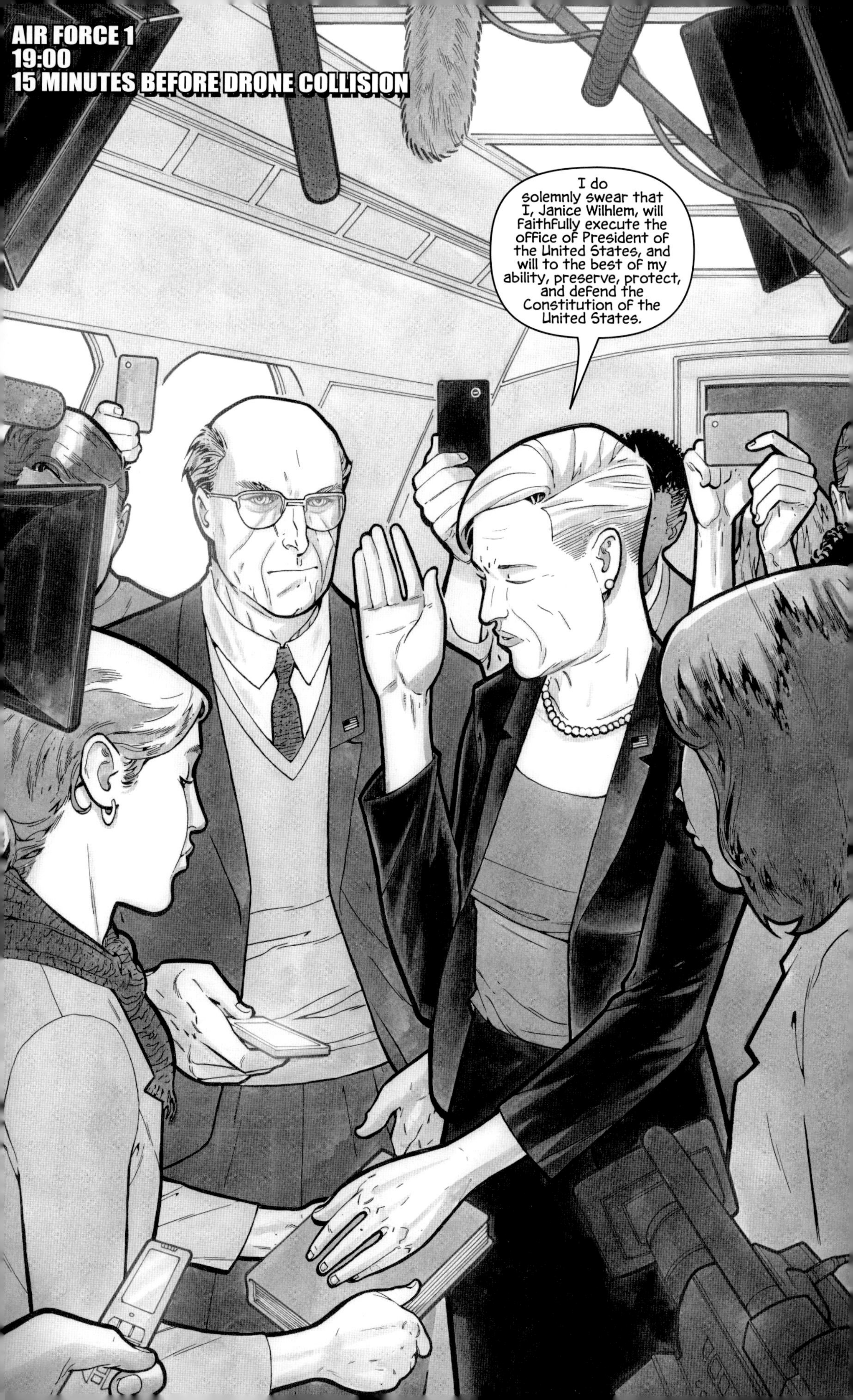
AIR FORCE 1
19:00
15 MINUTES BEFORE DRONE COLLISION
I do solemnly swear that I, Janice Wilhlem, will faithfully execute the office of President of the United States, and will to the best of my ability, preserve, protect, and defend the Constitution of the United States.

CHAPTER FOUR

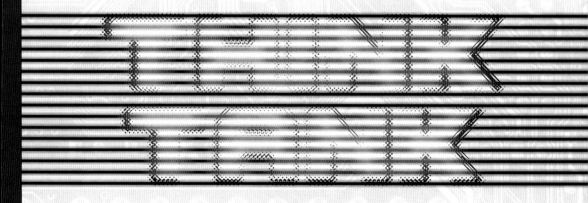

$$\oint \vec{E} \cdot d\vec{A} = \frac{1}{\varepsilon_0} q_{in} \qquad \oint \vec{B} \cdot d\vec{A} = 0 \qquad \oint \vec{E} \cdot d\vec{\ell} = -\frac{d}{dt}\int \vec{B} \, d\vec{A}$$

$$\oint \vec{B} \cdot d\vec{\ell} = \mu_0 I_{in} \qquad \vec{F} = q(\vec{v} \times \vec{B} + \vec{E}) \qquad i = \frac{dq}{dt}$$

point charge

$p = qd$

$V_f - V_i$

$\vec{\tau} = \vec{p} \times \vec{E}$

$C = \frac{Q}{V}$

$C = \varepsilon_0 \frac{A}{d}$

$R = \frac{V}{i}$

R_{eq}

$\frac{1}{R_{eq}}$

$d\vec{B} = \frac{\mu_0}{4\pi}$

$\vec{\tau} = \vec{\mu} \times$

"I SEE IN THE NEAR FUTURE A CRISIS APPROACHING THAT UNNERVES ME AND CAUSES ME TO TREMBLE FOR THE SAFETY OF MY COUNTRY. AS A RESULT OF THE WAR, CORPORATIONS HAVE BEEN ENTHRONED AND AN ERA OF CORRUPTION IN HIGH PLACES WILL FOLLOW, AND THE MONEY POWER OF THE COUNTRY WILL ENDEAVOR TO PROLONG ITS REIGN BY WORKING UPON THE PREJUDICES OF THE PEOPLE UNTIL ALL WEALTH IS AGGREGATED IN A FEW HANDS, AND THE REPUBLIC IS DESTROYED. I FEEL AT THIS MOMENT MORE ANXIETY FOR THE SAFETY OF MY COUNTRY THAN EVER BEFORE, EVEN IN THE MIDST OF WAR."

—ABRAHAM LINCOLN

$$\varepsilon = -\frac{d\Phi}{dt} \qquad \varepsilon = -N\frac{d\Phi}{dt} \qquad |\varepsilon| = \frac{N\Phi}{|dt|}$$

$$u_E = \frac{1}{2}\varepsilon_0 E^2 \qquad u_B = \frac{1}{2}\frac{B^2}{\mu_0} \qquad U_B = \frac{1}{2}Li^2$$

$$= q_0 e^{-t/\tau_c} \qquad q = C\varepsilon(1-e^{-t/\tau_c}) \qquad i = i_0 e^{-t/\tau_L} \qquad i = \frac{\varepsilon}{R}(1-e^{-t/\tau_L})$$

$$= \frac{L}{R} \qquad \tau_c = RC \qquad \mu = NiA \qquad \frac{1}{4\pi\varepsilon_0} = 9 \times 10^9 \qquad \frac{\mu_0}{4\pi} = 10^{-7}$$

M means 10^6 $\qquad$ μ means 10^{-6}

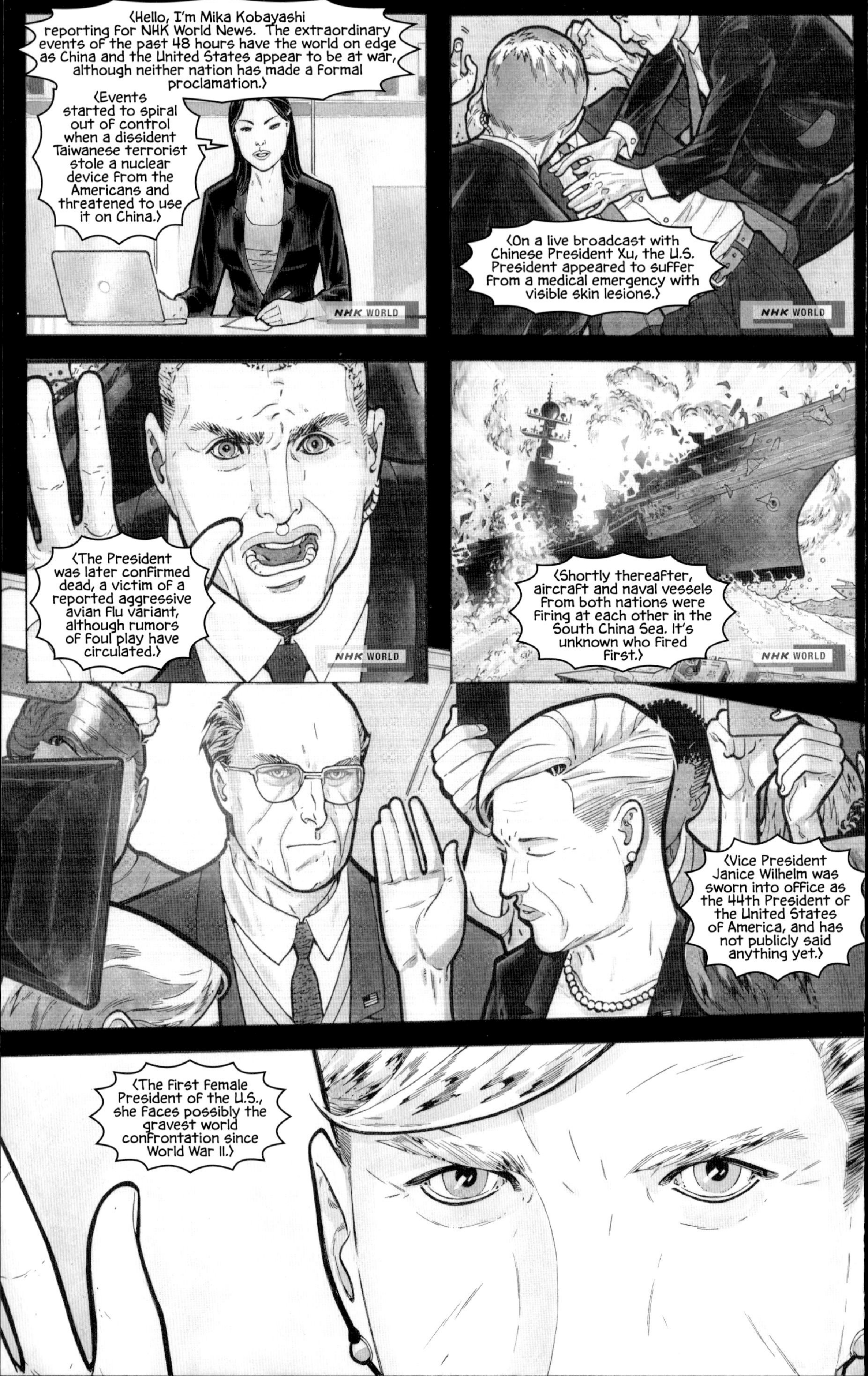

‹Hello, I'm Mika Kobayashi reporting for NHK World News. The extraordinary events of the past 48 hours have the world on edge as China and the United States appear to be at war, although neither nation has made a formal proclamation.›
‹Events started to spiral out of control when a dissident Taiwanese terrorist stole a nuclear device from the Americans and threatened to use it on China.›
NHK WORLD
‹On a live broadcast with Chinese President Xu, the U.S. President appeared to suffer from a medical emergency with visible skin lesions.›
NHK WORLD
‹The President was later confirmed dead, a victim of a reported aggressive avian flu variant, although rumors of foul play have circulated.›
NHK WORLD
‹Shortly thereafter, aircraft and naval vessels from both nations were firing at each other in the South China Sea. It's unknown who fired first.›
NHK WORLD
‹Vice President Janice Wilhelm was sworn into office as the 44th President of the United States of America, and has not publicly said anything yet.›
‹The first female President of the U.S., she faces possibly the gravest world confrontation since World War II.›

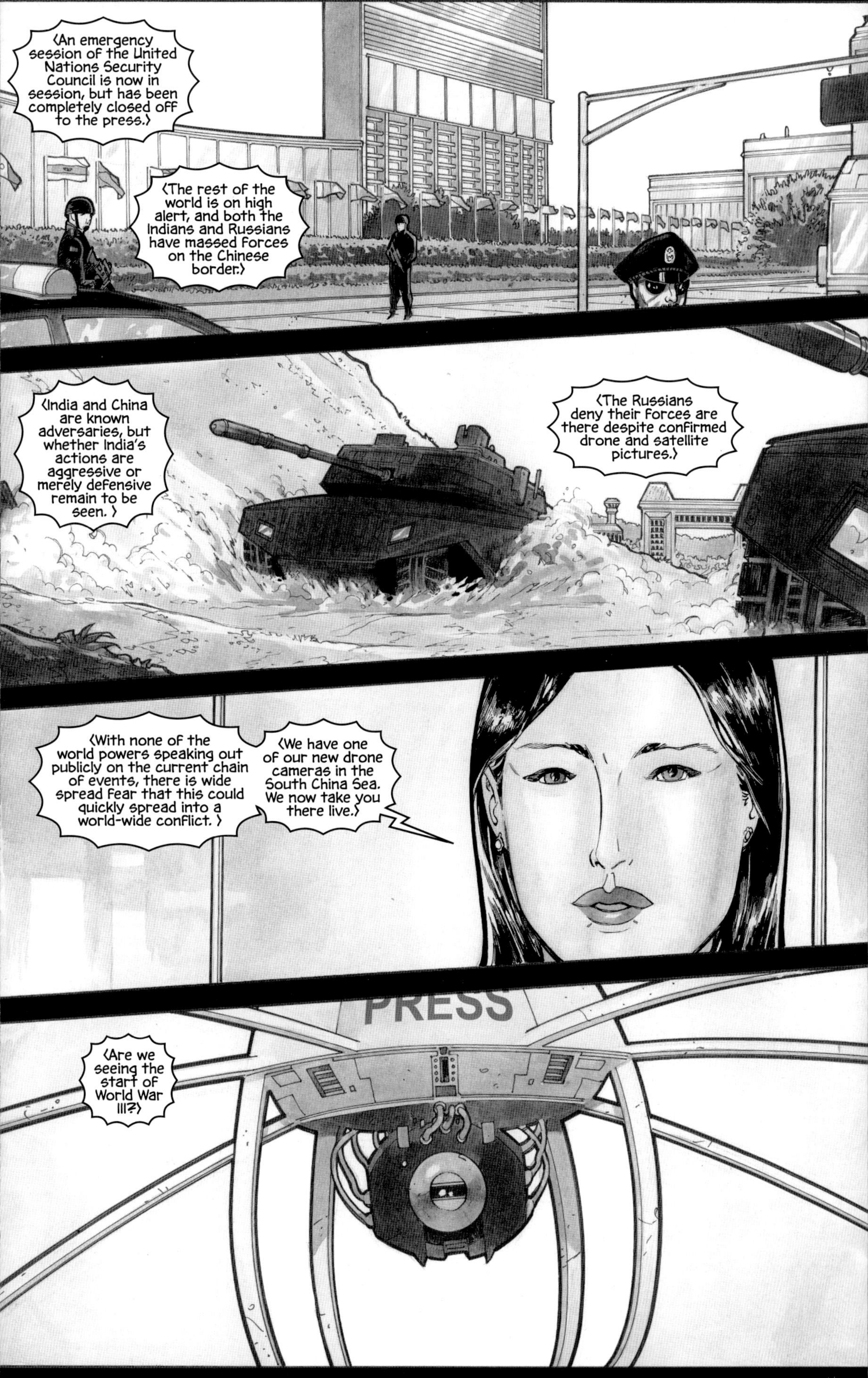

‹An emergency session of the United Nations Security Council is now in session, but has been completely closed off to the press.›
‹The rest of the world is on high alert, and both the Indians and Russians have massed forces on the Chinese border.›
‹India and China are known adversaries, but whether India's actions are aggressive or merely defensive remain to be seen. ›
‹The Russians deny their forces are there despite confirmed drone and satellite pictures.›
‹With none of the world powers speaking out publicly on the current chain of events, there is wide spread fear that this could quickly spread into a world-wide conflict. ›
‹We have one of our new drone cameras in the South China Sea. We now take you there live.›
PRESS
‹Are we seeing the start of World War III?›

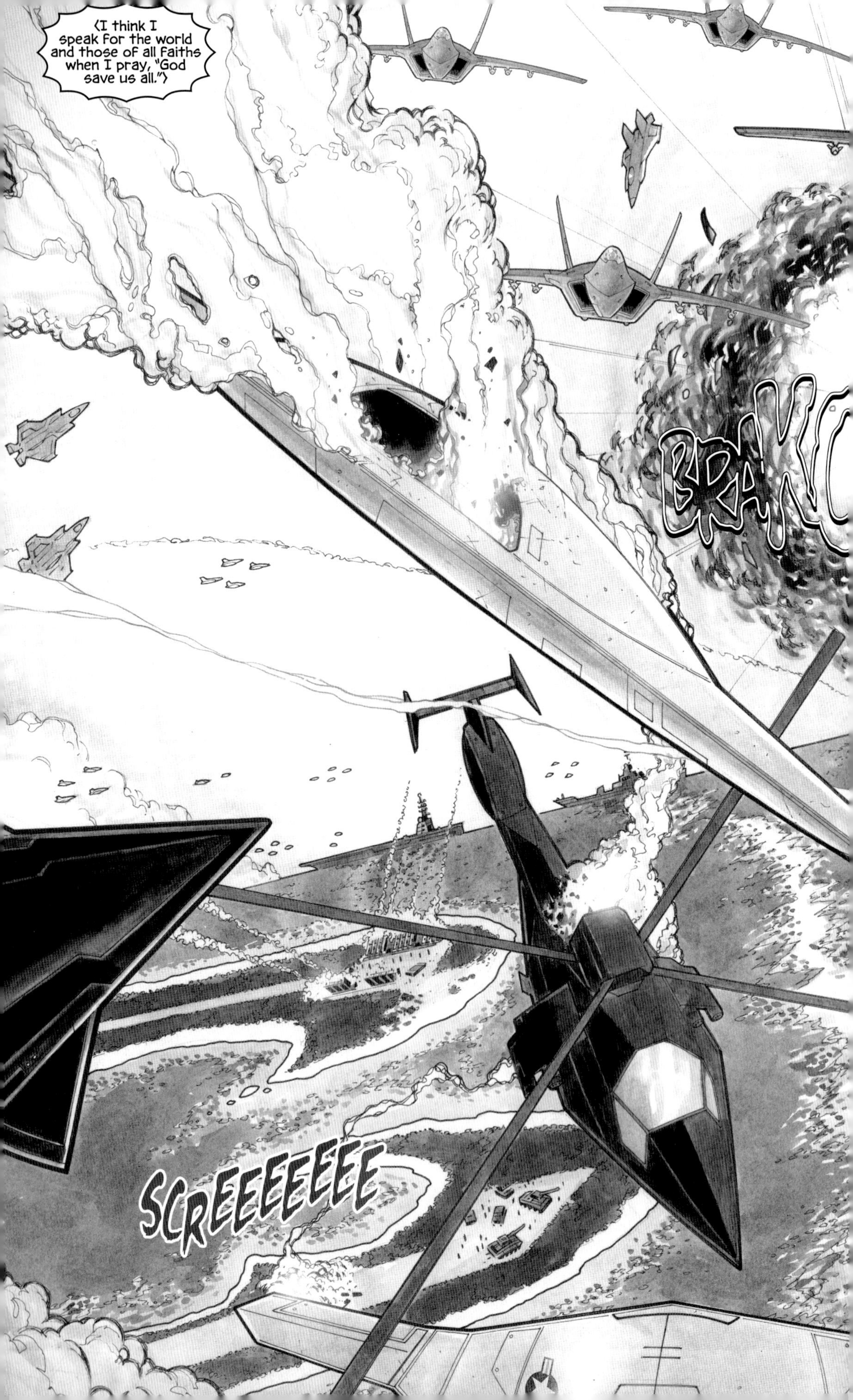
‹I think I speak for the world and those of all Faiths when I pray, "God save us all."›
BRAKO
SCREEEEEEE

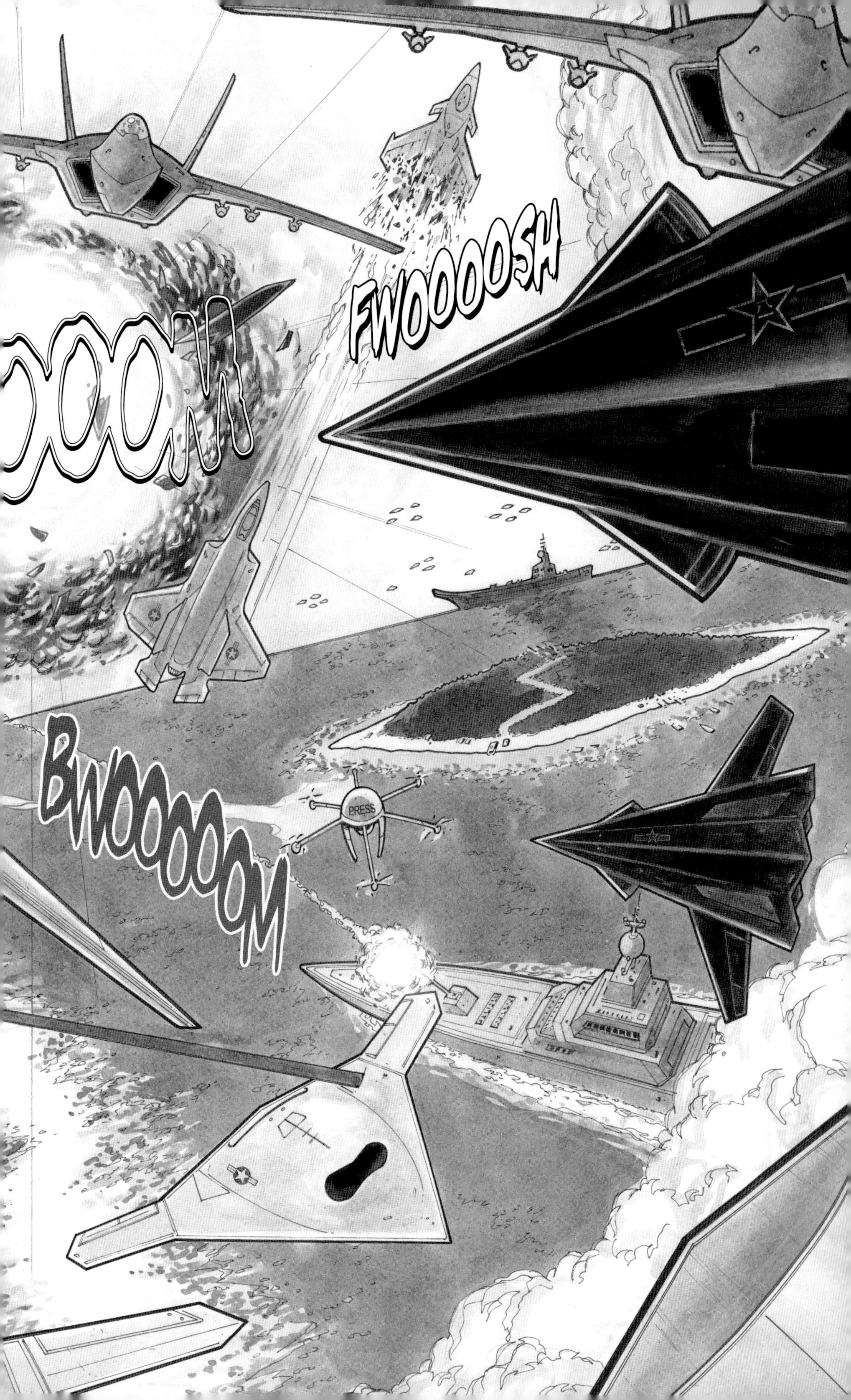
FWOOOOSH
OOOM
PRESS
BWOOOOOOM

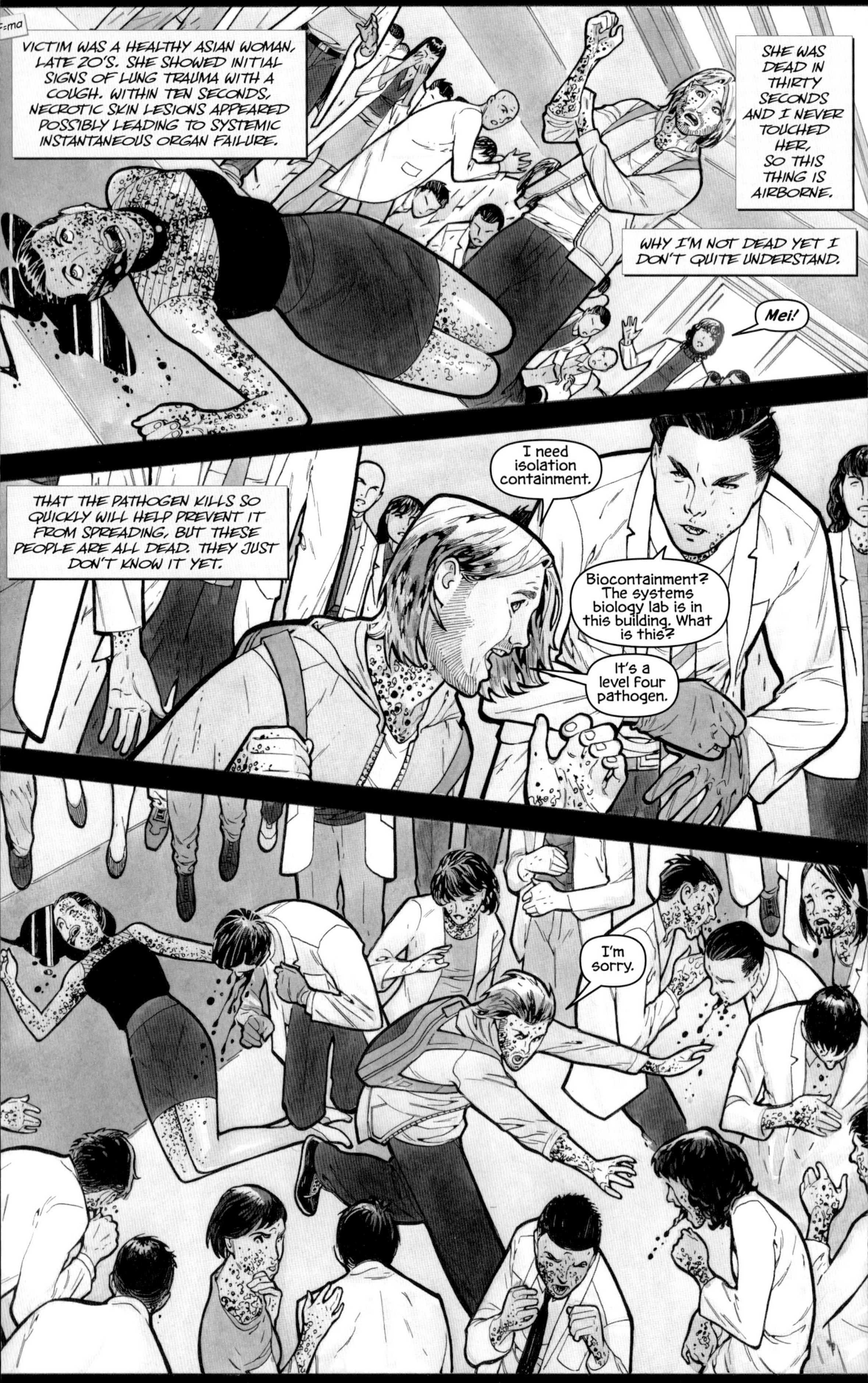
VICTIM WAS A HEALTHY ASIAN WOMAN, LATE 20'S. SHE SHOWED INITIAL SIGNS OF LUNG TRAUMA WITH A COUGH. WITHIN TEN SECONDS, NECROTIC SKIN LESIONS APPEARED POSSIBLY LEADING TO SYSTEMIC INSTANTANEOUS ORGAN FAILURE.
SHE WAS DEAD IN THIRTY SECONDS AND I NEVER TOUCHED HER, SO THIS THING IS AIRBORNE.
WHY I'M NOT DEAD YET I DON'T QUITE UNDERSTAND.
Mei!
THAT THE PATHOGEN KILLS SO QUICKLY WILL HELP PREVENT IT FROM SPREADING, BUT THESE PEOPLE ARE ALL DEAD. THEY JUST DON'T KNOW IT YET.
I need isolation containment.
Biocontainment? The systems biology lab is in this building. What is this?
It's a level four pathogen.
I'm sorry.

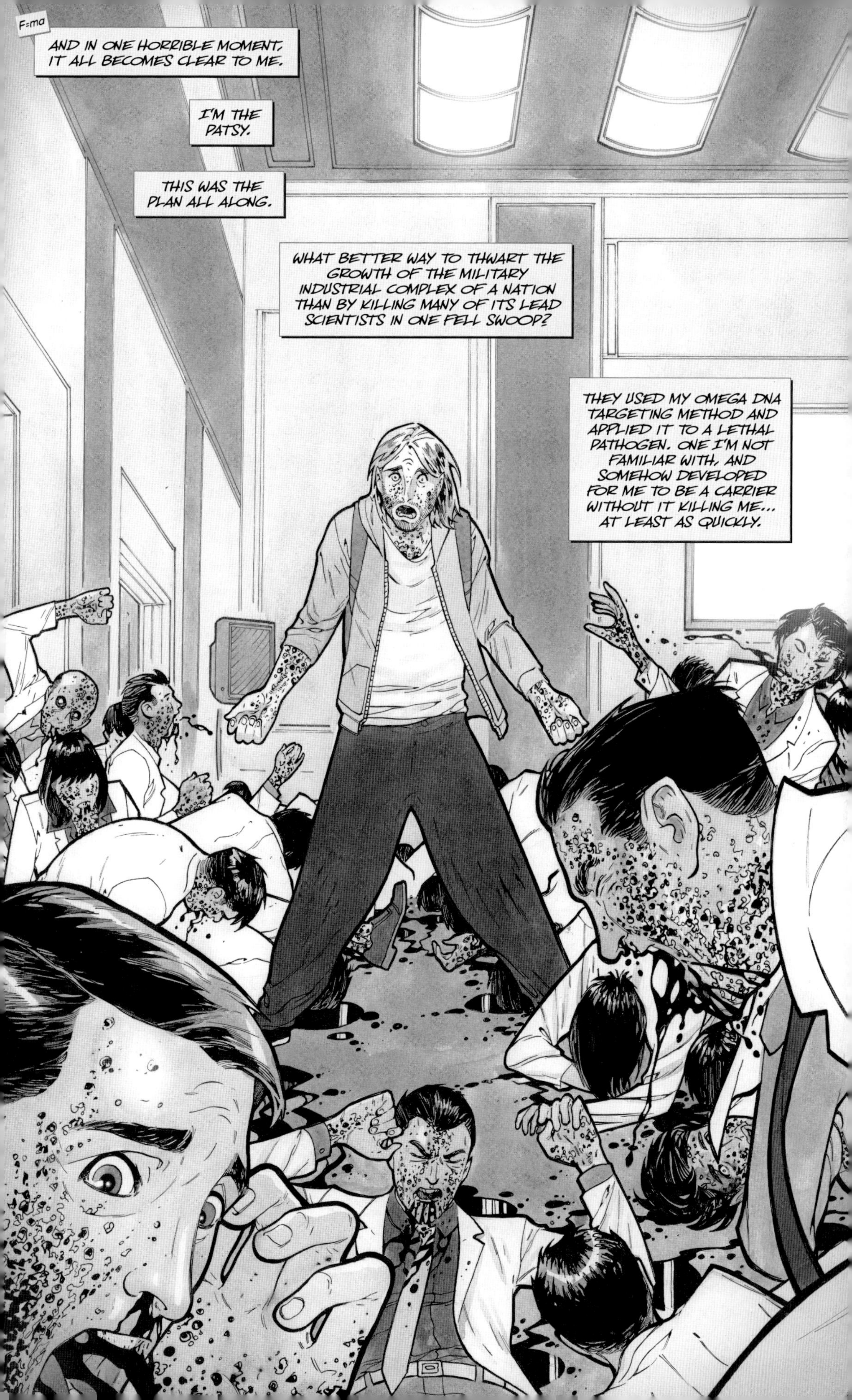

F=ma
AND IN ONE HORRIBLE MOMENT, IT ALL BECOMES CLEAR TO ME.
I'M THE PATSY.
THIS WAS THE PLAN ALL ALONG.
WHAT BETTER WAY TO THWART THE GROWTH OF THE MILITARY INDUSTRIAL COMPLEX OF A NATION THAN BY KILLING MANY OF ITS LEAD SCIENTISTS IN ONE FELL SWOOP?
THEY USED MY OMEGA DNA TARGETING METHOD AND APPLIED IT TO A LETHAL PATHOGEN. ONE I'M NOT FAMILIAR WITH, AND SOMEHOW DEVELOPED FOR ME TO BE A CARRIER WITHOUT IT KILLING ME... AT LEAST AS QUICKLY.

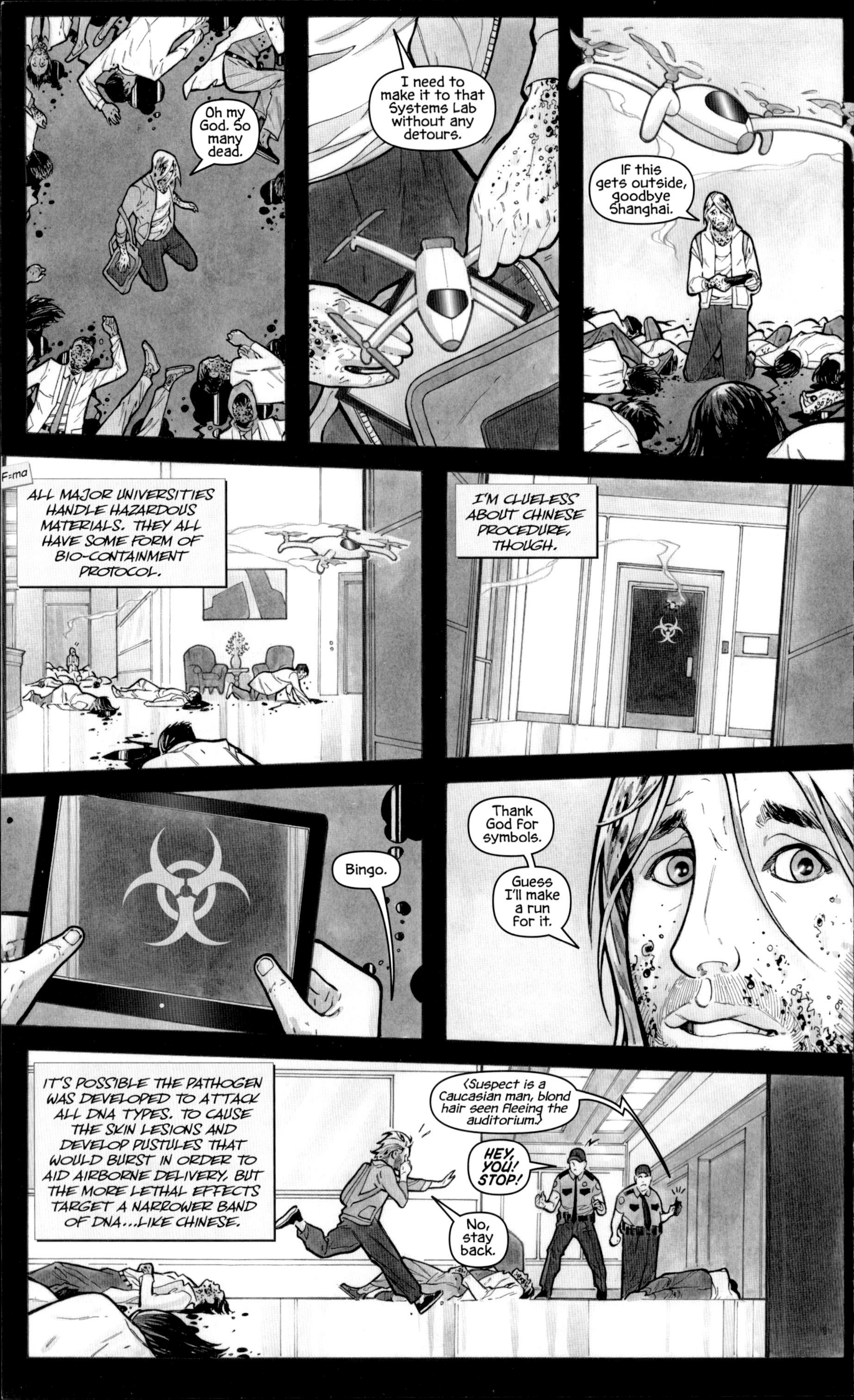
Oh my God. So many dead.
I need to make it to that Systems Lab without any detours.
If this gets outside, goodbye Shanghai.
F=ma
ALL MAJOR UNIVERSITIES HANDLE HAZARDOUS MATERIALS. THEY ALL HAVE SOME FORM OF BIO-CONTAINMENT PROTOCOL.
I'M CLUELESS ABOUT CHINESE PROCEDURE, THOUGH.
Bingo.
Thank God for symbols.
Guess I'll make a run for it.
IT'S POSSIBLE THE PATHOGEN WAS DEVELOPED TO ATTACK ALL DNA TYPES. TO CAUSE THE SKIN LESIONS AND DEVELOP PUSTULES THAT WOULD BURST IN ORDER TO AID AIRBORNE DELIVERY, BUT THE MORE LETHAL EFFECTS TARGET A NARROWER BAND OF DNA...LIKE CHINESE.
<Suspect is a Caucasian man, blond hair seen fleeing the auditorium.>
HEY, YOU! STOP!
No, stay back.

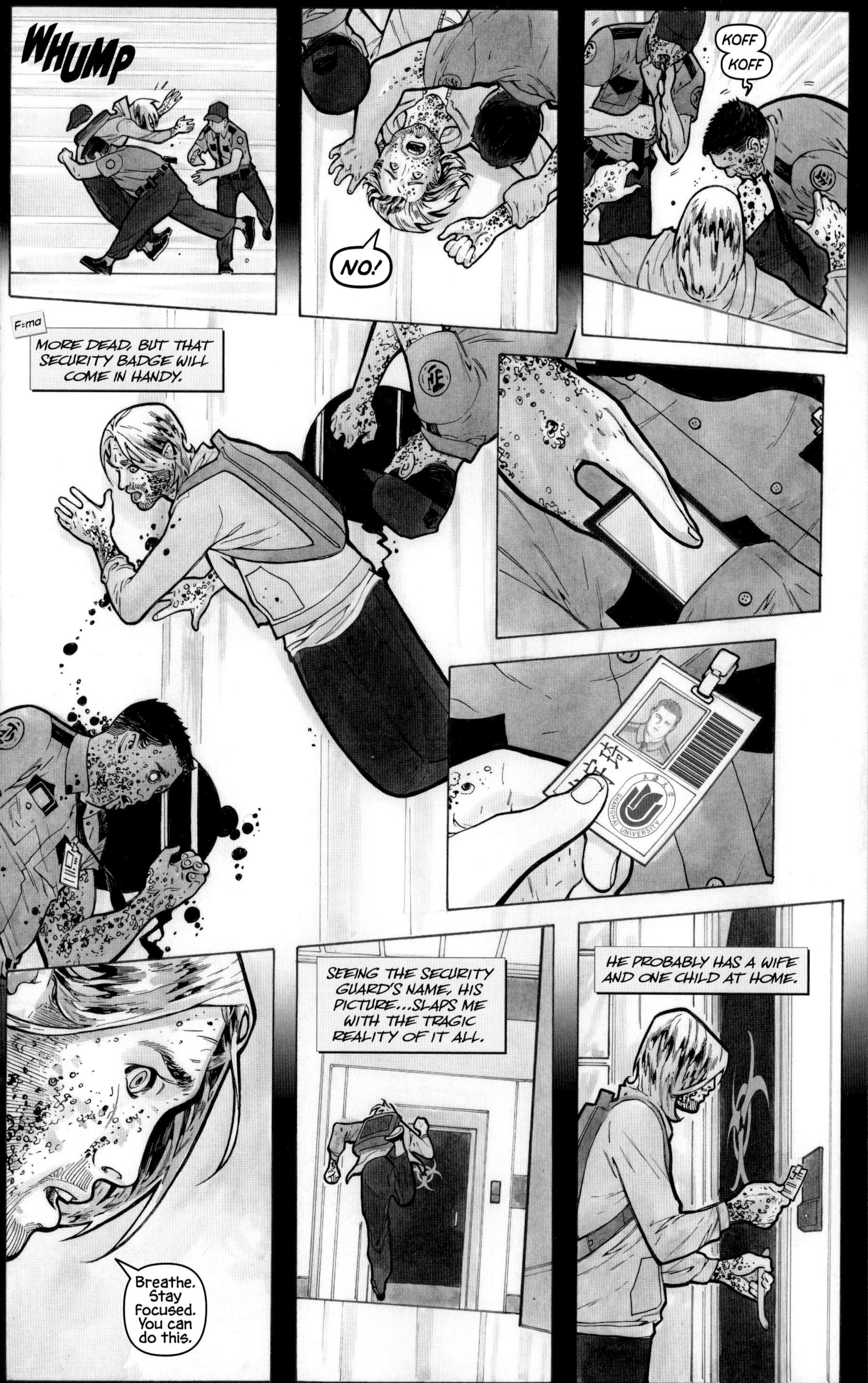
WHUMP
NO!
KOFF KOFF
F=ma
MORE DEAD, BUT THAT SECURITY BADGE WILL COME IN HANDY.
SHANGHAI UNIVERSITY
Breathe. Stay focused. You can do this.
SEEING THE SECURITY GUARD'S NAME, HIS PICTURE...SLAPS ME WITH THE TRAGIC REALITY OF IT ALL.
HE PROBABLY HAS A WIFE AND ONE CHILD AT HOME.

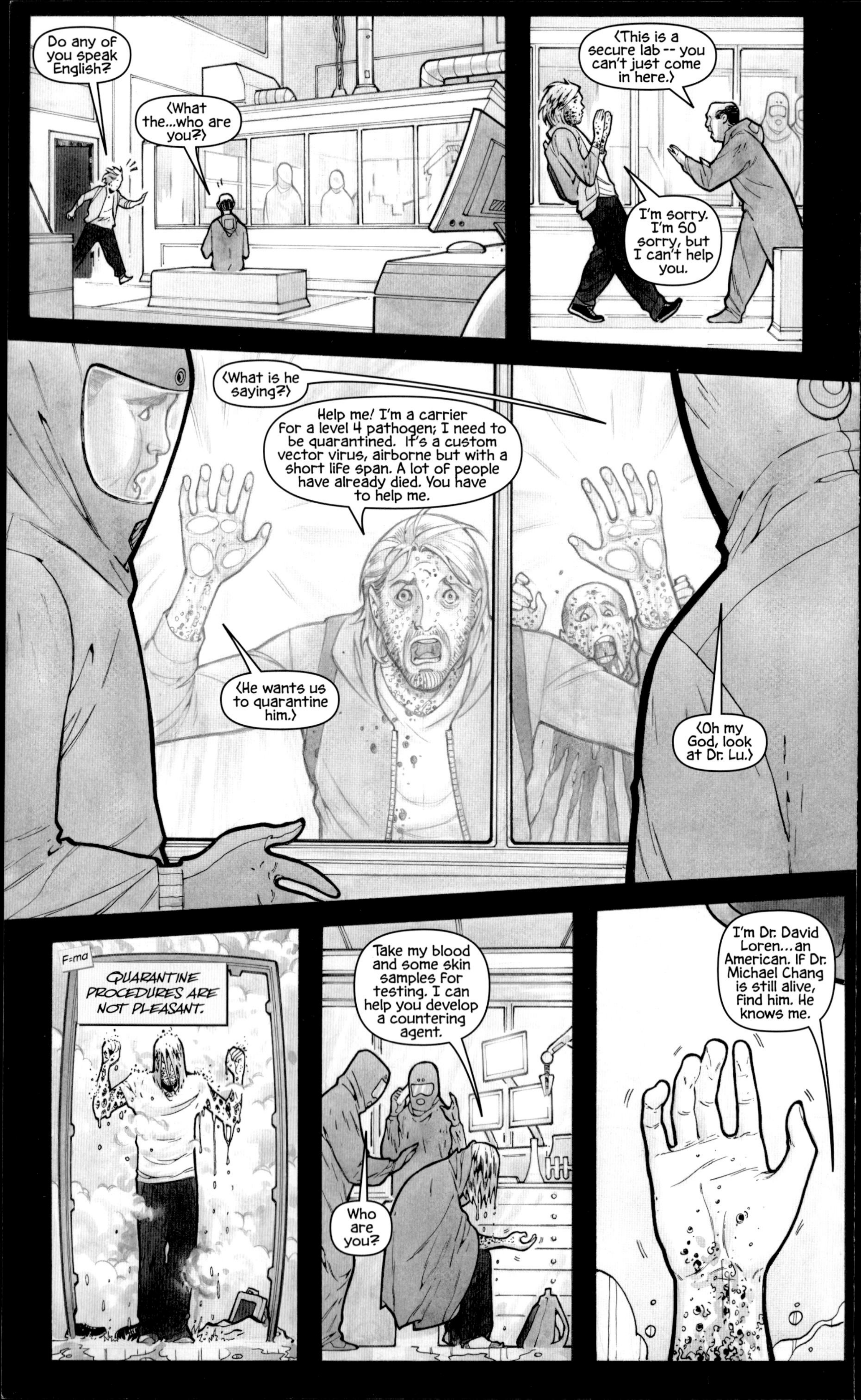
Do any of you speak English?
‹What the...who are you?›
‹This is a secure lab -- you can't just come in here.›
I'm sorry. I'm SO sorry, but I can't help you.
‹What is he saying?›
Help me! I'm a carrier for a level 4 pathogen; I need to be quarantined. It's a custom vector virus, airborne but with a short life span. A lot of people have already died. You have to help me.
‹He wants us to quarantine him.›
‹Oh my God, look at Dr. Lu.›
F=ma
QUARANTINE PROCEDURES ARE NOT PLEASANT.
Take my blood and some skin samples for testing. I can help you develop a countering agent.
Who are you?
I'm Dr. David Loren...an American. If Dr. Michael Chang is still alive, find him. He knows me.

**PHILIPPINES
GENERAL CLARKSON**

**WHITE HOUSE:
SITUATION ROOM
SENATOR
MITCHELL**

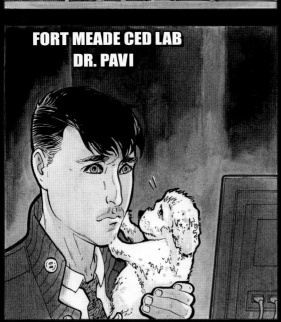

**FORT MEADE CED LAB
DR. PAVI**

HARRISON RESIDENCE:

MIRRA SWAY

TSANG ONG

This thing is wrapping up, boys. We should get her ready for transport back stateside.

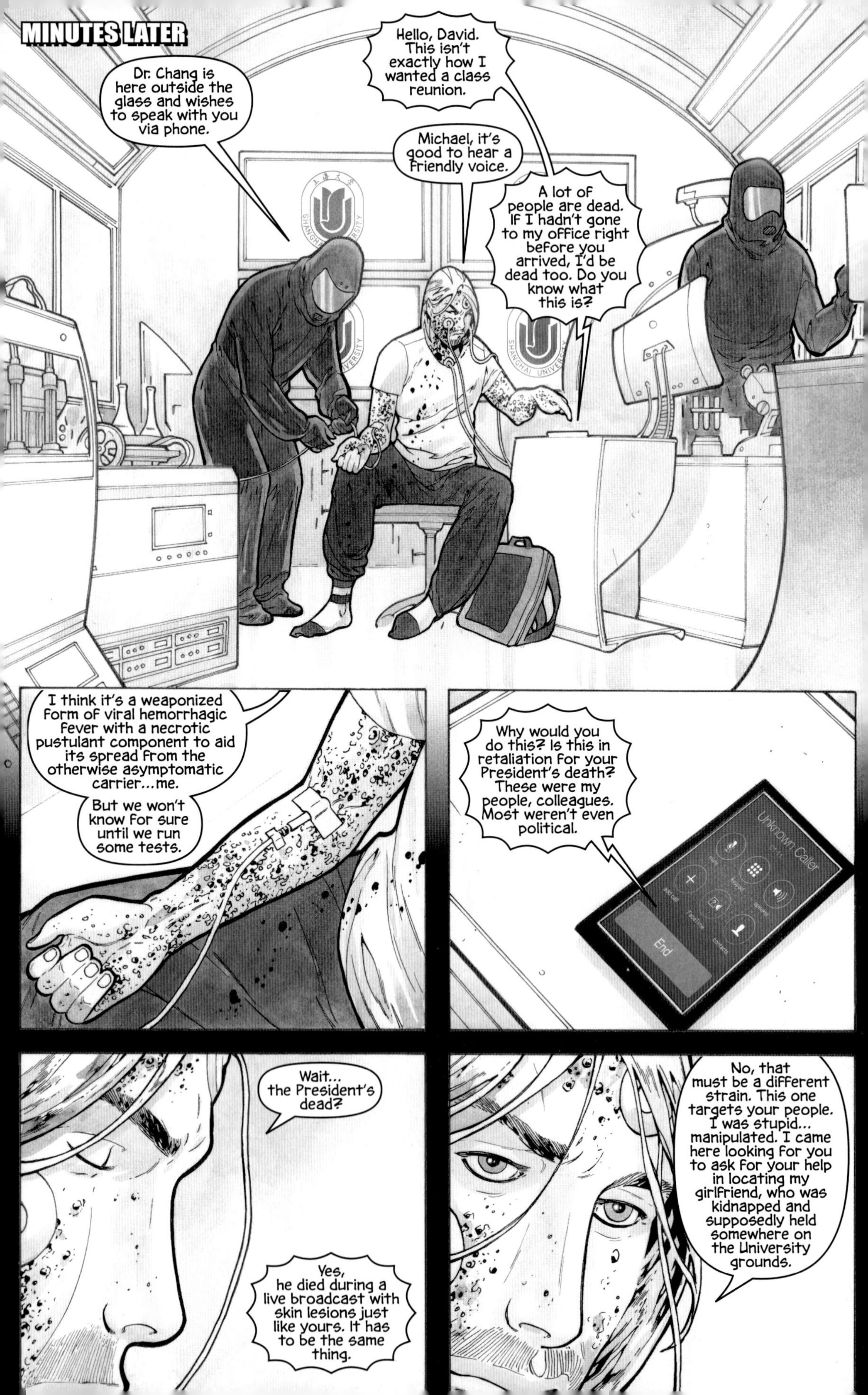
MINUTES LATER
Dr. Chang is here outside the glass and wishes to speak with you via phone.
Hello, David. This isn't exactly how I wanted a class reunion.
Michael, it's good to hear a friendly voice.
A lot of people are dead. If I hadn't gone to my office right before you arrived, I'd be dead too. Do you know what this is?
SHANGHAI UNIVERSITY
I think it's a weaponized form of viral hemorrhagic fever with a necrotic pustulant component to aid its spread from the otherwise asymptomatic carrier...me.
But we won't know for sure until we run some tests.
Why would you do this? Is this in retaliation for your President's death? These were my people, colleagues. Most weren't even political.
Unknown Caller
End
Wait... the President's dead?
Yes, he died during a live broadcast with skin lesions just like yours. It has to be the same thing.
No, that must be a different strain. This one targets your people. I was stupid... manipulated. I came here looking for you to ask for your help in locating my girlfriend, who was kidnapped and supposedly held somewhere on the University grounds.

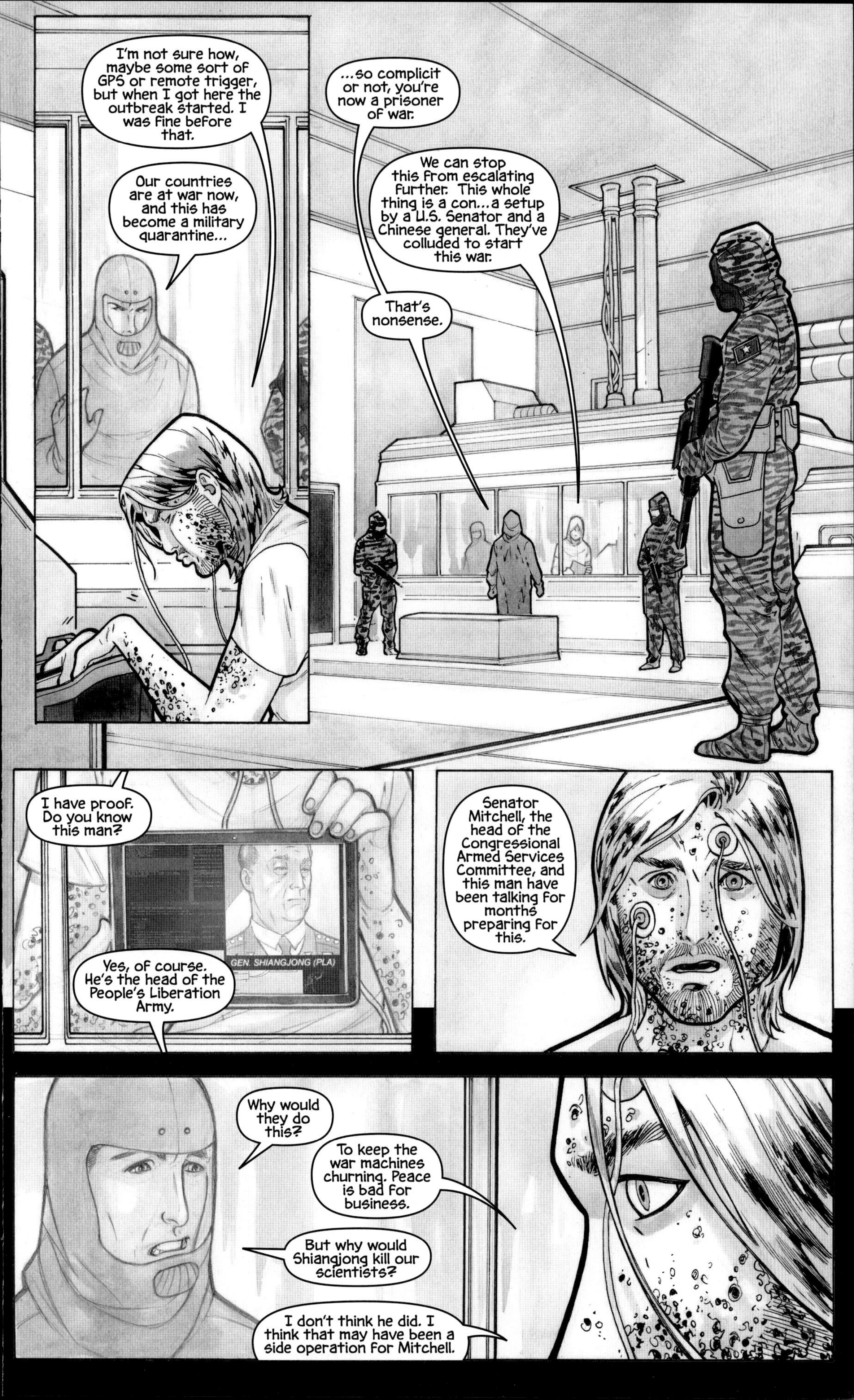
I'm not sure how, maybe some sort of GPS or remote trigger, but when I got here the outbreak started. I was fine before that.
Our countries are at war now, and this has become a military quarantine...
...so complicit or not, you're now a prisoner of war.
We can stop this from escalating further. This whole thing is a con...a setup by a U.S. Senator and a Chinese general. They've colluded to start this war.
That's nonsense.
I have proof. Do you know this man?
GEN. SHIANGJONG (PLA)
Yes, of course. He's the head of the People's Liberation Army.
Senator Mitchell, the head of the Congressional Armed Services Committee, and this man have been talking for months preparing for this.
Why would they do this?
To keep the war machines churning. Peace is bad for business.
But why would Shiangjong kill our scientists?
I don't think he did. I think that may have been a side operation for Mitchell.

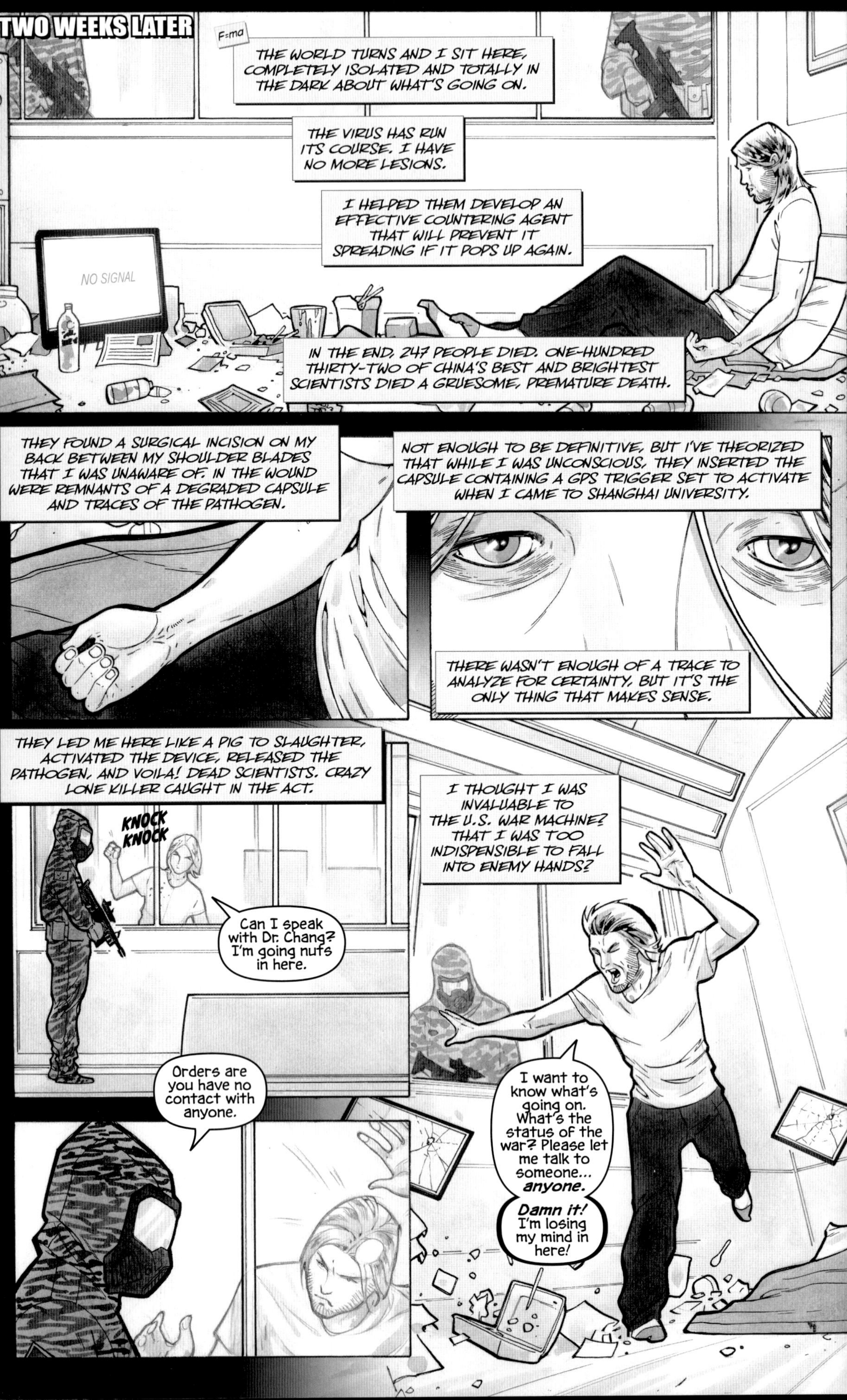
TWO WEEKS LATER
F=ma
THE WORLD TURNS AND I SIT HERE, COMPLETELY ISOLATED AND TOTALLY IN THE DARK ABOUT WHAT'S GOING ON.
THE VIRUS HAS RUN ITS COURSE. I HAVE NO MORE LESIONS.
I HELPED THEM DEVELOP AN EFFECTIVE COUNTERING AGENT THAT WILL PREVENT IT SPREADING IF IT POPS UP AGAIN.
NO SIGNAL
IN THE END, 247 PEOPLE DIED. ONE-HUNDRED THIRTY-TWO OF CHINA'S BEST AND BRIGHTEST SCIENTISTS DIED A GRUESOME, PREMATURE DEATH.
THEY FOUND A SURGICAL INCISION ON MY BACK BETWEEN MY SHOULDER BLADES THAT I WAS UNAWARE OF. IN THE WOUND WERE REMNANTS OF A DEGRADED CAPSULE AND TRACES OF THE PATHOGEN.
NOT ENOUGH TO BE DEFINITIVE, BUT I'VE THEORIZED THAT WHILE I WAS UNCONSCIOUS, THEY INSERTED THE CAPSULE CONTAINING A GPS TRIGGER SET TO ACTIVATE WHEN I CAME TO SHANGHAI UNIVERSITY.
THERE WASN'T ENOUGH OF A TRACE TO ANALYZE FOR CERTAINTY, BUT IT'S THE ONLY THING THAT MAKES SENSE.
THEY LED ME HERE LIKE A PIG TO SLAUGHTER, ACTIVATED THE DEVICE, RELEASED THE PATHOGEN, AND VOILA! DEAD SCIENTISTS. CRAZY LONE KILLER CAUGHT IN THE ACT.
KNOCK KNOCK
Can I speak with Dr. Chang? I'm going nuts in here.
I THOUGHT I WAS INVALUABLE TO THE U.S. WAR MACHINE? THAT I WAS TOO INDISPENSIBLE TO FALL INTO ENEMY HANDS?
Orders are you have no contact with anyone.
I want to know what's going on. What's the status of the war? Please let me talk to someone... *anyone*.
Damn it! I'm losing my mind in here!

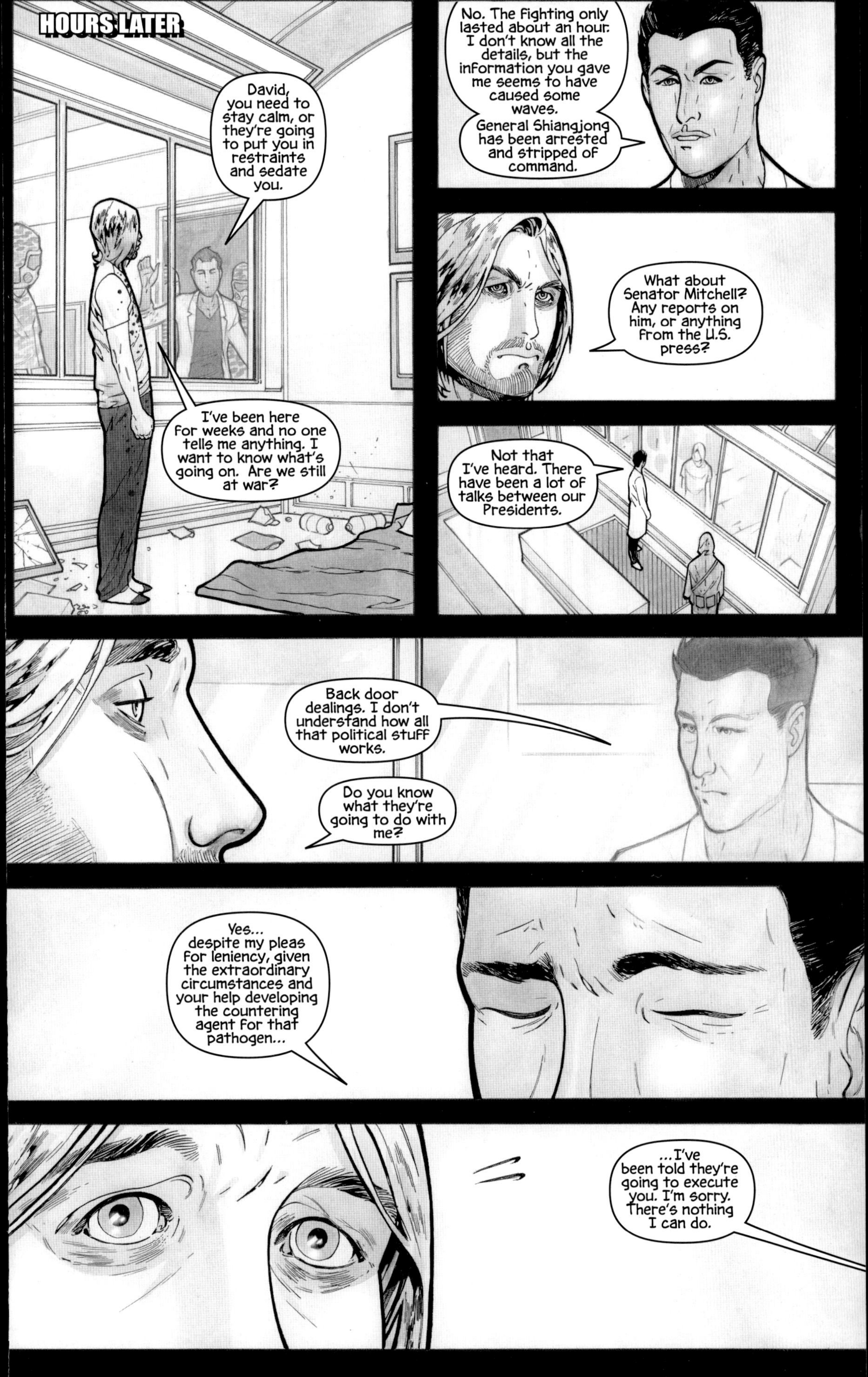
HOURS LATER
David, you need to stay calm, or they're going to put you in restraints and sedate you.
I've been here for weeks and no one tells me anything. I want to know what's going on. Are we still at war?
No. The fighting only lasted about an hour. I don't know all the details, but the information you gave me seems to have caused some waves.
General Shiangjong has been arrested and stripped of command.
What about Senator Mitchell? Any reports on him, or anything from the U.S. press?
Not that I've heard. There have been a lot of talks between our Presidents.
Back door dealings. I don't understand how all that political stuff works.
Do you know what they're going to do with me?
Yes... despite my pleas for leniency, given the extraordinary circumstances and your help developing the countering agent for that pathogen...
...I've been told they're going to execute you. I'm sorry. There's nothing I can do.

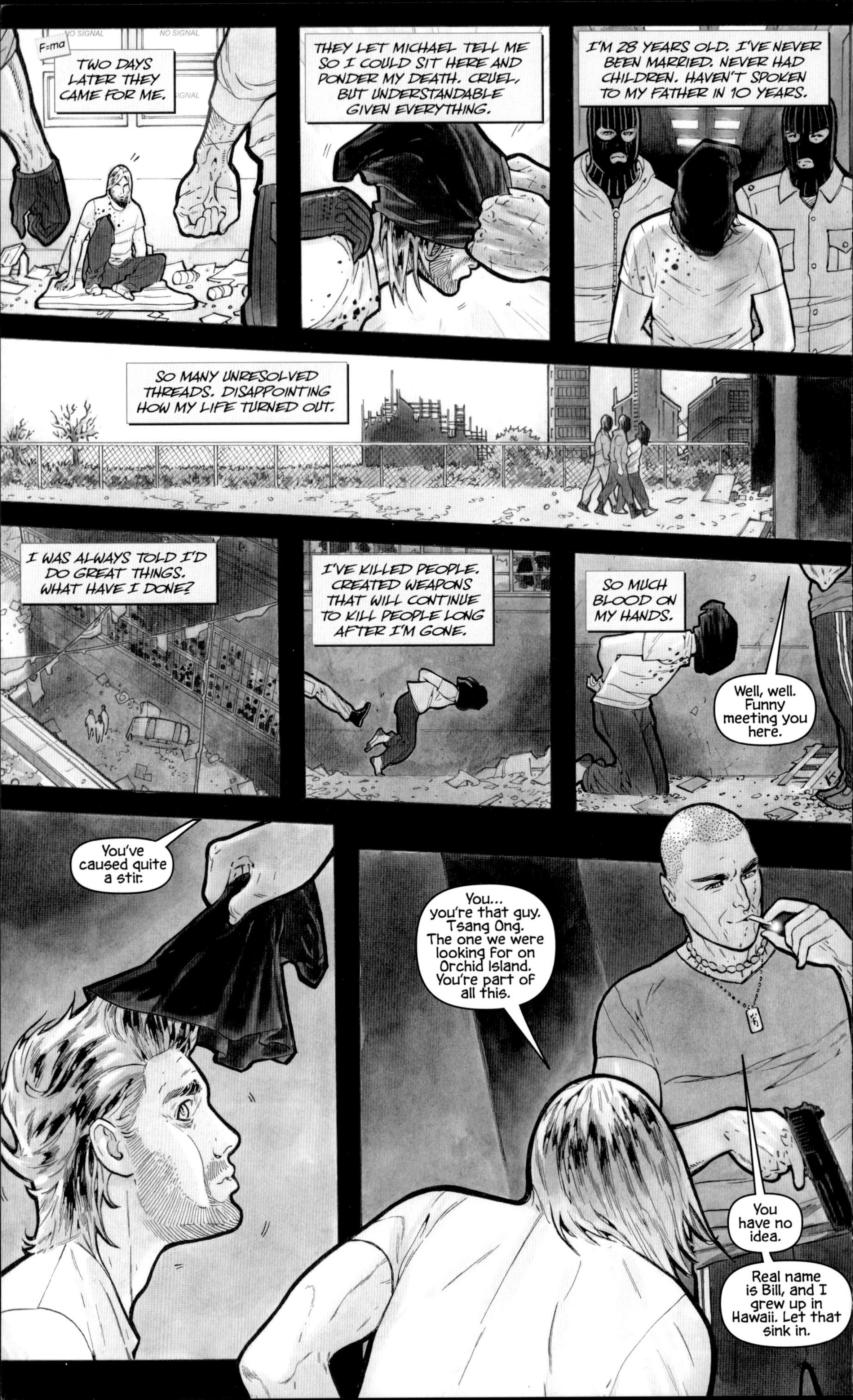
NO SIGNAL
NO SIGNAL
F=ma
TWO DAYS LATER THEY CAME FOR ME.
THEY LET MICHAEL TELL ME SO I COULD SIT HERE AND PONDER MY DEATH. CRUEL, BUT UNDERSTANDABLE GIVEN EVERYTHING.
I'M 28 YEARS OLD. I'VE NEVER BEEN MARRIED. NEVER HAD CHILDREN. HAVEN'T SPOKEN TO MY FATHER IN 10 YEARS.
SO MANY UNRESOLVED THREADS. DISAPPOINTING HOW MY LIFE TURNED OUT.
I WAS ALWAYS TOLD I'D DO GREAT THINGS. WHAT HAVE I DONE?
I'VE KILLED PEOPLE. CREATED WEAPONS THAT WILL CONTINUE TO KILL PEOPLE LONG AFTER I'M GONE.
SO MUCH BLOOD ON MY HANDS.
Well, well. Funny meeting you here.
You've caused quite a stir.
You... you're that guy. Tsang Ong. The one we were looking for on Orchid Island. You're part of all this.
You have no idea.
Real name is Bill, and I grew up in Hawaii. Let that sink in.

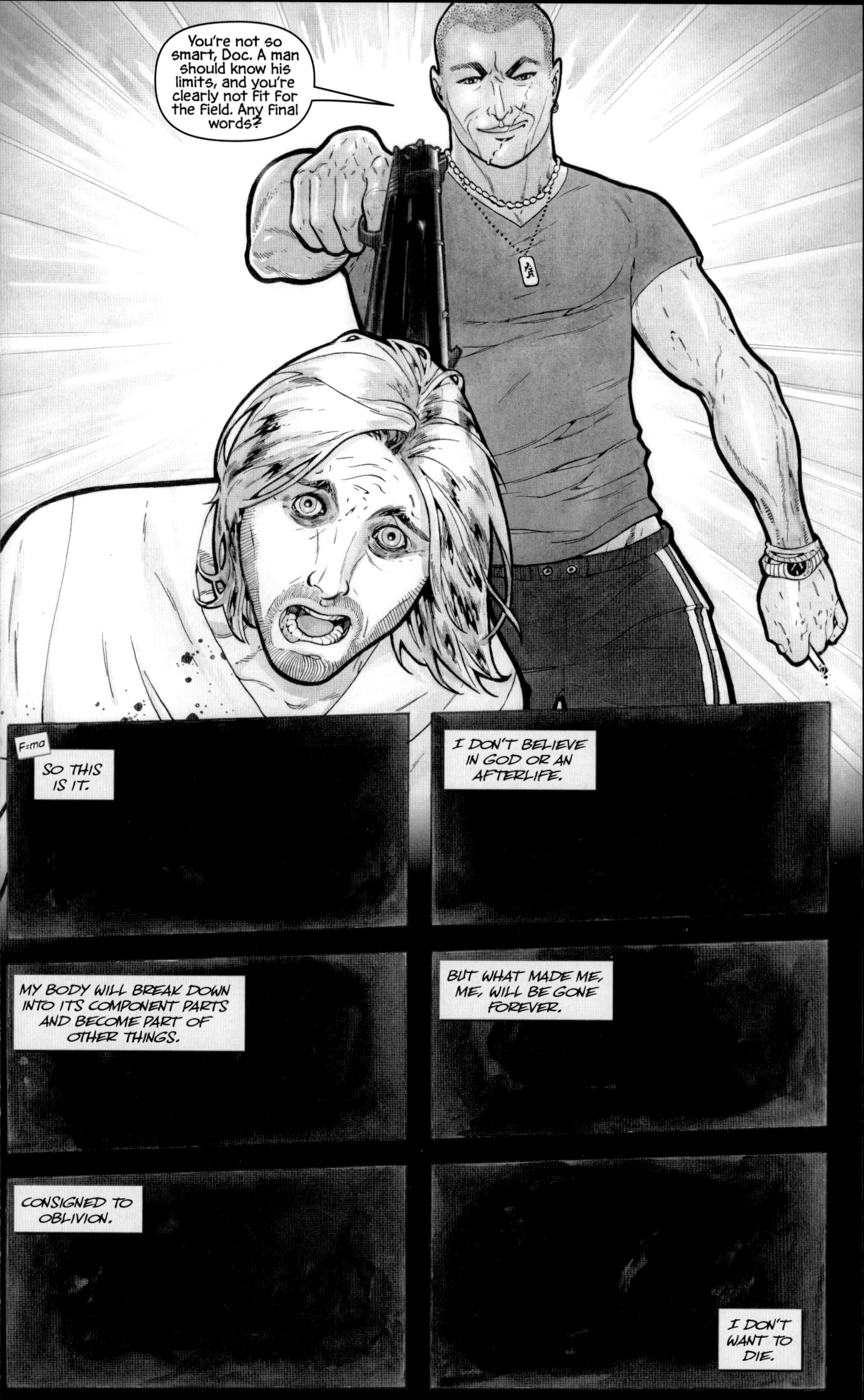
You're not so smart, Doc. A man should know his limits, and you're clearly not fit for the field. Any final words?
F=ma
SO THIS IS IT.
I DON'T BELIEVE IN GOD OR AN AFTERLIFE.
MY BODY WILL BREAK DOWN INTO ITS COMPONENT PARTS AND BECOME PART OF OTHER THINGS.
BUT WHAT MADE ME, ME, WILL BE GONE FOREVER.
CONSIGNED TO OBLIVION.
I DON'T WANT TO DIE.

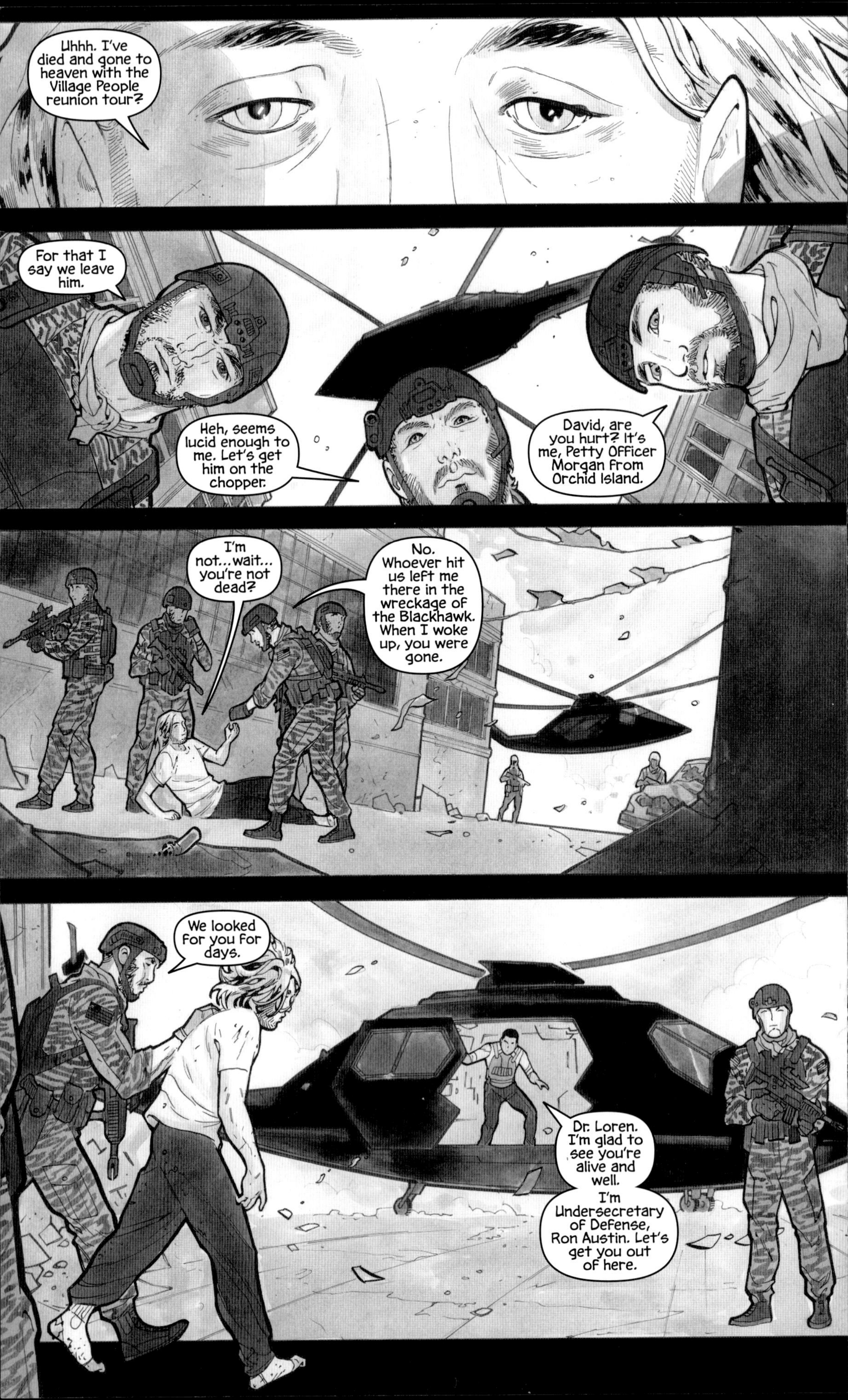
Uhhh. I've died and gone to heaven with the Village People reunion tour?
For that I say we leave him.
Heh, seems lucid enough to me. Let's get him on the chopper.
David, are you hurt? It's me, Petty Officer Morgan from Orchid Island.
I'm not...wait... you're not dead?
No. Whoever hit us left me there in the wreckage of the Blackhawk. When I woke up, you were gone.
We looked for you for days.
Dr. Loren. I'm glad to see you're alive and well.
I'm Undersecretary of Defense, Ron Austin. Let's get you out of here.

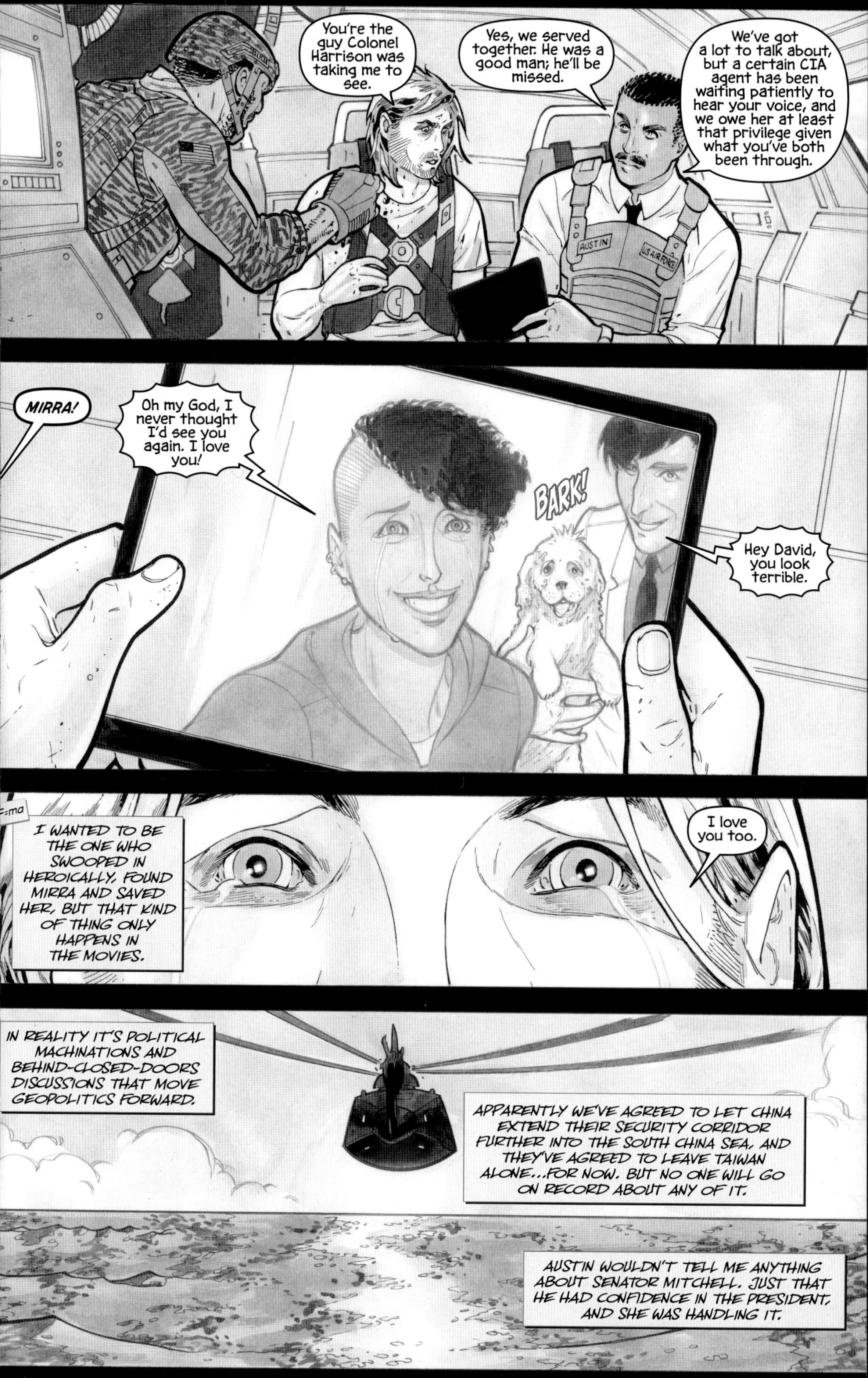
You're the guy Colonel Harrison was taking me to see.
Yes, we served together. He was a good man; he'll be missed.
We've got a lot to talk about, but a certain CIA agent has been waiting patiently to hear your voice, and we owe her at least that privilege given what you've both been through.
AUSTIN
U.S. AIR FORCE
MIRRA!
Oh my God, I never thought I'd see you again. I love you!
BARK!
Hey David, you look terrible.
I WANTED TO BE THE ONE WHO SWOOPED IN HEROICALLY, FOUND MIRRA AND SAVED HER, BUT THAT KIND OF THING ONLY HAPPENS IN THE MOVIES.
I love you too.
IN REALITY IT'S POLITICAL MACHINATIONS AND BEHIND-CLOSED-DOORS DISCUSSIONS THAT MOVE GEOPOLITICS FORWARD.
APPARENTLY WE'VE AGREED TO LET CHINA EXTEND THEIR SECURITY CORRIDOR FURTHER INTO THE SOUTH CHINA SEA, AND THEY'VE AGREED TO LEAVE TAIWAN ALONE...FOR NOW. BUT NO ONE WILL GO ON RECORD ABOUT ANY OF IT.
AUSTIN WOULDN'T TELL ME ANYTHING ABOUT SENATOR MITCHELL. JUST THAT HE HAD CONFIDENCE IN THE PRESIDENT, AND SHE WAS HANDLING IT.

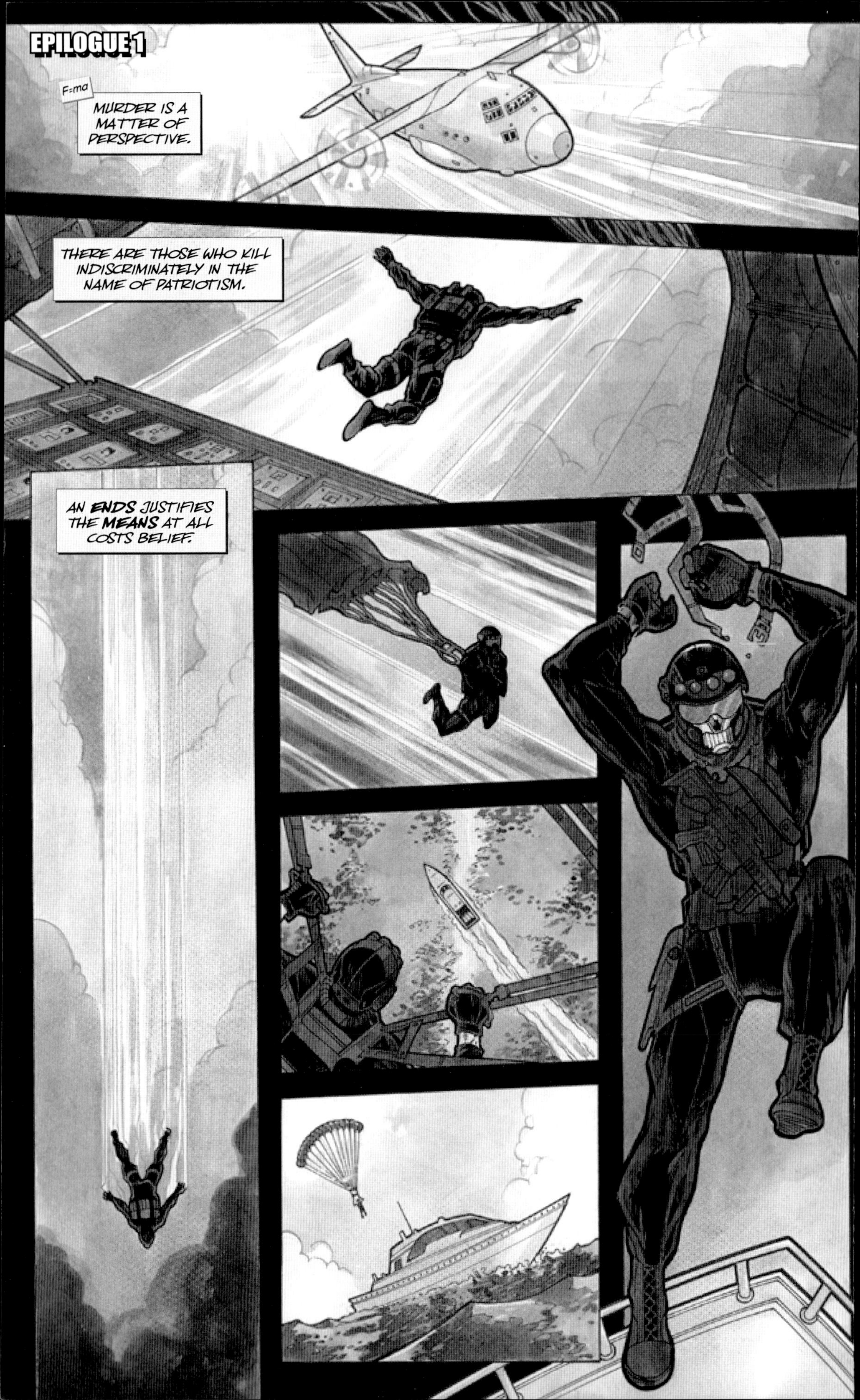
EPILOGUE 1
F=ma
MURDER IS A MATTER OF PERSPECTIVE.
THERE ARE THOSE WHO KILL INDISCRIMINATELY IN THE NAME OF PATRIOTISM.
AN ENDS JUSTIFIES THE MEANS AT ALL COSTS BELIEF.

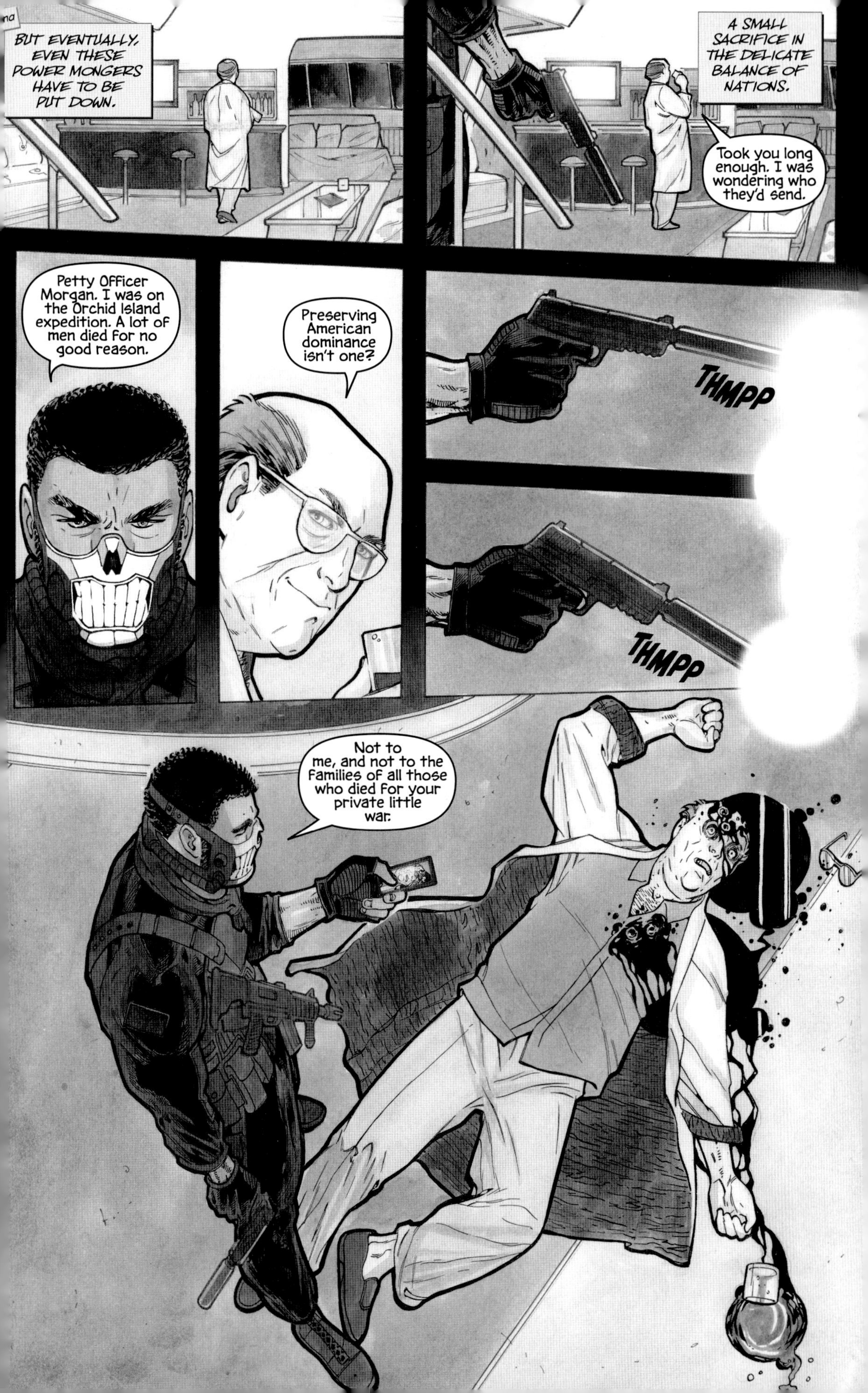

BUT EVENTUALLY, EVEN THESE POWER MONGERS HAVE TO BE PUT DOWN.
A SMALL SACRIFICE IN THE DELICATE BALANCE OF NATIONS.
Took you long enough. I was wondering who they'd send.
Petty Officer Morgan. I was on the Orchid Island expedition. A lot of men died for no good reason.
Preserving American dominance isn't one?
THMPP
THMPP
Not to me, and not to the families of all those who died for your private little war.

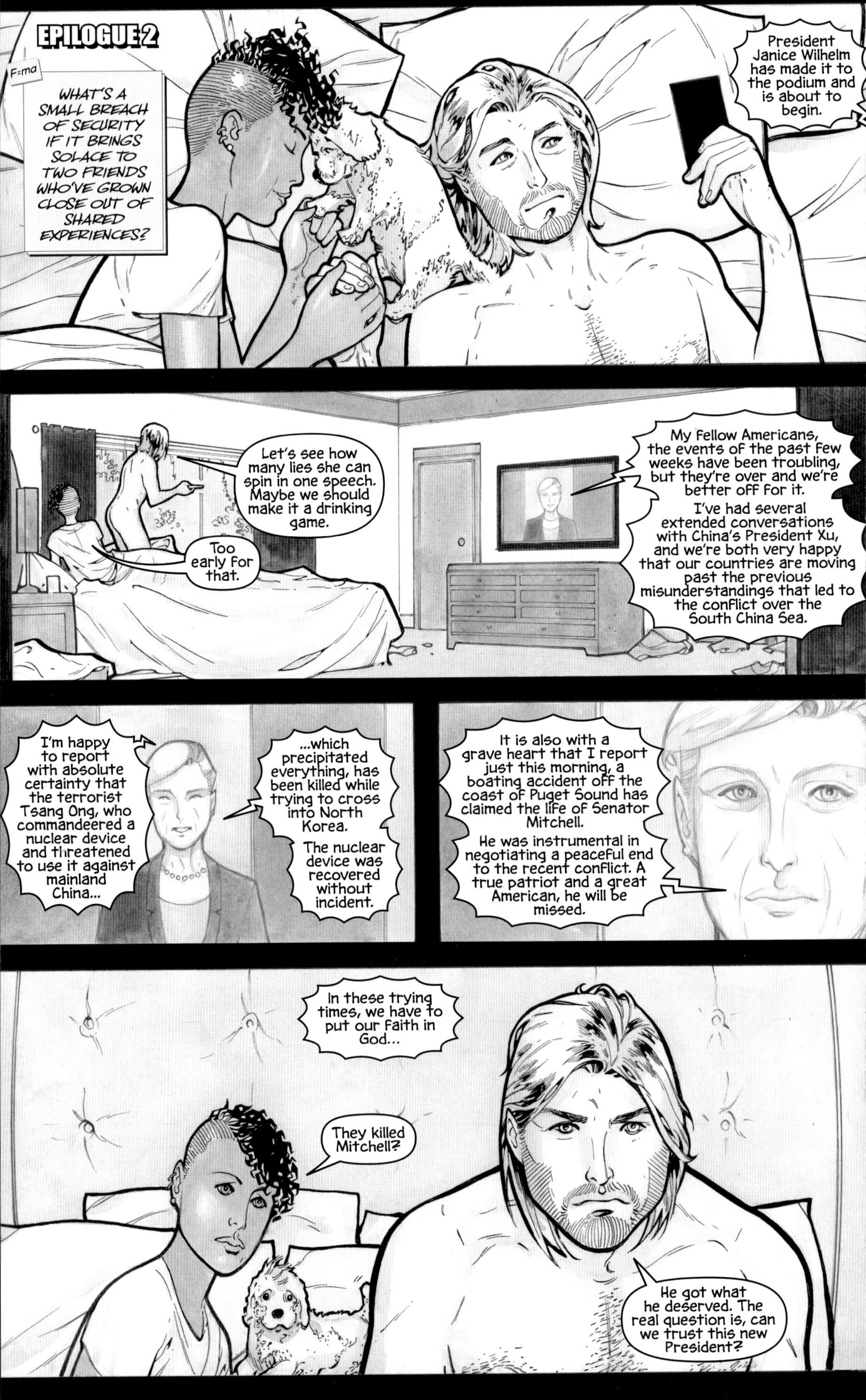
EPILOGUE 2
F=ma
WHAT'S A SMALL BREACH OF SECURITY IF IT BRINGS SOLACE TO TWO FRIENDS WHO'VE GROWN CLOSE OUT OF SHARED EXPERIENCES?
President Janice Wilhelm has made it to the podium and is about to begin.
Let's see how many lies she can spin in one speech. Maybe we should make it a drinking game.
Too early for that.
My Fellow Americans, the events of the past few weeks have been troubling, but they're over and we're better off for it.
I've had several extended conversations with China's President Xu, and we're both very happy that our countries are moving past the previous misunderstandings that led to the conflict over the South China Sea.
I'm happy to report with absolute certainty that the terrorist Tsang Ong, who commandeered a nuclear device and threatened to use it against mainland China...
...which precipitated everything, has been killed while trying to cross into North Korea.
The nuclear device was recovered without incident.
It is also with a grave heart that I report just this morning, a boating accident off the coast of Puget Sound has claimed the life of Senator Mitchell.
He was instrumental in negotiating a peaceful end to the recent conflict. A true patriot and a great American, he will be missed.
In these trying times, we have to put our faith in God...
They killed Mitchell?
He got what he deserved. The real question is, can we trust this new President?

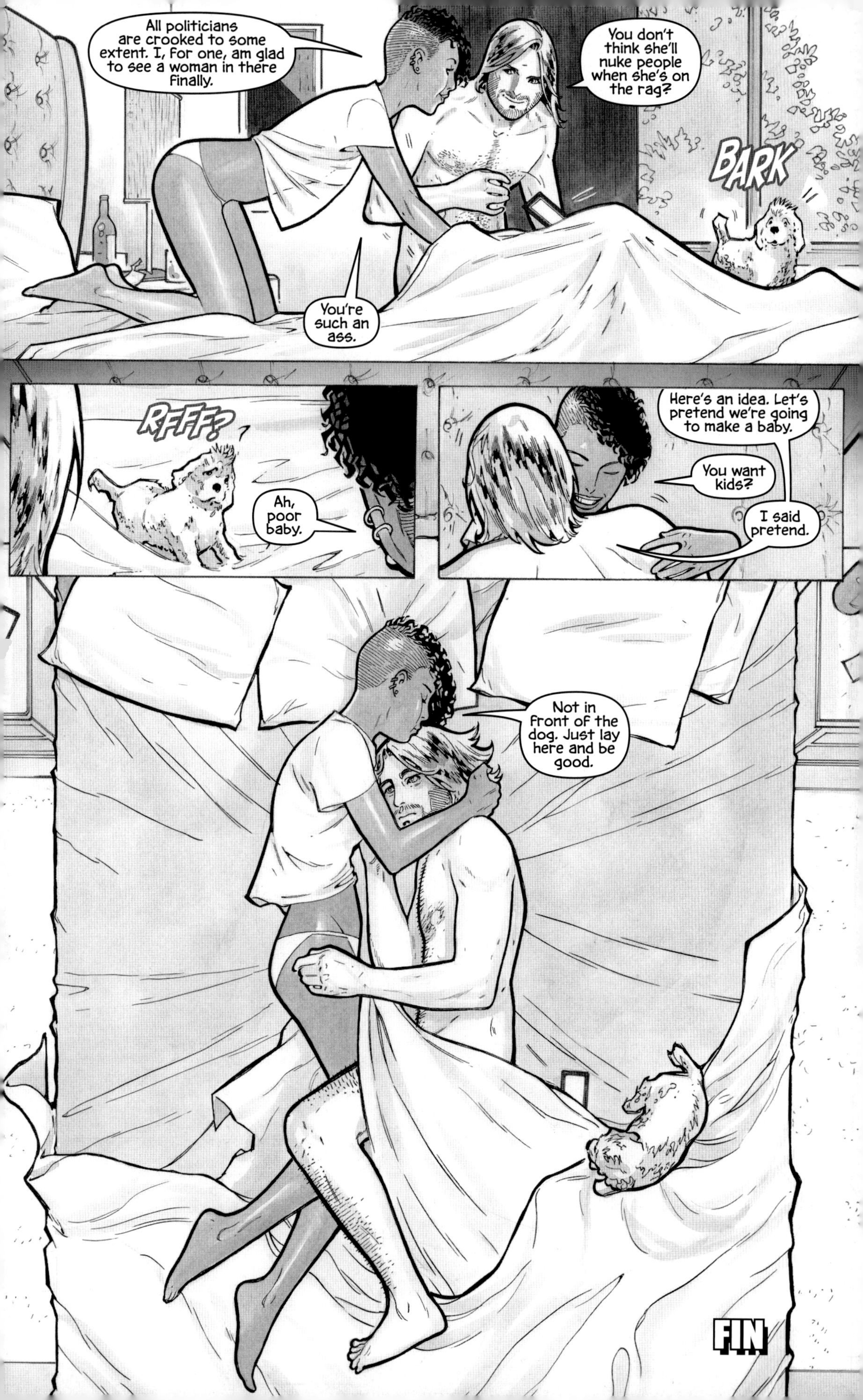

All politicians are crooked to some extent. I, for one, am glad to see a woman in there finally.
You don't think she'll nuke people when she's on the rag?
BARK
You're such an ass.
RFFF?
Ah, poor baby.
Here's an idea. Let's pretend we're going to make a baby.
You want kids?
I said pretend.
Not in front of the dog. Just lay here and be good.
FIN

米粉湯
101
旅社

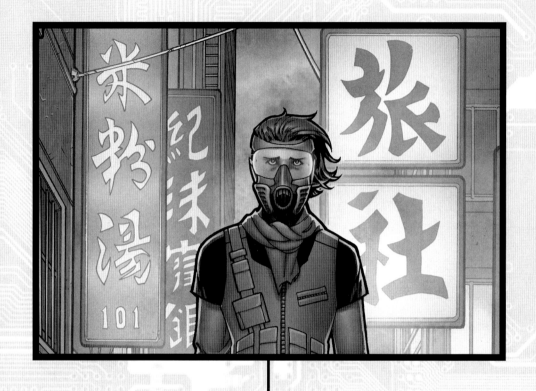

COVER GALLERY

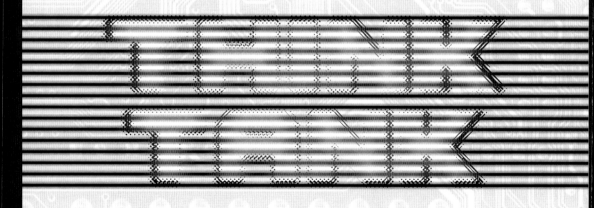

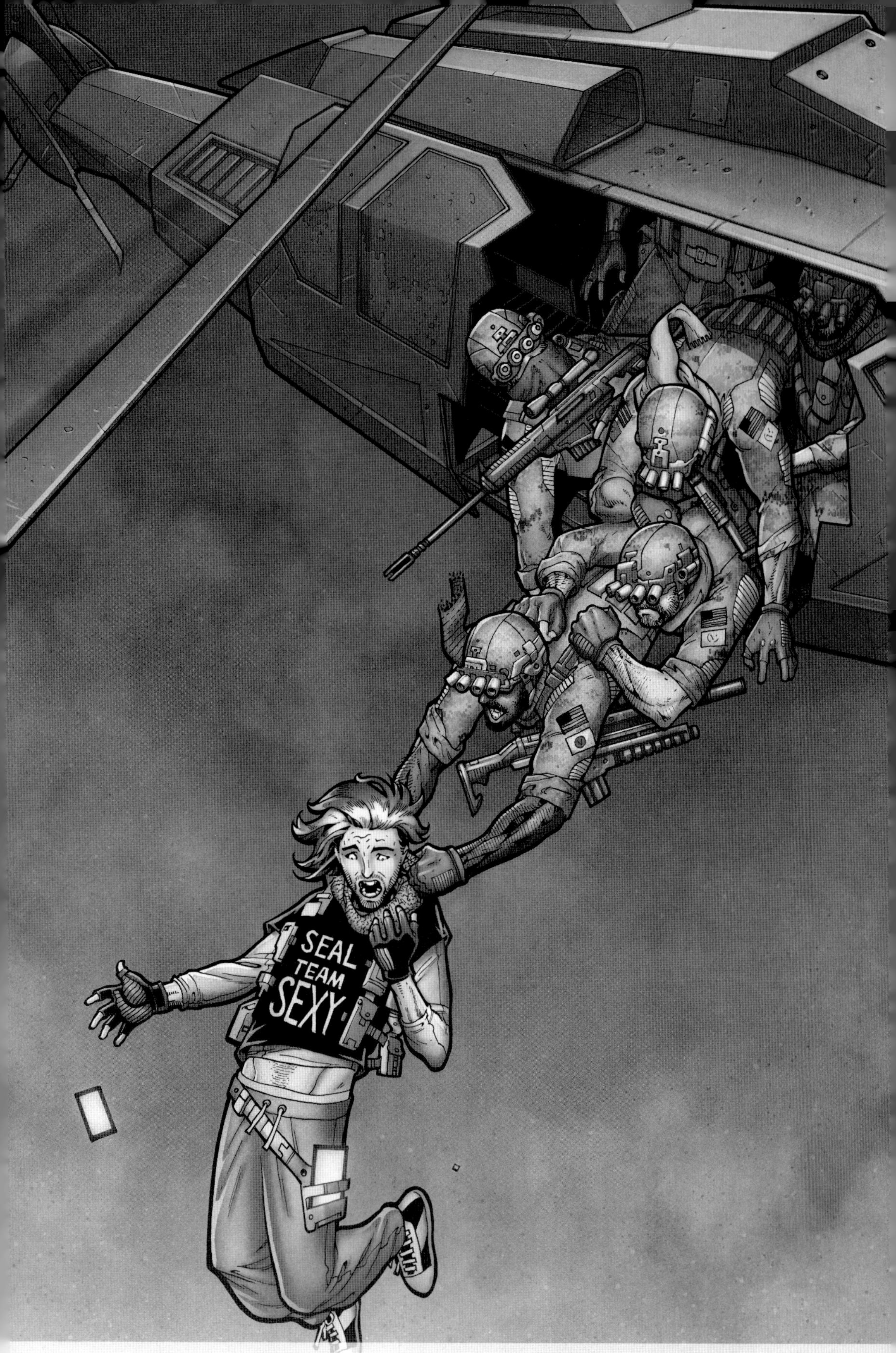
SEAL
TEAM
SEXY

Think Tank #9 cover A art by **Rahsan Ekedal** and **Bill Farmer**

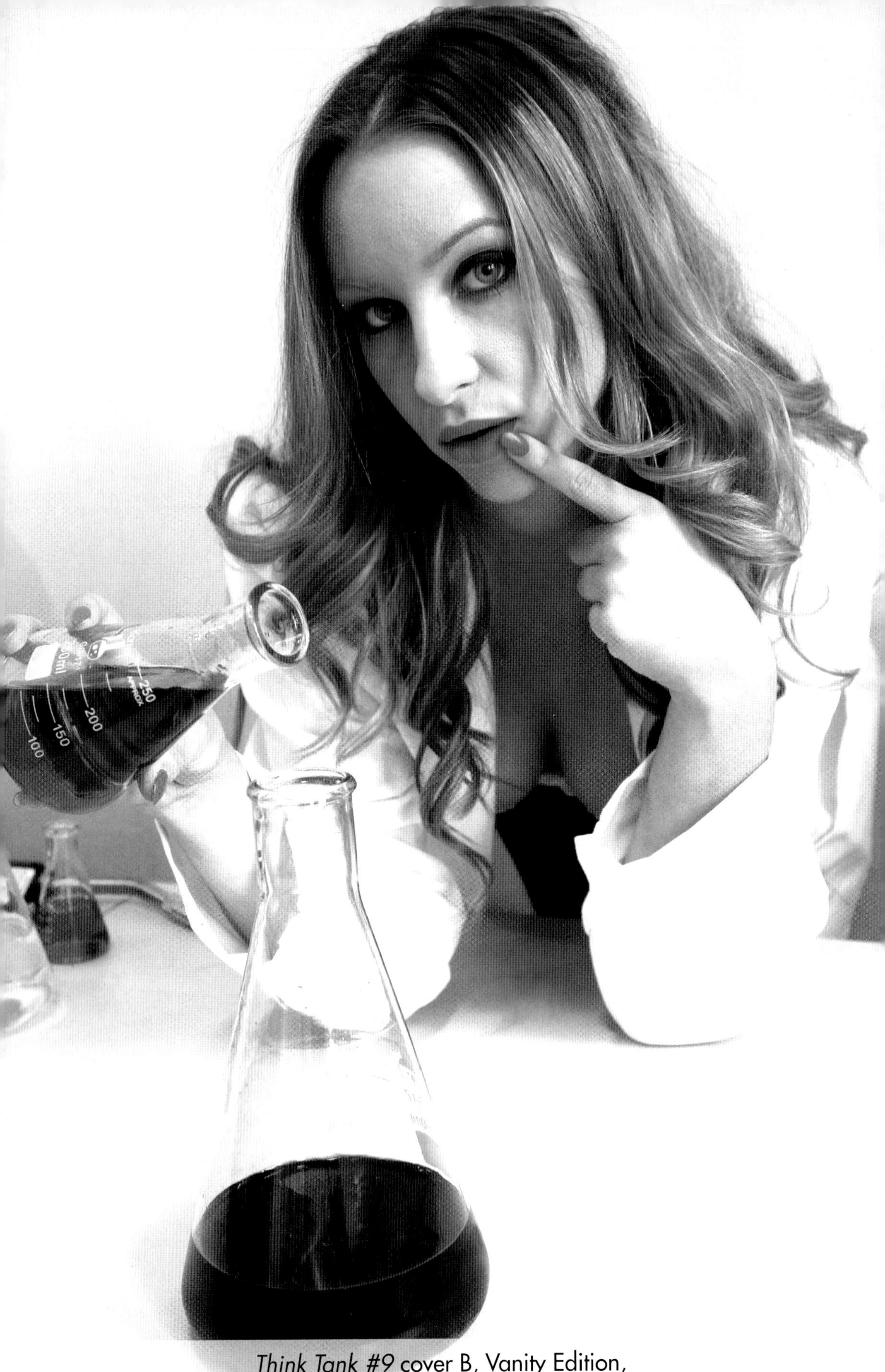
250
200
150
100

Think Tank #9 cover B, Vanity Edition,
by **C.J. Reddy Photography;** Model: **Danielle Jurik**

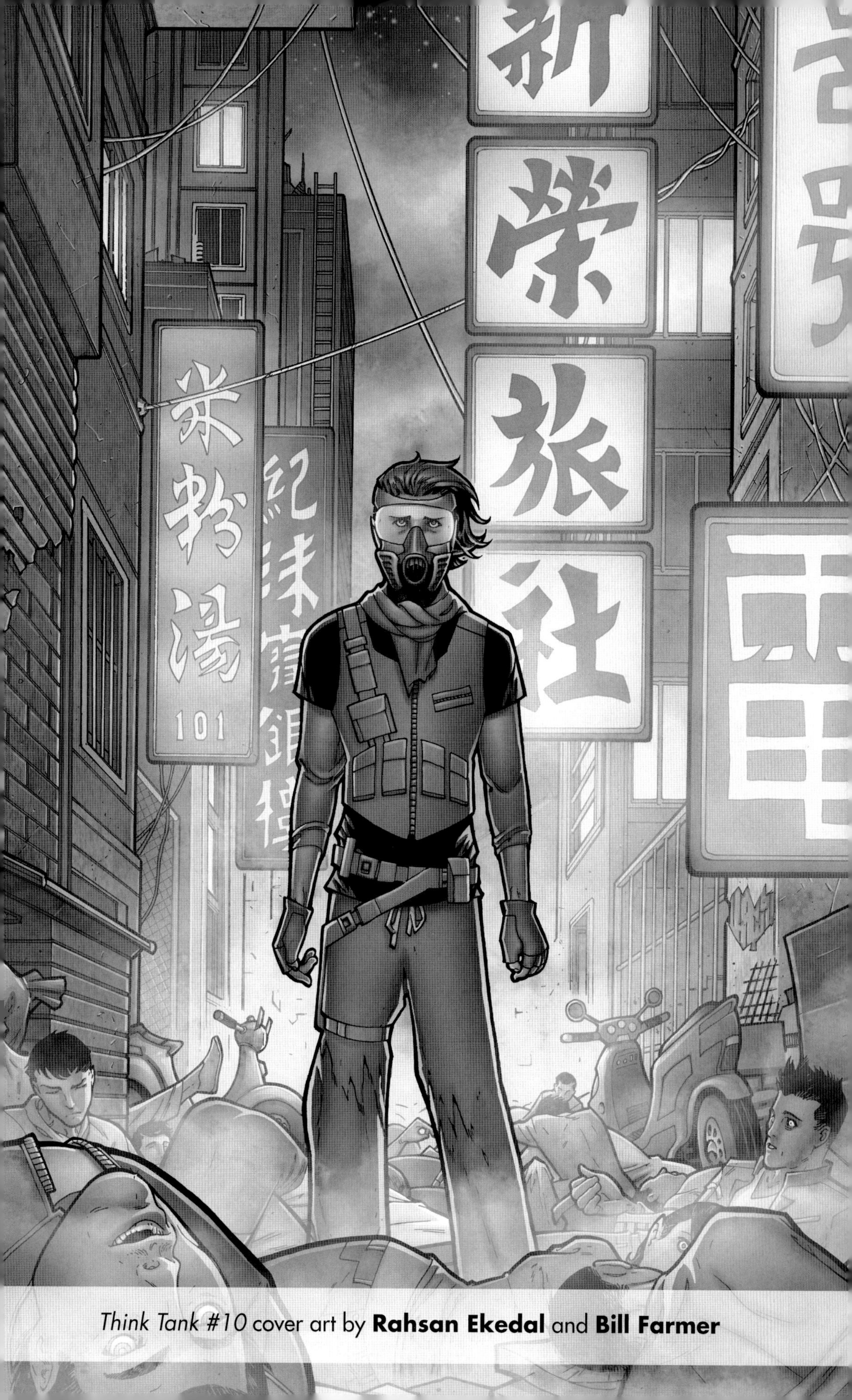
新榮旅社
米粉湯
101

Think Tank #10 cover art by **Rahsan Ekedal** and **Bill Farmer**

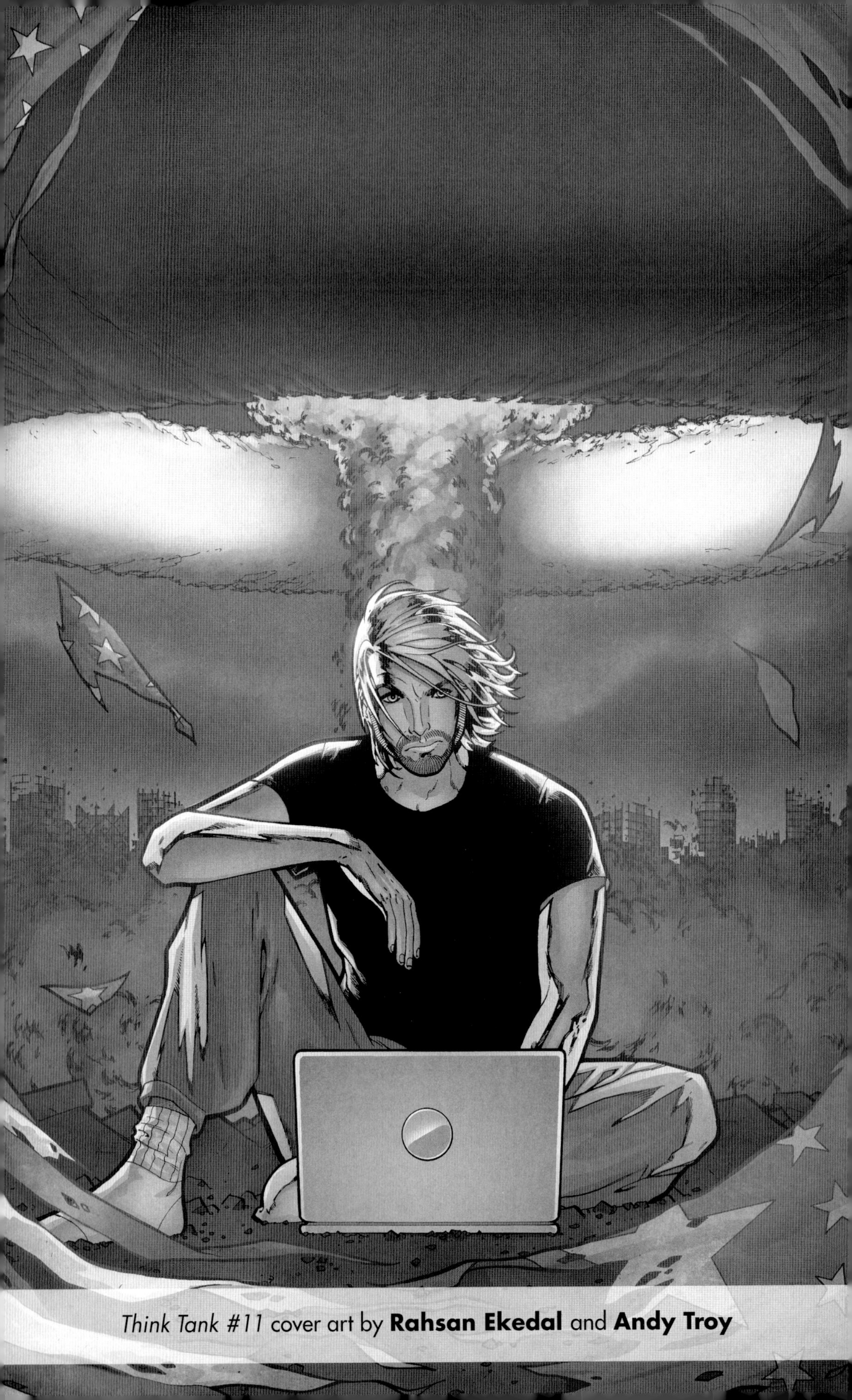

Think Tank #11 cover art by **Rahsan Ekedal** and **Andy Troy**

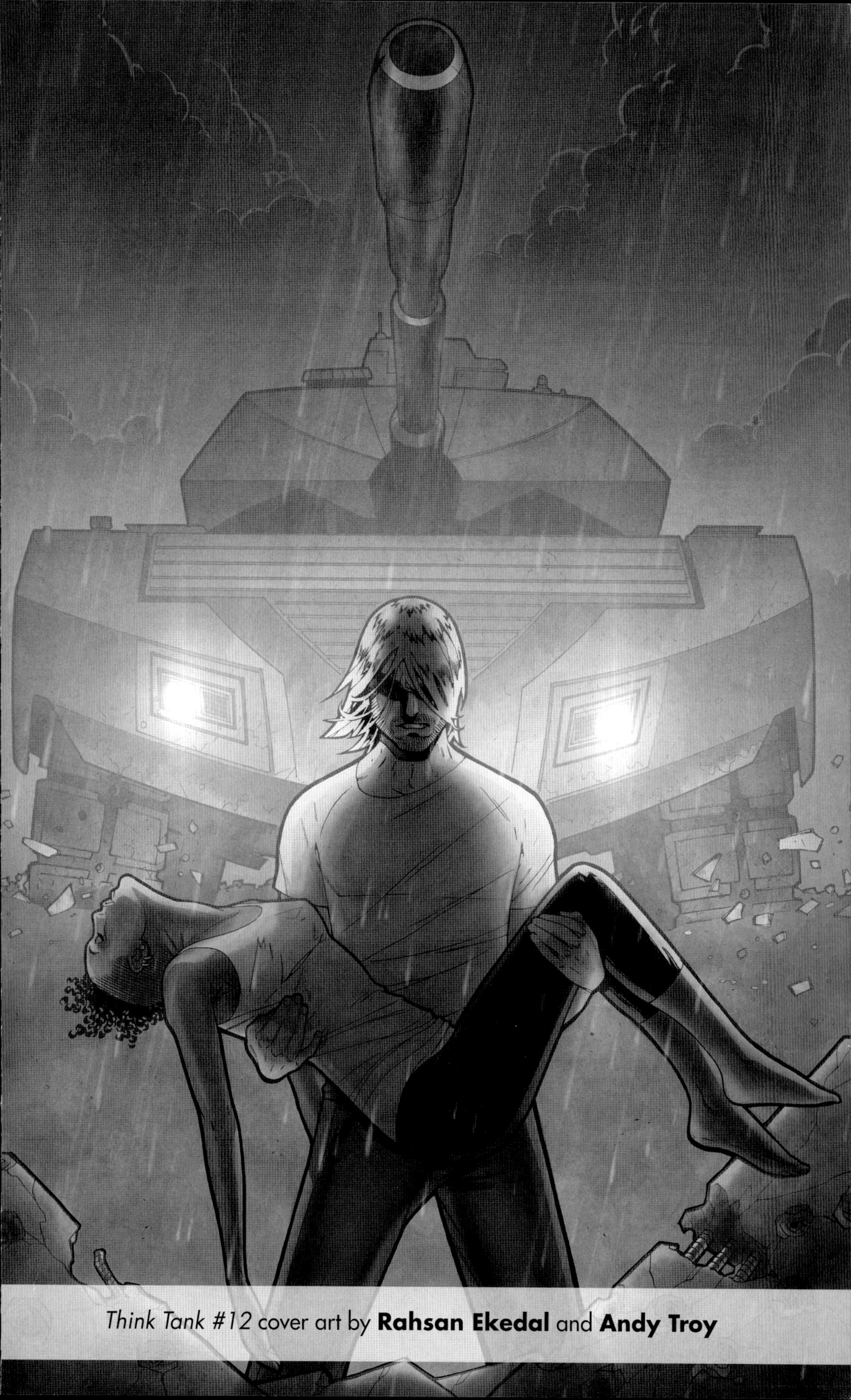

Think Tank #12 cover art by **Rahsan Ekedal** and **Andy Troy**

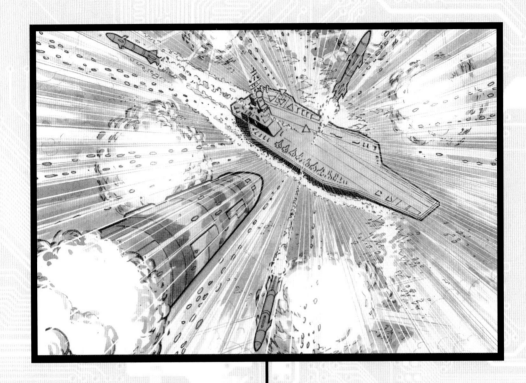

SCIENCE CLASS

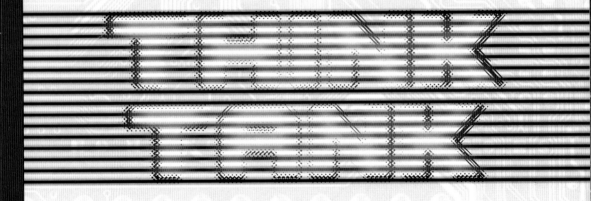

SCIENCE CLASS

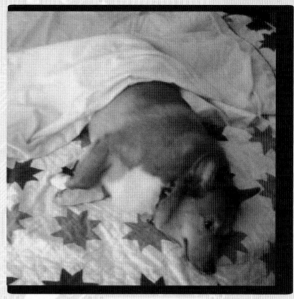

First thing I want to get out of the way is a R.I.P. for my dear dog Roman who died in the middle of the production on this book. Into the great unknown you go first, my friend. Maybe I'll see you again, who knows. I've been fairly open about my upbringing. I was raised Christian and attended church two to three times a week until I went off to college. Like most college students, I sort of lost track of the church while I was partying and trying to get laid. I found my faith again after college and went to church pretty regularly until I started doing the research for *Lady Pendragon*. That research tested my faith severely and after many unfulfilling discussions about it with pastors I turned my back on it. I was a self-proclaimed atheist for a long time but now have come back around to the agnostic side a bit. I'm open minded but unwilling to accept things that make no sense whatsoever. It always makes me laugh when Christians call Mormons a cult. As if Christianity is any easier to believe! Ultimately, I'm fine with anyone believing whatever they want as long as they aren't killing other people for their so-called faith.

Sorry for the side rant. On to the full intro!

The thing about David Loren you need to understand is that he's arrogant and that's his ultimate downfall. In the first arc (issues 1-4), he escaped the building and thought he outsmarted his superiors, but they let him go to test their defenses and to acquire tech they knew he had developed but not shared yet. In this third volume (issues 9-12), similar stuff seems to come to him with ease, but it's a trap. This is twice he's fallen for it, so he'll learn from his mistakes and be wiser for it in the future…but I've seen the discussion of the story online about how David gets away with things too easily. That was kind of the point, which moved the plot to the next point, then to the next move, counter-move, etc. Anyway, yes I'm pathetic enough to read what's written online, heh. =P

This is the last volume of the first "season." The season includes issues 1-12 and the Dossier, which has a standalone quick story in it, but not super important to the overall arc (but funny if you loathe *Twilight*). I want to thank the 5,000 or so of you who've been with us for every issue. The rest of you who've read it in the trades or digitally, I certainly appreciate that you've read the story as well, but those initial 5k people that gave this little black and white book a chance in print…I'll forever be in your debt. The thing you need to know about me, is that I do care what you think of the book. I want you to like it, to enjoy it, and to tell your friends about it.

See, I've had an issue with comic books for a long time. I've read thousands of them in my life and I don't remember 99.9% of them. Comics I bought and read last week I don't recall what happened in them. Paying $3-$4 for something you can read in 5 minutes and never think about again seems like not a good value for your dollar. It's the reason I do heavy narration, the research, the Science Class…I want you to get more for your money. I want you to put down one of these books and think about it for a minute. I want you to be looking at news articles online and read one you may never have considered looking at before because of what you read about in one of these stories. Maybe I'm a fool as I see books with forgettable, rehashed, done-a-thousand-times-before stories selling literally twenty times what this book does. I'm not bitter, just determined. Every time I go to a convention I meet about 50-100 people (depending on size of show) that try my book for the first time. Do that enough times and it adds up. It's also why you don't see me frequently do the same show two years in a row. I try to spread out and hit as much geographically as I can.

I'll jump into some Science Class topics here in a second, but first a reminder that *Think Tank: Fun with PTSD*. It's a one shot book that will make you laugh until I kill off a semi-major character, then you won't laugh as much! Bwah ha ha! And just an advance FYI, I am NOT making fun of PTSD, quite the contrary.

Now, on to the real science stuff.

GENERAL RESEARCHING TIPS

I get asked a lot how I do my research. It usually starts with a simple Google search. Usually in the top few links is a Wikipedia page. It is a great resource, but not all that reliable. It does, however, frequently list out a TON of other links and even a couple books. Depending on how deep I want to get into the topic, I'll start clicking on the links (which usually have other links) and peruse those as well. Eventually you'll see a pattern of these sites all making reference to a single book or a single person and, for intense research, I'll get that book, read it, and start following that person on social media. In some cases I'll reach out to that person and see if they'll talk to me. I've done that with geneticists and had some pretty amazing conversations. There are a few scientists that are leading men or women in their field that I can openly call friends. I met them either through the Science and Entertainment Exchange (see link) or from emailing them. People love to talk about what they do. I've always been shocked when well-published, top scientists only have 60 twitter followers. I always look to see whom THEY follow too; you can find out about even more awesome people that way. One warning about researching some military things is to be careful that you're not looking at a video game discussion page. I spent HOURS going through a forum the other day, completely mesmerized...up until I realized it wasn't real.

http://goo.gl/Woyylk

NAVAL SPECIAL WARFARE GROUP 4 SBT -12 ●

I just assumed there was SEAL Team 1-10, or something like that, since SEAL Team Six was popularized. They aren't formed like that and, although technically the SEALs and the Special Warfare Units (like the one I feature) are different, I've lumped them in together. I initially wrote an in-detail narrative explaining the difference, but it was too much. Only super crazed military nerds (like me) would know the difference and I'm allowed some creative license! These groups all have various specializations, which makes sense. If you're going to be the best at something, you have to specialize.

Basic info on SEALs taken from the first site link:

There are eight SEAL teams. Each team has six platoons and a headquarters element. SEAL platoons consist of 16 SEALs -- two officers, one chief, and 13 enlisted men. A platoon is generally the largest operational element assigned to a mission. The platoon may also be divided into two squads or four elements. Every member of a SEAL platoon is qualified in diving, parachuting, and demolitions.

http://goo.gl/6f9KqB
http://goo.gl/kAc3HJ

UNITED STATES ARMS DEALER TO THE WORLD

The U.S. is the salesman for 44% of the worlds whopping one trillion a year spent on the militaries around the world. We sell submarines, tanks, planes, systems, guns – you name it, we sell it. The first link below at globalissues. com has detailed charts and graphs on what we sell and whom we sell it to. We have made the same mistakes over the centuries by arming people that eventually come back to bite us in the ass (Iran, Iraq, Afghanistan, etc.). The Middle East is my favorite quagmire of unrest. Can you think of a time in your life when there wasn't "trouble in the Middle East"? In this specific story, I've certainly taken creative liberty with the situation between Taiwan and China, but it's only a possible scenario. I'll talk about that more in the next issue.

chart by amCharts.com
Arms sales (agreements), by Supplier, 2004-2011 (in billions of constant 2011 U.S. dollars)

- Others: 5%
- Other European: 10%
- Italy: 3%
- Germany: 4%
- China: 4%
- United Kingdom: 5%
- France: 8%
- Russia: 17%
- United States: 44%

Source: Richard F. Grimmett, CRS Report for Congress; Conventional Arms Transfers to Developing Nations, 2004-2011. August 24, 2012

If you've not seen the movie *Lord of War* by Andrew Niccol and starring Nicholas Cage (in one of his 1-in-4 awesome films) you should watch it, it's pretty scary awesome.

http://goo.gl/IWXQOS
http://goo.gl/tkOI5N

ECM AND ECCM

Electronic countermeasures and electronic counter-countermeasures! Try saying that five times fast. Electronic warfare (EW) and the use of ECM and ECCM is all about using the electromagnetic spectrum to gain or block advantages in battle. Useful in aerial confrontations and missile attacks, it's how targets are identified and locked onto. ECM allows an attacking aircraft to mask its movements and signature from their target's radar. In this story, the missiles used ECM to try and prevent the Blackhawk from being aware that they were locking onto them. The Blackhawk engaged countering measures (ECCM) to overcome that. Not your typical use, it's usually applied the other way around, but it works. Bottom line is, whoever has the better equipment for EW will win the encounter. The irony I'm trying to get across in this story is that, since we sell so many weapons overseas, too frequently we're confronted with our own weapons...whether by friendly fire or by someone simply using our own stuff against us.

http://goo.gl/wx55Tz
http://goo.gl/YnEJIS

ROCKWELL ARC-220 AND RAYTHEON'S MIM-HAWK

These are both real things as well. The link below will take you to where you can buy the one from Rockwell. I couldn't find a sales slip for the Raytheon one, but the second link shows more info about it.

http://goo.gl/I9k1YJ
http://goo.gl/tbBMdc

SURFACE TO AIR MISSILES (SAM)

These have been around in concept since 1931. People discussed them prior to that, but the first conceptual drawing was completed that year by Dr. Gustav Prasmus. The modern versions, including the well-known Patriot system, are vastly better with significant improvements in the aforementioned electronic warfare department. Looking at those early sketches, however, the basic design and appearance of these is the same and hasn't changed much in 80 years. The first effectively used SAM was during the Vietnam War by the Soviets against the U.S.

http://goo.gl/HNUmkZ
http://goo.gl/6oUfqQ

BODY LOSING MASS AT DEATH

The first I'd ever heard of this was reading one of Dan Brown's books where he talks about the Noetic Sciences and how the body loses a small amount of mass when it dies and that a lot of people have "theorized" that it's the soul departing the body. In 1901 (or 1907, from other conflicting reports) Dr. Duncan MacDougall researched weight loss at the precise moment of death by putting people who were about to die on a specially designed scale and weighing them as they died. There was a measurable weight loss for humans but NOT for a subsequent experiment with dogs. So pseudo-science started claiming that this was the soul and that the soul had weight. This is a discredited study, but fun to talk about. A movie about this came out in 2003 called *21 Grams*; it's worth watching on Netflix.

http://goo.gl/pYRSA0
http://goo.gl/G5IOkl
http://goo.gl/c62MKU
http://goo.gl/rkr6Mi

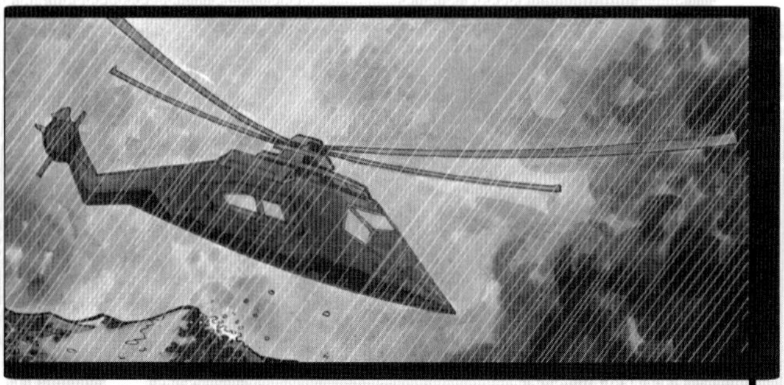

BLACKHAWK SIKORSKY

I love these things. Here's a link to a site where you can buy one if you have millions of liquid cash to spare. I especially love the optional weapons kits they offer. The 2nd link has some of the photographs taken at Bin Laden's compound where the stealth Sikorsky crashed.

http://goo.gl/ddv6Vq
http://goo.gl/2j5XFc

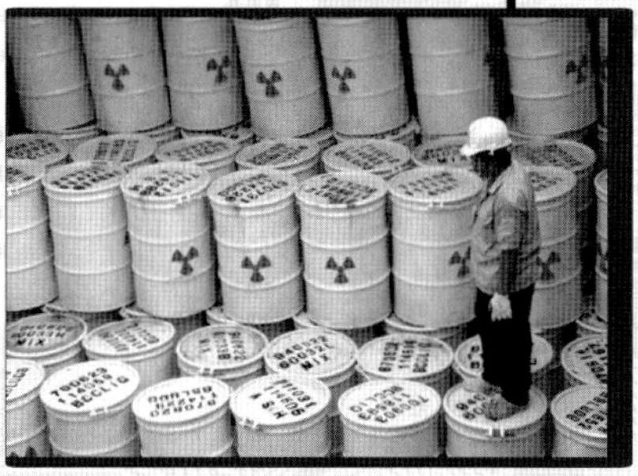

ORCHID ISLAND

This is a real place. I included it primarily because of its location and that it really does have that nuclear waste facility on it. There's lots of controversy surrounding it; I know our country has a bleak history of this kind of action as well.

http://goo.gl/iT85H5
http://goo.gl/PKWcZp
http://goo.gl/EWFQzx
http://goo.gl/WxqDsP

PROPAGANDA

Propaganda is kind of like marketing a brand, except the brand is an idea or a government. Propaganda gets a bad rap, but it's not all that different from how companies advertise product to us on a daily basis. The Nazis are frequently associated with propaganda and Hitler's "Triumph of the Will" is considered the first propaganda film. Lots of glittering troops, shiny uniforms, and upward angles to make him appear majestic:

http://goo.gl/RWJns3

The Nazis had an agenda, obviously, and some of their more grotesque posters can be found here:

http://goo.gl/pKPYNw

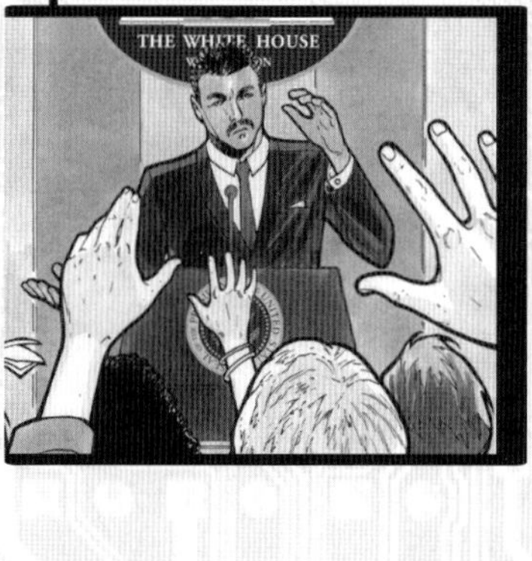
THE WHITE HOUSE

I link to this stuff only because it's good to see evil for what it is. No one should shy away from confronting a wrong because we might see the confrontation as going against our civic duty. That's what happened to a lot of Germans. But propaganda is used in *every* war. Colin Powell's presentation to the UN on Iraq WMDs is great propaganda theater:

http://goo.gl/bHKvLV

There were no WMDs, but we all thought there were! This was manipulation and deceit of the highest order. I liken some of what I've done with *Think Tank* to how this situation was handled, as I personally believe that Colin Powell was tricked into doing this. The first link has a detailed explanation of how propaganda works.

http://goo.gl/kifpdb
http://goo.gl/I01nmq

TAIWAN-CHINA

When I started looking into where I wanted to set the third arc of *Think Tank* and where David would go out into the field, I realized I knew very little about the situation in Taiwan and its relationship to China. I've always said "write what you **want** to know" so I set it there and proceeded to dig in and find out all I could. Living in the U.S., we don't often see foreign militaries. If you live in Taiwan, you'll see naval vessels and planes from a variety of different countries…all the time. That has to be disconcerting. Also, to be a part of the Pacific Pivot, as Obama is now calling it, doesn't help:

http://goo.gl/pftVmx
http://goo.gl/Tawxoq

For decades, the U.S. had been able to keep China down by limiting its access to broader energy supplies. Restricting the flow of oil stalled their economic engine. That changed about 15 years ago and we've seen the resulting boom in the Chinese economy. As any economist will tell you, however, it's not that simple and there are a lot of other factors involved. For some very interesting stats comparing the U.S. to China, check out the link below:

http://goo.gl/Js0t92

The Taiwanese situation is a complicated one and has to do with civil war, regime change, and a fleeing dictator who wanted to regain his glory on the mainland. Stanford has a pretty detailed timeline/history of Taiwan worth a look:

http://goo.gl/BjaNNT
http://goo.gl/14zBzw
http://goo.gl/ioa6bu

U.S. ARMS SALES TO TAIWAN

Our military's greatest fear regarding China is that we'll lose Taiwan as an "ally." It's weird that we call them an ally when, technically, we don't recognize them as a country. In fact, our government has a policy of "strategic ambiguity" when it comes to Taiwan. We've armed them and have vowed to protect them from the Chinese for decades. Here's a list of the weapons we sell them:

http://goo.gl/veLneg

PRESIDENTIAL DEATH THREATS

Obama gets 30 death threats a day compared to Bush, who got about six a day. The Secret Service investigates ALL of these as if they're real, so don't be a chucklehead and spout off on twitter.

http://goo.gl/410mh5
http://goo.gl/HEdSyQ

It is against the law to threaten the president and you will be prosecuted. This link shows the actual law:

http://goo.gl/oy9o8R

WAR

The study of war is one you can lose decades in. What causes war? What are the stated reasons versus what we find out, years later, to be the actual reasons? The dictionary definition of war is, "a state of armed conflict between different nations or states or different groups within a nation or state." The 2nd link below is the more interesting one and breaks down the possible causes of war and how it might be prevented. My father was an Air Force officer and during Vietnam, stationed in a missile silo prepared to nuke the Soviets. I remember him telling me a story about the movie *War Games* and how that "turning of the key" thing was totally overplayed. In reality, they "turned the key" all the time in drills so, if the order was real, they wouldn't have even thought about it.

http://goo.gl/2j9evF
http://goo.gl/vdc9vq
http://goo.gl/txH1cP

DREAMS

I have weird dreams. I get some of my best ideas from dreams. I do keep a dream journal and write down anything that is of passing interest. You lose your dreams very quickly, but if you write down even part of it you can roll it back, almost like a movie in your mind. Again, I hit VERY broad strokes on a lot of this stuff, but here is a passage I took from the first link below:

METAPHYSICS OF DREAMS: What is your subconscious trying to tell you? One good way to find out is through your dreams. When we sleep, our subconscious doesn't need to battle with our conscious mind. Our emotional side is not challenged by our logic, so it's easy for our subconscious to break through barriers. But it isn't always easy to understand what it is trying to tell us. The subconscious relays messages in the form of dream symbols, or sometimes even bizarre dreams in which we are participants or observers. Think of a dream as a private movie screening of a film in which you play the leading role, or perhaps just sit in the front row of the theater.

The study of dreams is broad and there are as many legit scientists and psychiatrists who are dedicated to this as there are crackpot fortuneteller-types who are also into it. I've included links for both types!

http://goo.gl/6ieyn7
http://goo.gl/6Hy0J0
http://goo.gl/5PrZum
http://goo.gl/6ZSPlc

PSYCHOLOGY OF DREAMS

Dreams are so rich and have such an authentic feeling that scientists have long assumed they must have a crucial psychological purpose. To Freud, dreaming provided a playground for the unconscious mind; to Jung, it was a stage where the psyche's archetypes acted out primal themes. Newer theories hold that dreams help the brain to consolidate emotional memories or to work though current problems, like divorce and work frustrations.

SCIENCE OF DREAMS

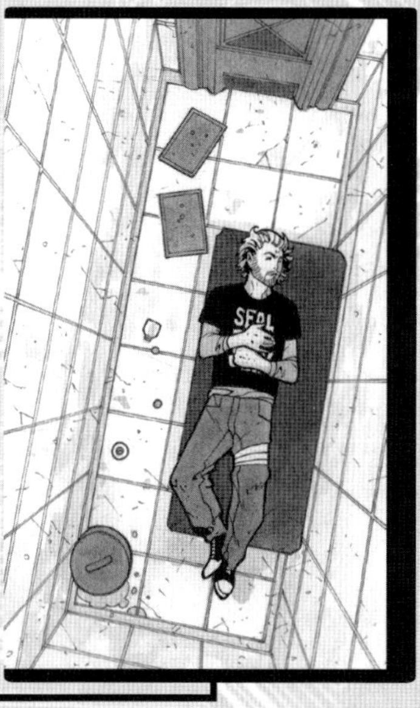

In a paper published last month in the journal *Nature Reviews Neuroscience*, Dr. J. Allan Hobson, a psychiatrist and longtime sleep researcher at Harvard, argues that the main function of rapid-eye-movement sleep, or REM, when most dreaming occurs, is physiological. The brain is warming its circuits, anticipating the sights and sounds and emotions of waking.

Physiological theories are based on the idea that we dream in order to exercise various neural connections that some researchers believe affect certain types of learning. Psychological theories are based on the idea that dreaming allows us to sort through problems, events of the day, or things that are requiring a lot of our attention. Some of these theorists think dreams might be prophetic. Many researchers and scientists also believe that perhaps it is a combination of the two theories.

http://goo.gl/8wwBNk

ISOLATION

Extreme isolation is considered torture by most countries around the world… including some that we consider to be incubators of terrorists. I'm not 100% on how I feel about this, but some of the research I did showed that isolation can mess people up. I also find it interesting that our own intelligence people call it "white torture" but the government doesn't classify it as such.

http://goo.gl/kQup63
http://goo.gl/hrvssb
http://goo.gl/OIXjGe

CHINESE DRONES

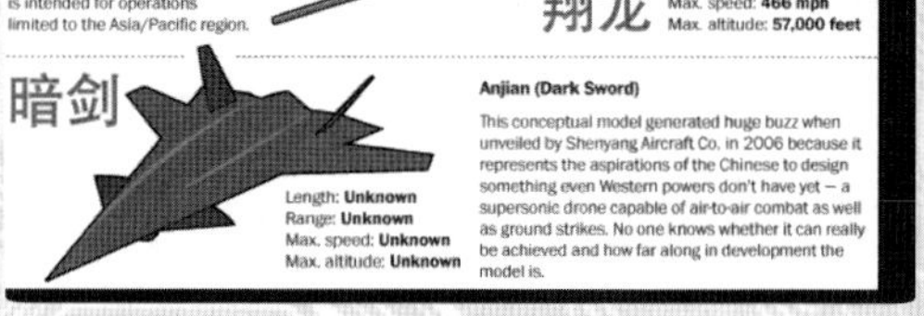
Yilong (Pterodactyl)
This medium-sized, propeller-driven drone is China's answer to the U.S. Predator and MQ-9 Reaper drones — with a similar V-tail configuration. Its manufacturer, Aviation Industry Corp., says the Yilong has undergone test flights and is now the only drone being freely sold on the international market that can be used for both reconnaissance and strikes.
Length: 29.5 feet
Range: 2,485.5 miles
Maximum speed: 174 mph
Maximum altitude: 16,404 feet
翼龙
Xianglong (Soaring Dragon)
Produced by Aviation Industry Corp., this is the Chinese version of the U.S. RQ-4 Global Hawk — an advanced, high-altitude, long-duration drone designed for reconnaissance. The main difference is that the Xianglong has only a fraction of the Global Hawk's range; its manufacturer says it is intended for operations limited to the Asia/Pacific region.
翔龙
Length: 45.9 feet
Range: 4,660 miles
Max. speed: 466 mph
Max. altitude: 57,000 feet
暗剑
Anjian (Dark Sword)
This conceptual model generated huge buzz when unveiled by Shenyang Aircraft Co. in 2006 because it represents the aspirations of the Chinese to design something even Western powers don't have yet — a supersonic drone capable of air-to-air combat as well as ground strikes. No one knows whether it can really be achieved and how far along in development the model is.
Length: Unknown
Range: Unknown
Max. speed: Unknown
Max. altitude: Unknown

When people think of drone technology they think of the United States, but there are currently 96 countries with some form of UAV technology in place. Only the bigger players have weaponized systems though. There are going to be a lot more of these birds in the air, and accidents are bound to happen. Countries are much more likely to risk unmanned vessels for risky reconnaissance flights. The U2 spy plane debacles from the Cold War are a thing of the past.

One report from the third link states;

> "The majority of foreign UAVs that countries have acquired fall within the tactical category. Tactical UAVs primarily conduct intelligence, surveillance, and reconnaissance missions and typically have a limited operational range of at most 300 kilometers. However, some more advanced varieties are capable of performing intelligence collection, targeting, or attack missions. Mini UAVs were also frequently acquired across the globe during this period."

http://goo.gl/3yZ6k1

http://goo.gl/K5avUP

http://goo.gl/W3k90

This picture shows the various Chinese Drones that are currently in use.

CHINESE NAVY AND MILITARY CAPABILITIES

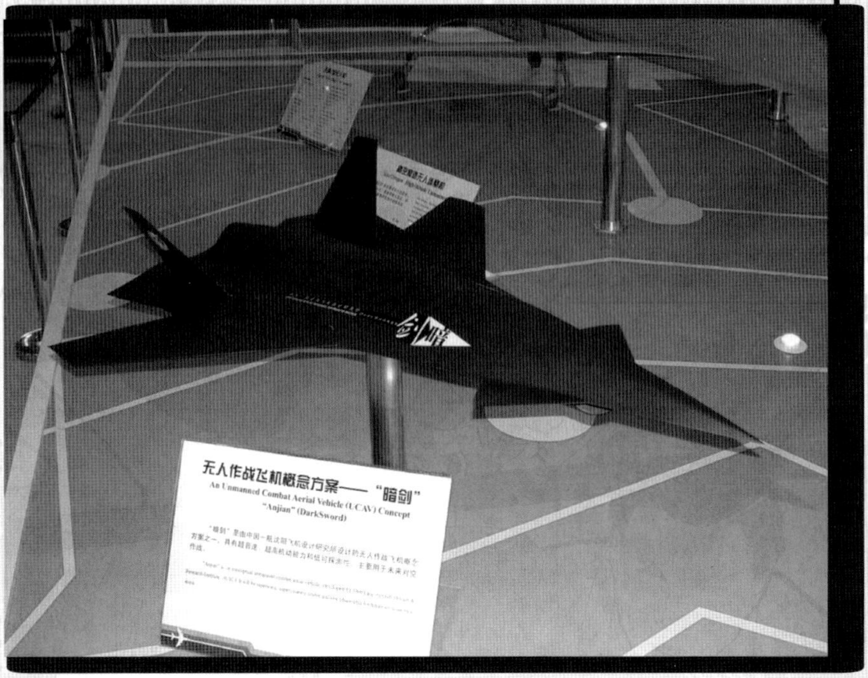

无人作战飞机概念方案——“暗剑”
An Unmanned Combat Aerial Vehicle (UCAV) Concept
“Anjian” (DarkSword)

China has the largest Navy in the world now. The US Navy is more technologically advanced, but the Chinese are closing that gap every year. I've been criticized for showing scenarios where China and the US might go to war. The irony of this is that I'm pulling many of those concepts from research. There's a very real chance that the US and China will have some sort of conflict over energy and oil. There's only so much of it, and we both drink it up like mad with all our machines and toys.

DAVID ROAMING SHANGHAI/PENINSULA SCENE

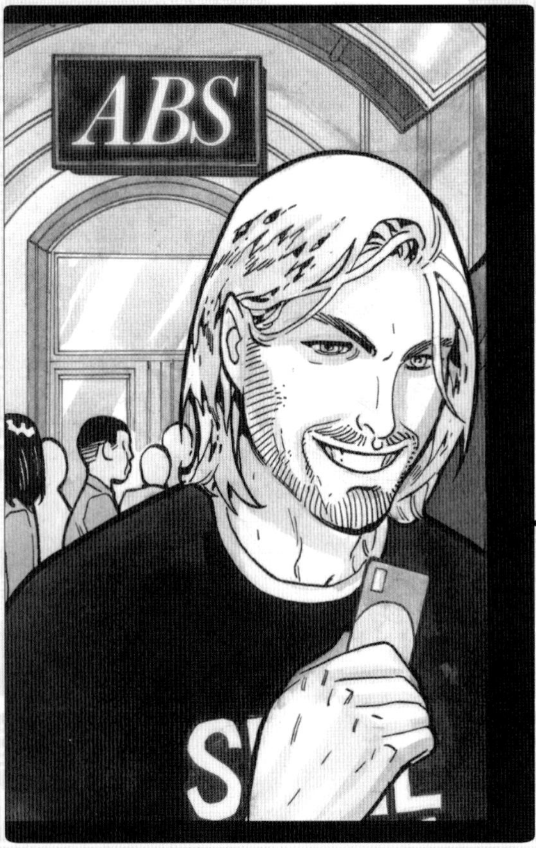

ABS

China's border security and access points for trains, planes, etc. are all insanely regulated. Once you get past all that, it's much easier to get around as it is in most countries. China has millions of foreigners within its borders on a daily basis, so it's not that difficult to blend in if you look busy, or if you wave money around.

Before you cry implausible for any of these things that are happening in the book, know that I have snuck into several science conferences without any identification of any kind in three different countries. Not that hard if you know the lingo.

DIFFERENT RULES FOR PEOPLE WITH MONEY

If you don't believe this I don't know what to tell you. Maybe you live in your own little world. Read this:

http://goo.gl/lIB2j

NUMBERED BANK ACCOUNTS

These are real, and you can have one! You can put money in that's not tracked by your government for taxes, and they allow you to retrieve it at any of their branches around the world.

http://goo.gl/hJhYt

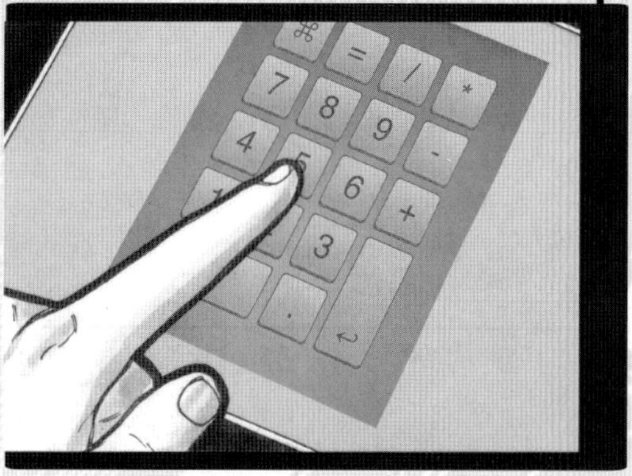
7
8
9
4
5
6
+
3
*
=
/
-

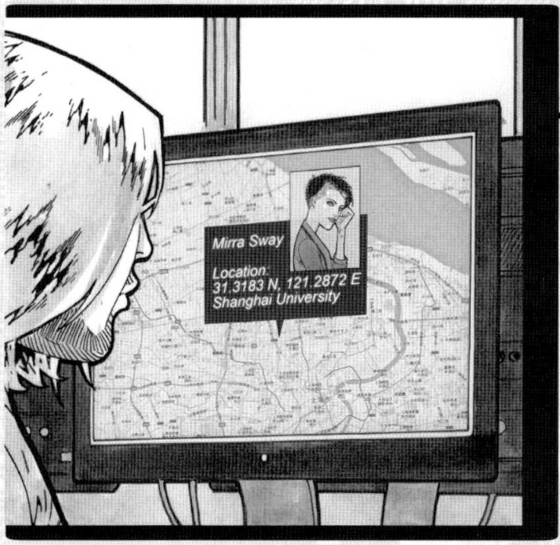
Mirra Sway
Location:
31.3183 N, 121.2872 E
Shanghai University

TRACKING YOUR TABLET

I know this is a throwaway line in here, but it's 100% true. You can be tracked even when your phone or tablet is off. You probably shouldn't care; who wants to track you anyway? But if you want to scratch your conspiracy itch, check out Flyware tracking apps.

http://goo.gl/DtWYbW

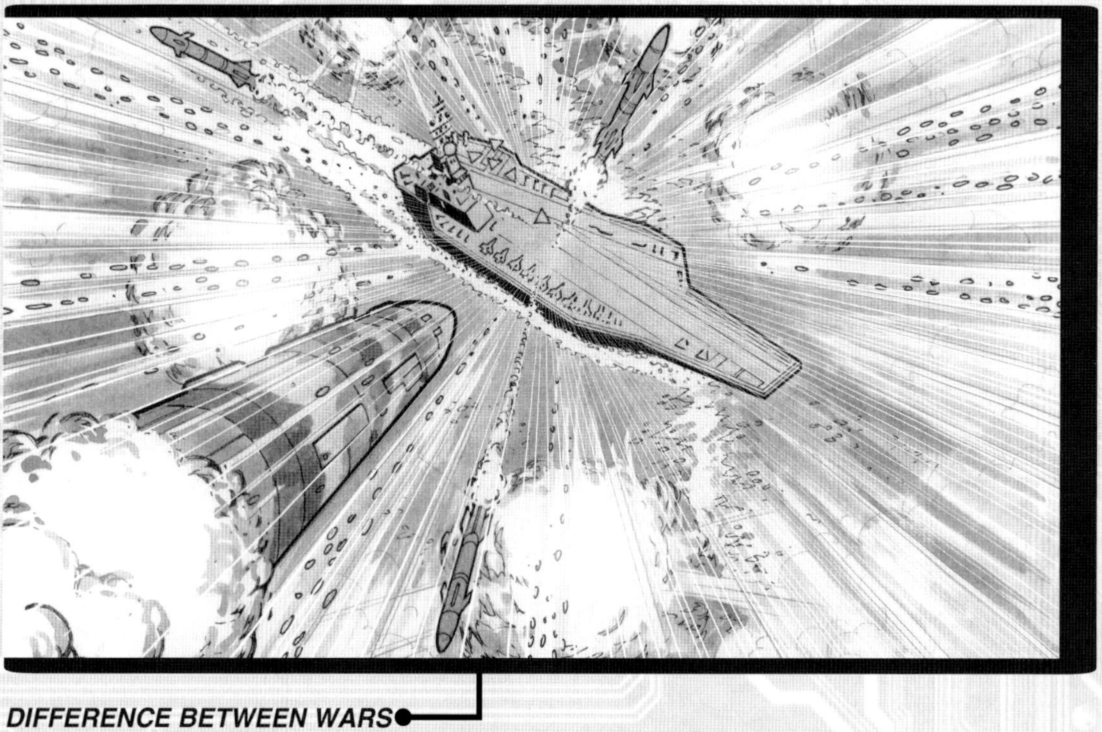

DIFFERENCE BETWEEN WARS

This link is worth checking. It shows the difference between various wars, body counts, etc. Fun stuff.

http://goo.gl/cYYsu

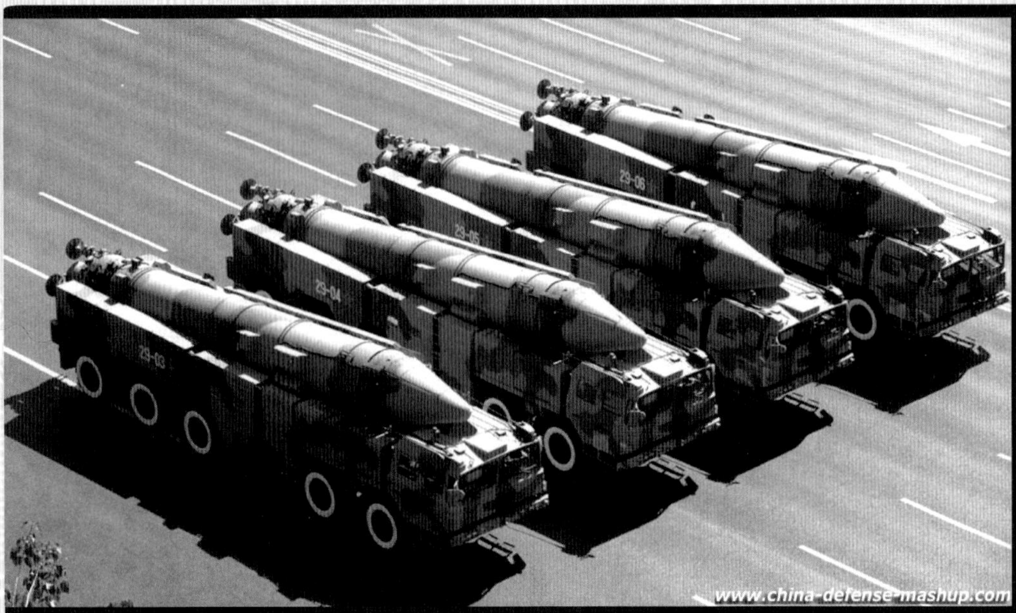
www.china-defense-mashup.com

DF21D ANTI-CARRIER MISSILE

These are real of course. It's scary stuff that it's possible now to take out one of our aircraft carriers in a single shot.

http://goo.gl/O5ZrU2

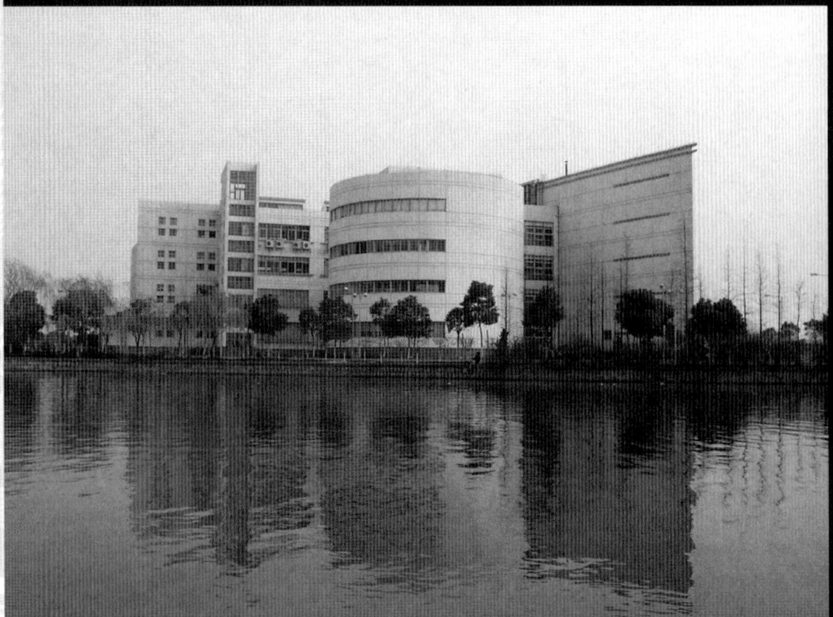

SHANGHAI UNIVERSITY

It's one of the best science and research universities in Asia. As always, we try to give it a real world flare, even though we're doing our fictional fun stuff.

http://goo.gl/bmPahP

NEWS DRONE CAMS

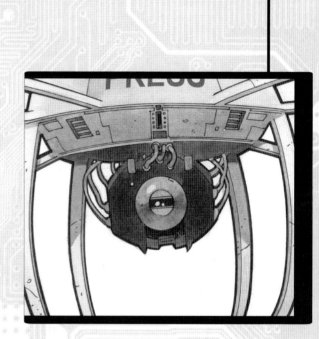

I added this scene at the beginning to frame the introduction, but I only saw these news drones about a week before I gave Rahsan the plot. I was watching some Japanese news program with subtitles, and they went live to some drone over the ocean and I was like, "WHAT?!?!?!" In the U.S., we always think we're the cutting edge of everything, but the Japanese have some interesting uses of tech that we don't. We use drones for football games - I guess we have our priorities. BTW, I recommend on occasion watching foreign news programs. It will open your eyes and broaden your outlook. Don't just listen to your own nation's rhetoric.

10 VIRAL EPIDEMICS THAT ALMOST WIPED US OUT

This too will scare you, worth checking out:

http://goo.gl/V6gL3e

About 400 million people worldwide have Hepatitis B, and show no symptoms or may not show symptoms for years:

http://goo.gl/zlPKiG

DAVID AS A "CARRIER" OF OMEGA

People "carry" viruses and germs all the time without ever realizing it. A true asymptomatic carrier is a person who has contracted an infectious disease or viral contamination, but displays no symptoms. These people can transmit the disease or virus without ever having any manifest signs of it themselves. In some cases, given the severity of a viral infection, it can cause lesser symptoms to the carrier. That's clearly what I've gone for in the story as David (injected with an OMEGA variant while he was under) gets some of the effects of the infectious agent that causes almost instantaneous death in the Chinese. They would have to make it a broad effect for it to kill so many, but the transmission time and length to death (seconds) would prevent it from spreading too broadly. Viruses are spread by skin contact or airborne through sneezing, talking, or floating off skin. Weaponized viruses and pathogens can be tailored to seek out the warm, watery humans that they munch on with such glee. Crashing in a plane and getting eaten by a shark scares us, but what we really should be scared of are viruses.

If you want to read some scary shit about viruses read this:

http://goo.gl/6YVbsD

VIRUS FACTOIDS

There are 10,000,000,000,000,000,000,000,000,000,000 different viruses on earth alone. I wrote it that way instead of 1 x 10^31 because it looks longer and makes the point. They evolve 10'000 faster than mammals. They reproduce to the tune of billions an hour. In every way, from a pure and rational perspective, you could make the claim that viruses are the dominant life form on Earth.

http://goo.gl/PS9PS3
http://goo.gl/bHWT4

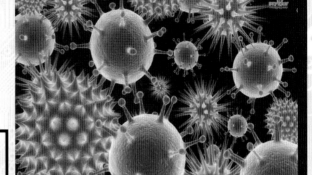

VIRAL SPREAD AND FOMITES

A fomite is defined by Merriam Webster as, "an inanimate object (as a dish, toy, book, doorknob, or clothing) that may be contaminated with infectious organisms and serve in their transmission."

Viruses spread by various means. The most common are (from the link below):

Droplet contact – This is the respiratory route in which the virus is transmitted when the infected person coughs or sneezes. The virus remains suspended in droplets of water and mucous that leave the body and can enter another person through the nose, mouth, or eyes.

- Viral droplet nuclei transmission – In this horizontal transmission, the virus is generally shed by the infected person in a mucous filled droplet. If the humidity in the environment is low, the mucous shell evaporates quickly allowing the virus nuclei to remain airborne for a longer period of time. This is possible because the virus nuclei are extremely light and can float in air traveling with air currents for a long time.

- Fecal-oral transmission – This is one of the virus transmission types that is generally not direct in the case of humans. However, improper washing of hands can lead to the spread of virus from the feces.

- Sexual transmission – One of the most common routes for viruses to spread is through sexual transmission. This can occur during vaginal or anal sex, and the actual transmission is either through exchange of body fluids, or infectious sores, or cuts. Oral sexual transmission can also spread by kissing.

- Direct contact or vector borne – Diseases that are spread by direct contact are generally called contagious diseases. Indirect contact can occur through touching common objects like public telephones.

http://goo.gl/HkDoHt

WARNING
Biohazard
警告
生物危害

BIOHAZARD

Basically if you see this sign anywhere, stay away. It's likely medical waste, but chances are there's something in there that won't react well to your skin.

BIO-SAFETY LEVELS ●━━━━━━━━━━━━━━

Basically these are the precautionary levels that scientists and researchers use when testing or evaluating different lethality of infectious agents. It's all about bio-containment, which is a whole industry itself. BS1 (biosafety level 1) has your easy stuff like canine hepatitis and non-pathogenic e-coli, to BS4 which has hemorraghic fevers and Ebola. Basically 1 is no fun, but easy to deal with, and 4 will kill you.

http://goo.gl/puxtw5

GPS TRIGGERING DEVICES/RELEASING THE PATHOGEN

Okay, I don't know if these exist but they should. Museums use them, so I don't see why we couldn't create one as a trigger for a bomb, or in this case for a very small sealed container that has been injected subcutaneously, that would then be absorbed by the blood stream and transmitted throughout the body very quickly. There is NOTHING online about this; I googled for hours. So, I think it's possible, even if I can't prove it.

We have GPS triggering devices all over the place now:

http://goo.gl/kiqY2N
http://goo.gl/vSKTQJ

We have the ability to have something activate or trigger when the location of the object on the GPS was reached. Whether this was a soluble container that when triggered would release a separate chemical that would dissolve it, or if it was just a very small container that was opened and the pathogen moved out on its own –doesn't matter! Both methodologies, both equally plausible, would result in David being hit with the pathogen. He would be affected, but not to the full extent as it was not specifically targeting him (not fully asymptomatic), and then the virus would transmit to others in his proximity. In this situation, David would be the most dangerous, not the people that die. They would die very quickly, but David would continue to carry and transmit the disease until it fully ran its course…or was countered. I went with enteric coating; easy way out.

Well people, that's it for now. Thanks again for joining Rahsan and I on this journey for these 12 issues. I'm looking forward to the next season, although there will be some months without the book. =(

Please hit me up online at my various feeds, or Rahsan at his:

Matt Hawkins
Please pester me on any of my feeds...or Rahsan on his!
@topcowmatt   @RahsanEkedal
https://www.facebook.com/Selfloathingnarcissist   http://www.rahsanekedal.com/
https://www.facebook.com/thinktankcomic   http://rekedal.blogspot.com/

A VOICE IN THE DARK
PREVIEW

BY LARIME TAYLOR

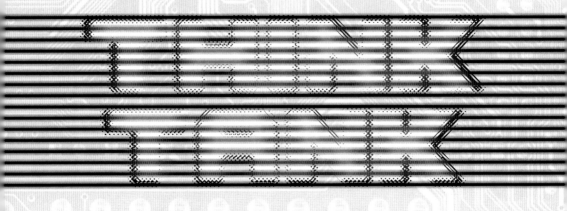

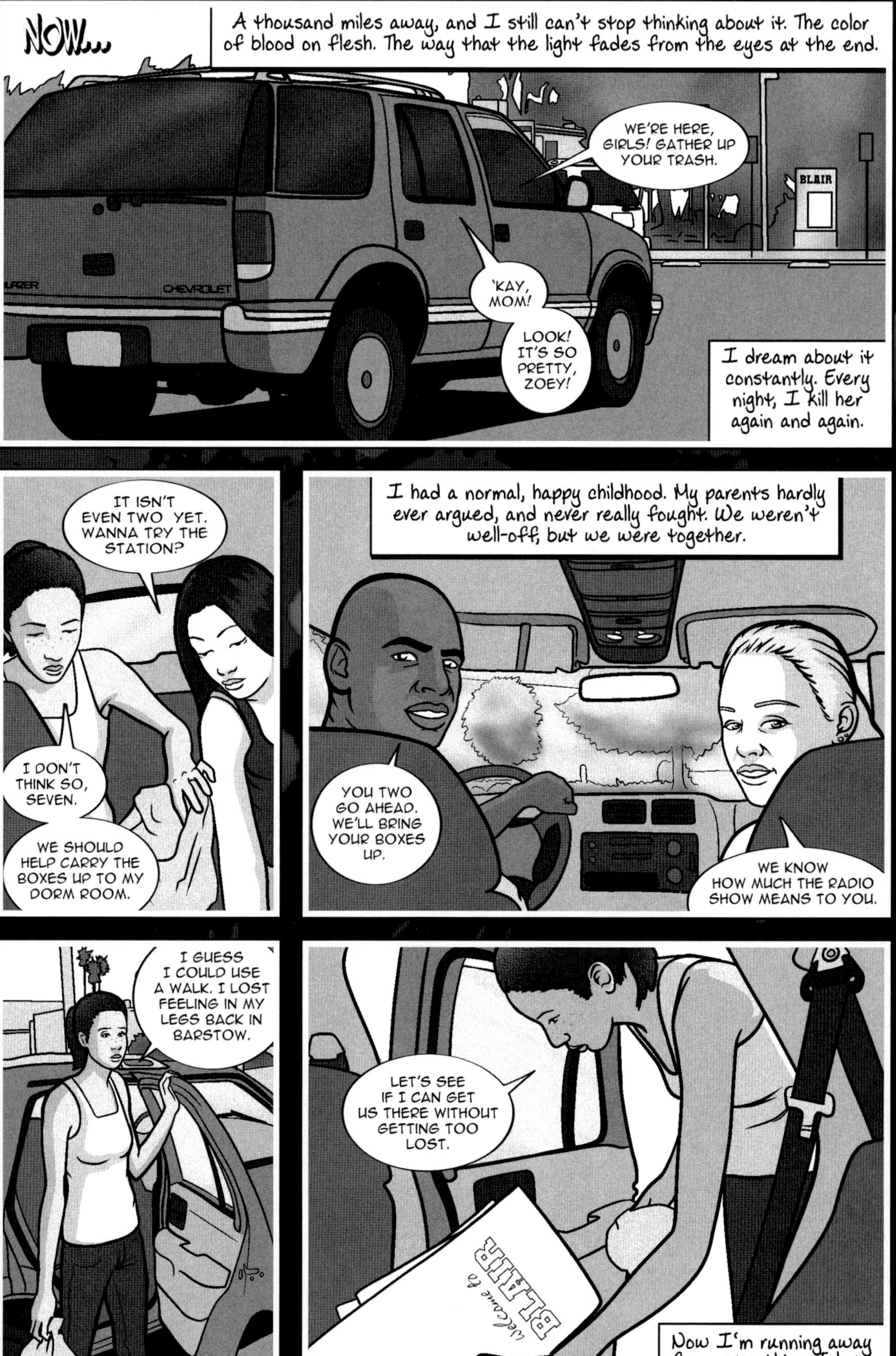
NOW...
A thousand miles away, and I still can't stop thinking about it. The color of blood on flesh. The way that the light fades from the eyes at the end.
WE'RE HERE, GIRLS! GATHER UP YOUR TRASH.
BLAIR
CHEVROLET
'KAY, MOM!
LOOK! IT'S SO PRETTY, ZOEY!
I dream about it constantly. Every night, I kill her again and again.
IT ISN'T EVEN TWO YET. WANNA TRY THE STATION?
I DON'T THINK SO, SEVEN.
WE SHOULD HELP CARRY THE BOXES UP TO MY DORM ROOM.
I had a normal, happy childhood. My parents hardly ever argued, and never really fought. We weren't well-off, but we were together.
YOU TWO GO AHEAD. WE'LL BRING YOUR BOXES UP.
WE KNOW HOW MUCH THE RADIO SHOW MEANS TO YOU.
I GUESS I COULD USE A WALK. I LOST FEELING IN MY LEGS BACK IN BARSTOW.
LET'S SEE IF I CAN GET US THERE WITHOUT GETTING TOO LOST.
Welcome to BLAIR
Now I'm running away from everything I love.

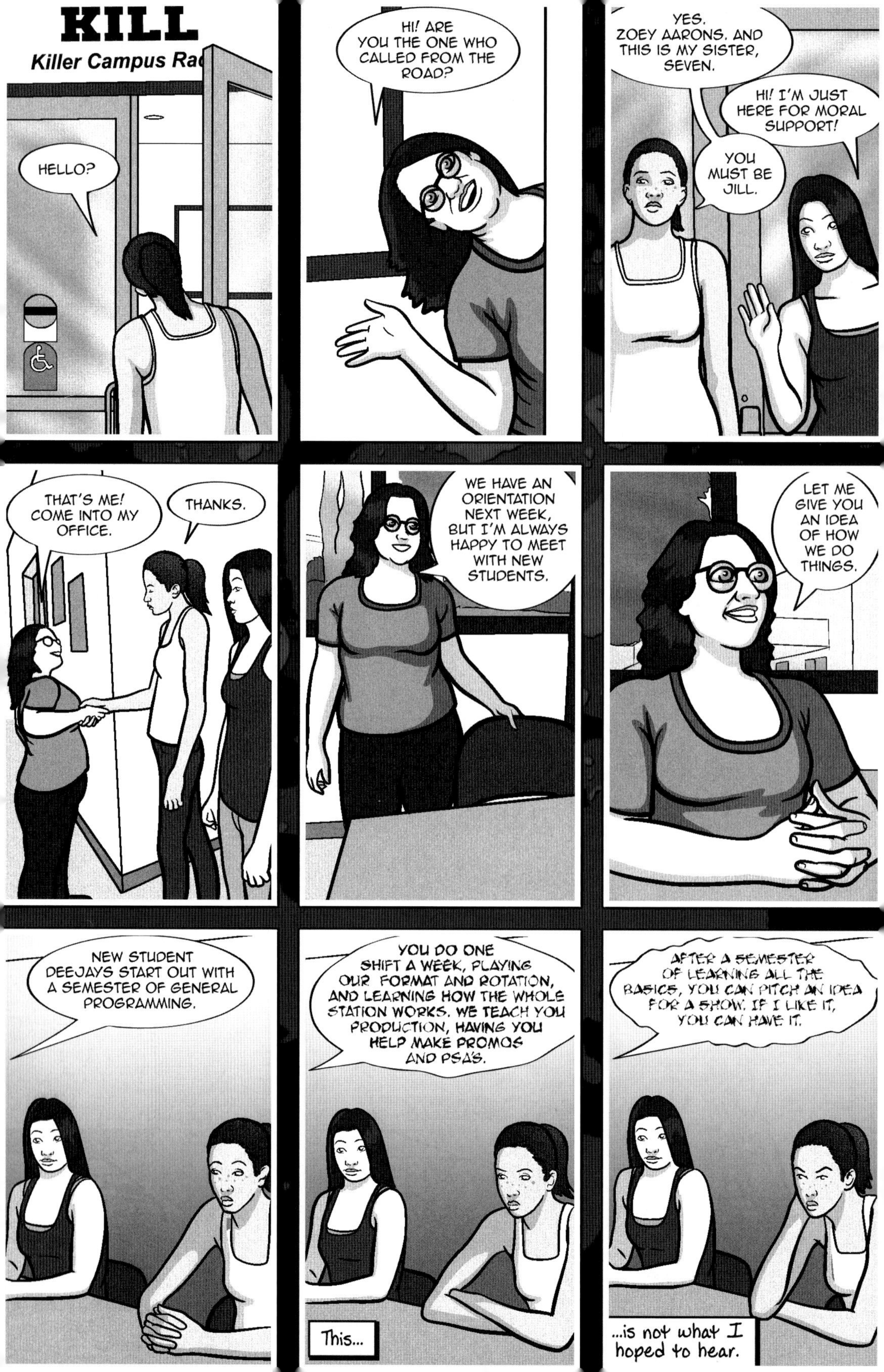
KILL
Killer Campus Ra
HELLO?
HI! ARE YOU THE ONE WHO CALLED FROM THE ROAD?
YES. ZOEY AARONS. AND THIS IS MY SISTER, SEVEN.
HI! I'M JUST HERE FOR MORAL SUPPORT!
YOU MUST BE JILL.
THAT'S ME! COME INTO MY OFFICE.
THANKS.
WE HAVE AN ORIENTATION NEXT WEEK, BUT I'M ALWAYS HAPPY TO MEET WITH NEW STUDENTS.
LET ME GIVE YOU AN IDEA OF HOW WE DO THINGS.
NEW STUDENT DEEJAYS START OUT WITH A SEMESTER OF GENERAL PROGRAMMING.
YOU DO ONE SHIFT A WEEK, PLAYING OUR FORMAT AND ROTATION, AND LEARNING HOW THE WHOLE STATION WORKS. WE TEACH YOU PRODUCTION, HAVING YOU HELP MAKE PROMOS AND PSA'S.
This...
AFTER A SEMESTER OF LEARNING ALL THE BASICS, YOU CAN PITCH AN IDEA FOR A SHOW. IF I LIKE IT, YOU CAN HAVE IT.
...is not what I hoped to hear.

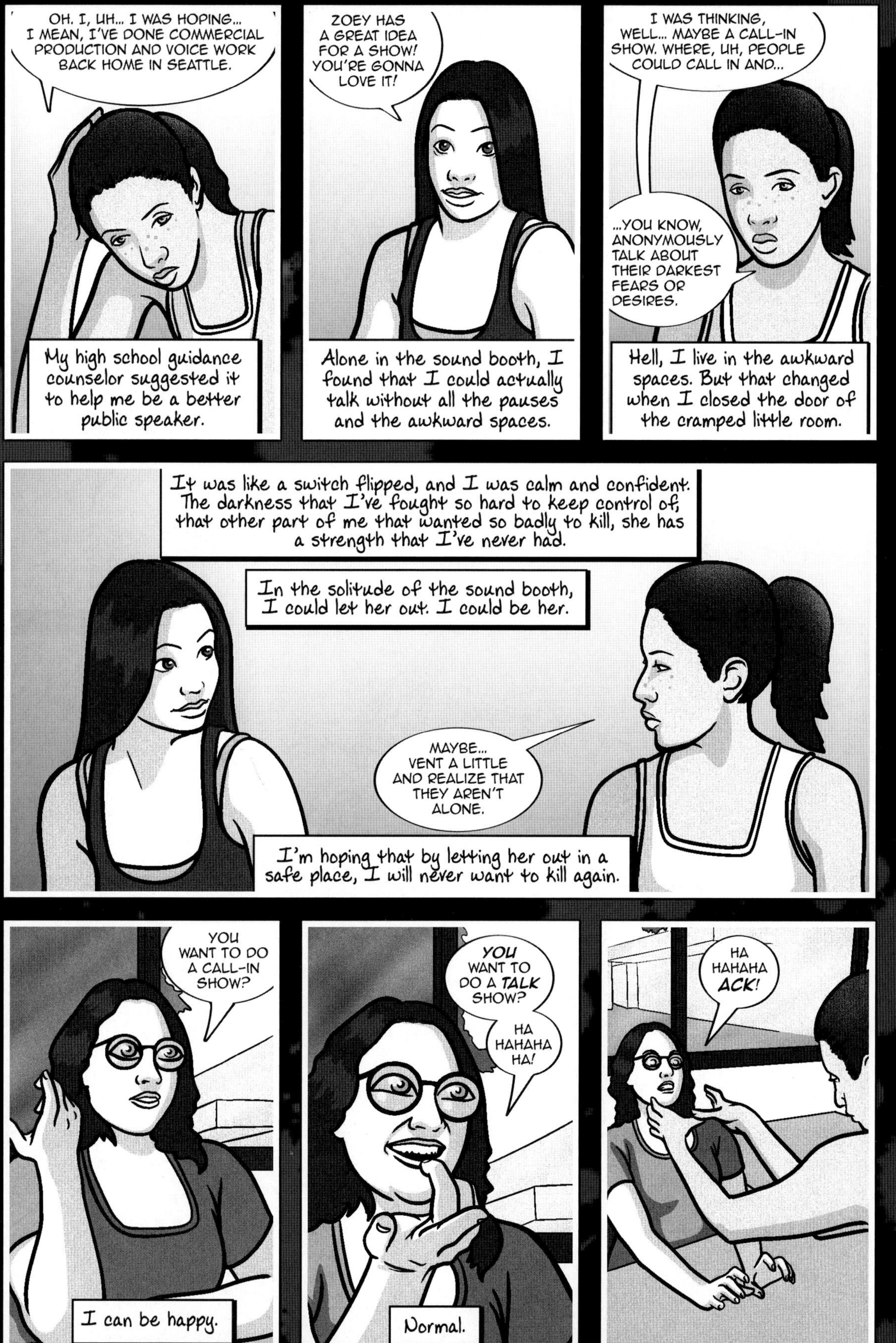
OH. I, UH... I WAS HOPING... I MEAN, I'VE DONE COMMERCIAL PRODUCTION AND VOICE WORK BACK HOME IN SEATTLE.
My high school guidance counselor suggested it to help me be a better public speaker.
ZOEY HAS A GREAT IDEA FOR A SHOW! YOU'RE GONNA LOVE IT!
Alone in the sound booth, I found that I could actually talk without all the pauses and the awkward spaces.
I WAS THINKING, WELL... MAYBE A CALL-IN SHOW. WHERE, UH, PEOPLE COULD CALL IN AND...
...YOU KNOW, ANONYMOUSLY TALK ABOUT THEIR DARKEST FEARS OR DESIRES.
Hell, I live in the awkward spaces. But that changed when I closed the door of the cramped little room.
It was like a switch flipped, and I was calm and confident. The darkness that I've fought so hard to keep control of, that other part of me that wanted so badly to kill, she has a strength that I've never had.
In the solitude of the sound booth, I could let her out. I could be her.
MAYBE... VENT A LITTLE AND REALIZE THAT THEY AREN'T ALONE.
I'm hoping that by letting her out in a safe place, I will never want to kill again.
YOU WANT TO DO A CALL-IN SHOW?
I can be happy.
YOU WANT TO DO A TALK SHOW?
HA HAHAHA HA!
Normal.
HA HAHAHA ACK!

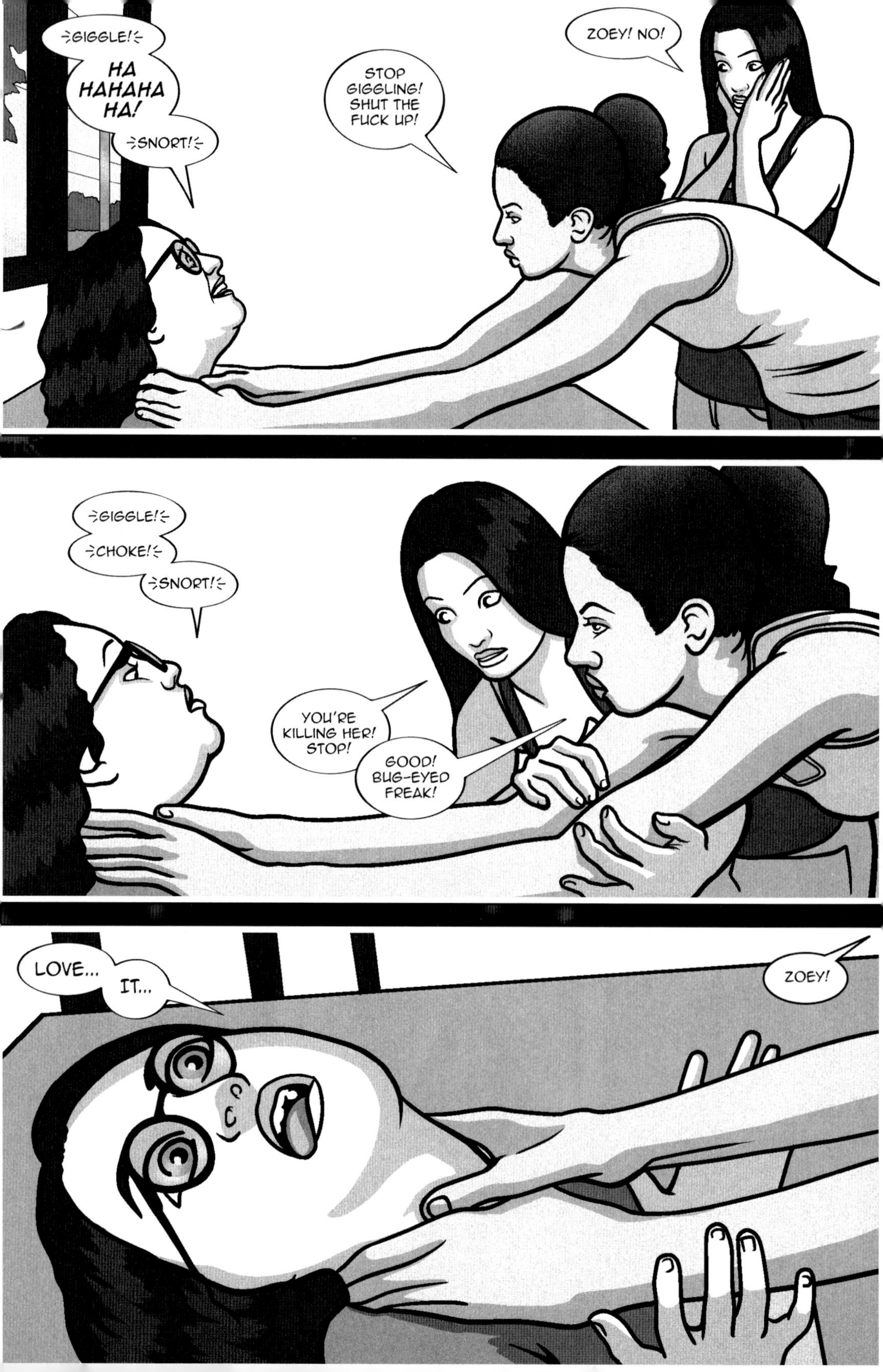

GIGGLE!
HA HAHAHA HA!
SNORT!
STOP GIGGLING! SHUT THE FUCK UP!
ZOEY! NO!
GIGGLE!
CHOKE!
SNORT!
YOU'RE KILLING HER! STOP!
GOOD! BUG-EYED FREAK!
LOVE... IT...
ZOEY!

It was all in my head.

ZOEY! DID YOU HEAR THAT? SHE SAID SHE LOVES IT!

...YOU DO?

I DO! NO ONE EVER WANTS TO DO A TALK SHOW. AND SINCE YOU HAVE SOME EXPERIENCE, I DON'T SEE THE POINT IN MAKING YOU DO GENERAL FORMAT.

I HAVE A MEETING AT TWO, BUT COME BACK DURING THE WEEK AND I'LL GO OVER OUR SETUP. YOU CAN START AS SOON AS YOU'RE READY.

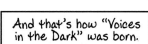

I... THANK YOU. I WILL.

AWESOME!

And that's how "Voices in the Dark" was born.

SEE? I KNEW YOU'D GET IT!

ON AIR

THANKS. I NEED A MINUTE. WAIT HERE?

'KAY! CAN WE GET DRINKS ON THE WAY BACK? I'M THIRSTY.

SURE.

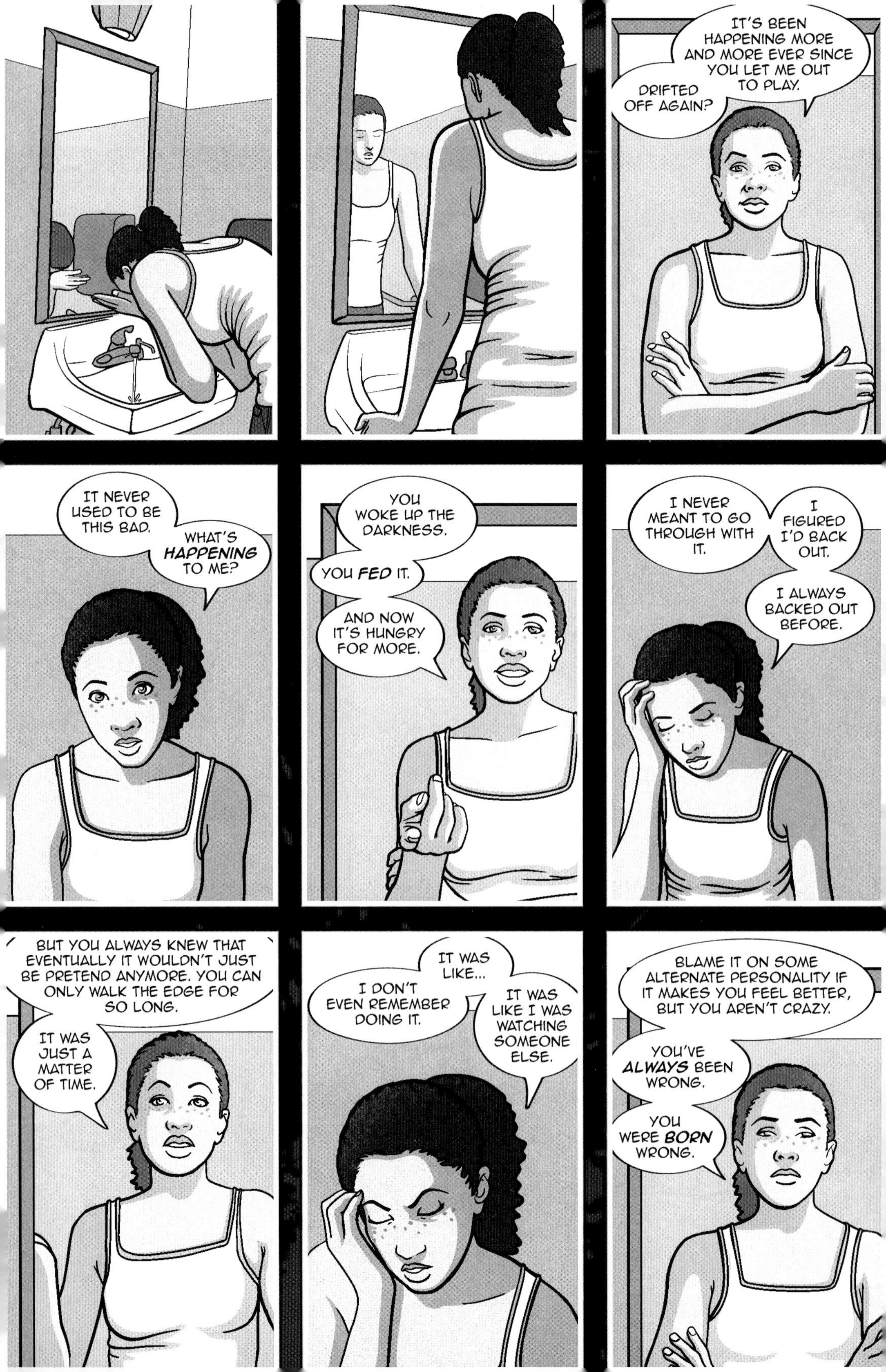
DRIFTED OFF AGAIN?
IT'S BEEN HAPPENING MORE AND MORE EVER SINCE YOU LET ME OUT TO PLAY.
IT NEVER USED TO BE THIS BAD.
WHAT'S HAPPENING TO ME?
YOU WOKE UP THE DARKNESS.
YOU FED IT.
AND NOW IT'S HUNGRY FOR MORE.
I NEVER MEANT TO GO THROUGH WITH IT.
I FIGURED I'D BACK OUT.
I ALWAYS BACKED OUT BEFORE.
BUT YOU ALWAYS KNEW THAT EVENTUALLY IT WOULDN'T JUST BE PRETEND ANYMORE. YOU CAN ONLY WALK THE EDGE FOR SO LONG.
IT WAS JUST A MATTER OF TIME.
I DON'T EVEN REMEMBER DOING IT.
IT WAS LIKE...
IT WAS LIKE I WAS WATCHING SOMEONE ELSE.
BLAME IT ON SOME ALTERNATE PERSONALITY IF IT MAKES YOU FEEL BETTER, BUT YOU AREN'T CRAZY.
YOU'VE ALWAYS BEEN WRONG.
YOU WERE BORN WRONG.

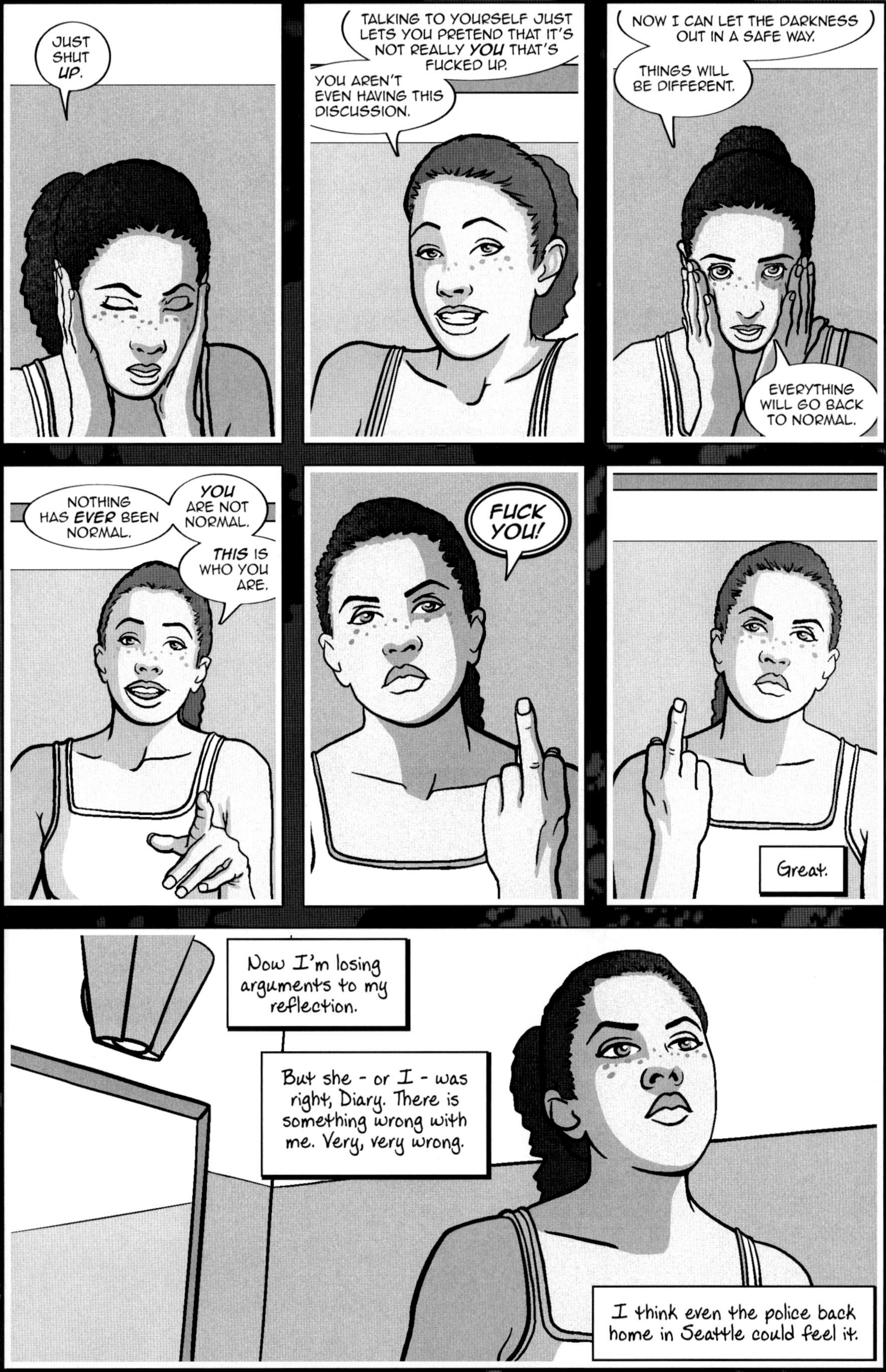
JUST SHUT *UP*.
TALKING TO YOURSELF JUST LETS YOU PRETEND THAT IT'S NOT REALLY *YOU* THAT'S FUCKED UP.
YOU AREN'T EVEN HAVING THIS DISCUSSION.
NOW I CAN LET THE DARKNESS OUT IN A SAFE WAY.
THINGS WILL BE DIFFERENT.
EVERYTHING WILL GO BACK TO NORMAL.
NOTHING HAS *EVER* BEEN NORMAL.
YOU ARE NOT NORMAL.
THIS IS WHO YOU ARE.
FUCK YOU!
Great.
Now I'm losing arguments to my reflection.
But she - or I - was right, Diary. There is something wrong with me. Very, very wrong.
I think even the police back home in Seattle could feel it.

THEN...

THANK YOU FOR COMING DOWN, MISS AARONS. I'M DETECTIVE YATES. SORRY TO KEEP YOU WAITING.

IT'S FINE, DETECTIVE. I HOPE I CAN HELP.

I was never an official suspect in the murder.

But early on, I was a "Person of Interest."

I WASN'T SURE HOW YOU TAKE YOUR COFFEE...

...SO I JUST GOT YOU SOME WATER.

I had just turned eighteen. I was a harmless kid.

I'M NOT MUCH OF A COFFEE DRINKER, UNLESS ICE AND CHOCOLATE ARE INVOLVED. THANKS.

IF ICE AND CHOCOLATE ARE INVOLVED, IT'S NOT COFFEE, MISS AARONS.

IT'S A MILKSHAKE. I WONDER ABOUT YOU KIDS.

See?

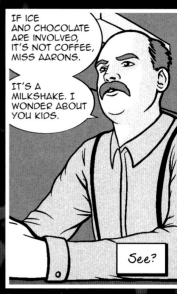

AS YOU SAY.

WHAT CAN I DO FOR YOU, DETECTIVE?

WELL, AS I SAID, WE APPRECIATE YOUR COOPERATION.

OF COURSE.

I JUST WANT TO VERIFY A FEW THINGS WITH YOU IN REGARDS TO ANNABELLE TURNER AND THE DAY OF HER DEATH.

SUCH AS...?

How I did it? Why I did it?

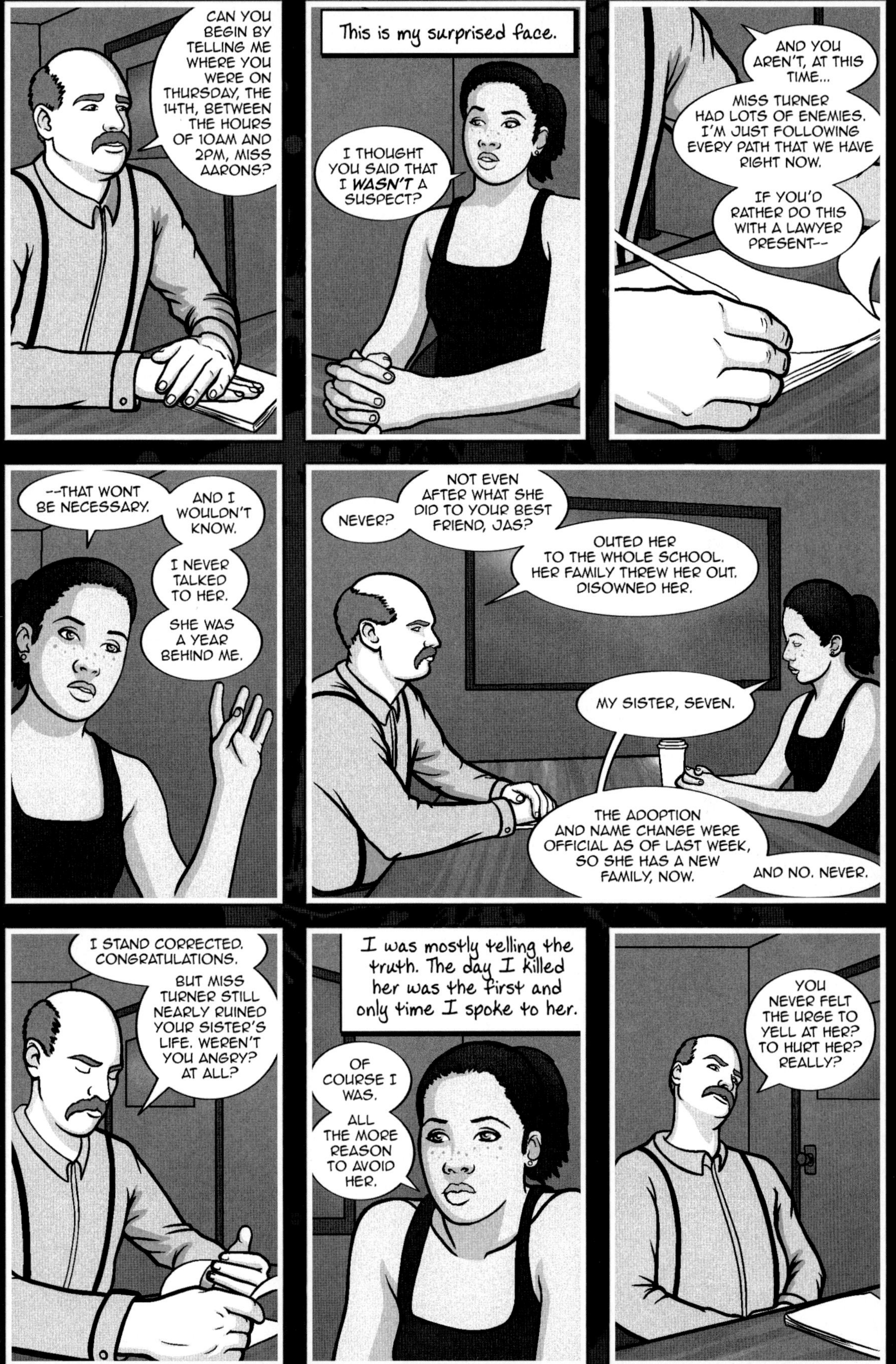
CAN YOU BEGIN BY TELLING ME WHERE YOU WERE ON THURSDAY, THE 14TH, BETWEEN THE HOURS OF 10AM AND 2PM, MISS AARONS?
This is my surprised face.
I THOUGHT YOU SAID THAT I WASN'T A SUSPECT?
AND YOU AREN'T, AT THIS TIME...
MISS TURNER HAD LOTS OF ENEMIES. I'M JUST FOLLOWING EVERY PATH THAT WE HAVE RIGHT NOW.
IF YOU'D RATHER DO THIS WITH A LAWYER PRESENT--
--THAT WONT BE NECESSARY.
AND I WOULDN'T KNOW.
I NEVER TALKED TO HER.
SHE WAS A YEAR BEHIND ME.
NEVER?
NOT EVEN AFTER WHAT SHE DID TO YOUR BEST FRIEND, JAS?
OUTED HER TO THE WHOLE SCHOOL. HER FAMILY THREW HER OUT. DISOWNED HER.
MY SISTER, SEVEN.
THE ADOPTION AND NAME CHANGE WERE OFFICIAL AS OF LAST WEEK, SO SHE HAS A NEW FAMILY, NOW.
AND NO. NEVER.
I STAND CORRECTED. CONGRATULATIONS.
BUT MISS TURNER STILL NEARLY RUINED YOUR SISTER'S LIFE. WEREN'T YOU ANGRY? AT ALL?
I was mostly telling the truth. The day I killed her was the first and only time I spoke to her.
OF COURSE I WAS.
ALL THE MORE REASON TO AVOID HER.
YOU NEVER FELT THE URGE TO YELL AT HER? TO HURT HER? REALLY?

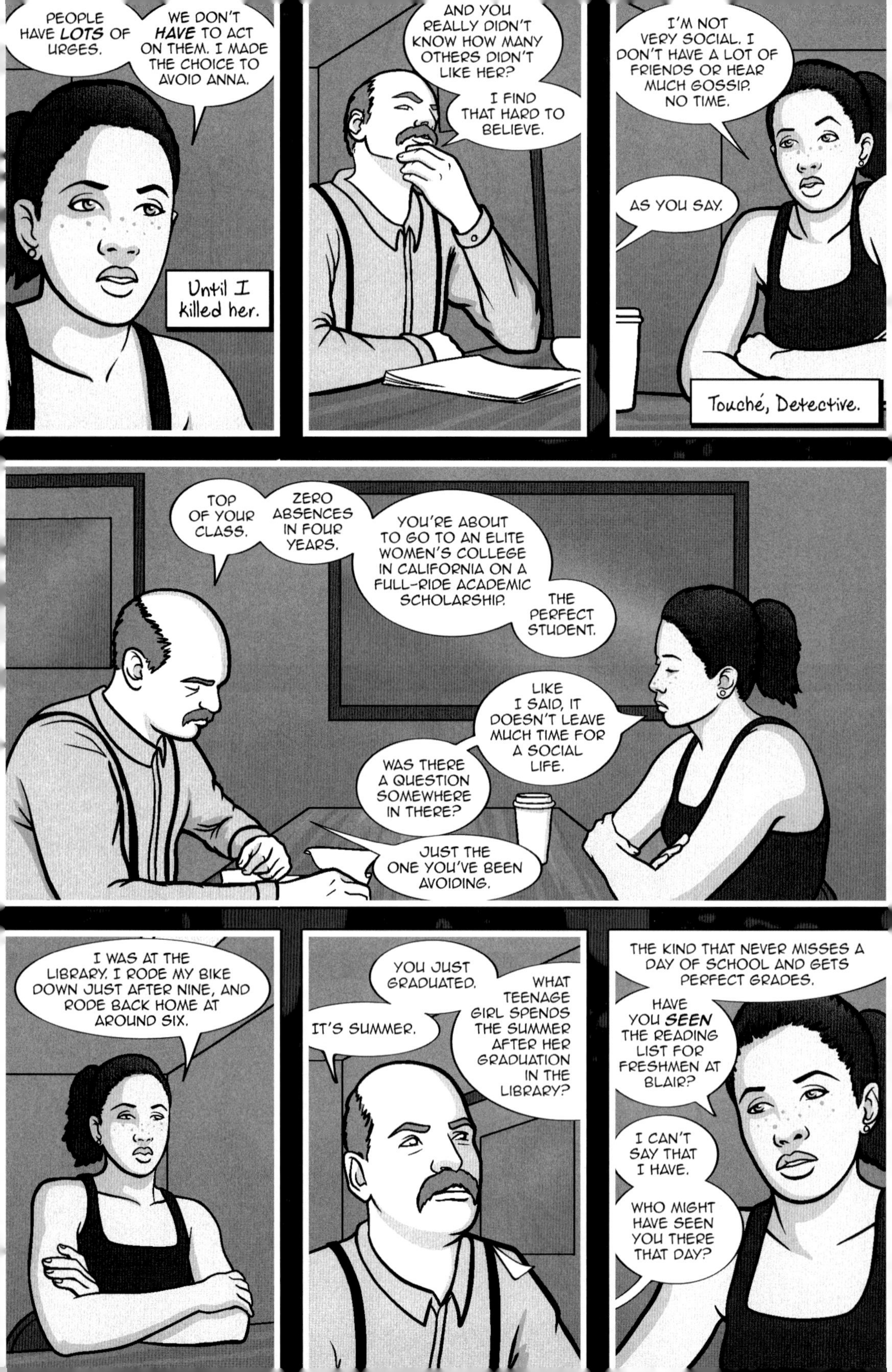
PEOPLE HAVE LOTS OF URGES.
WE DON'T HAVE TO ACT ON THEM. I MADE THE CHOICE TO AVOID ANNA.
Until I killed her.
AND YOU REALLY DIDN'T KNOW HOW MANY OTHERS DIDN'T LIKE HER?
I FIND THAT HARD TO BELIEVE.
I'M NOT VERY SOCIAL. I DON'T HAVE A LOT OF FRIENDS OR HEAR MUCH GOSSIP. NO TIME.
AS YOU SAY.
Touché, Detective.
TOP OF YOUR CLASS.
ZERO ABSENCES IN FOUR YEARS.
YOU'RE ABOUT TO GO TO AN ELITE WOMEN'S COLLEGE IN CALIFORNIA ON A FULL-RIDE ACADEMIC SCHOLARSHIP.
THE PERFECT STUDENT.
LIKE I SAID, IT DOESN'T LEAVE MUCH TIME FOR A SOCIAL LIFE.
WAS THERE A QUESTION SOMEWHERE IN THERE?
JUST THE ONE YOU'VE BEEN AVOIDING.
I WAS AT THE LIBRARY. I RODE MY BIKE DOWN JUST AFTER NINE, AND RODE BACK HOME AT AROUND SIX.
YOU JUST GRADUATED.
IT'S SUMMER.
WHAT TEENAGE GIRL SPENDS THE SUMMER AFTER HER GRADUATION IN THE LIBRARY?
THE KIND THAT NEVER MISSES A DAY OF SCHOOL AND GETS PERFECT GRADES.
HAVE YOU SEEN THE READING LIST FOR FRESHMEN AT BLAIR?
I CAN'T SAY THAT I HAVE.
WHO MIGHT HAVE SEEN YOU THERE THAT DAY?

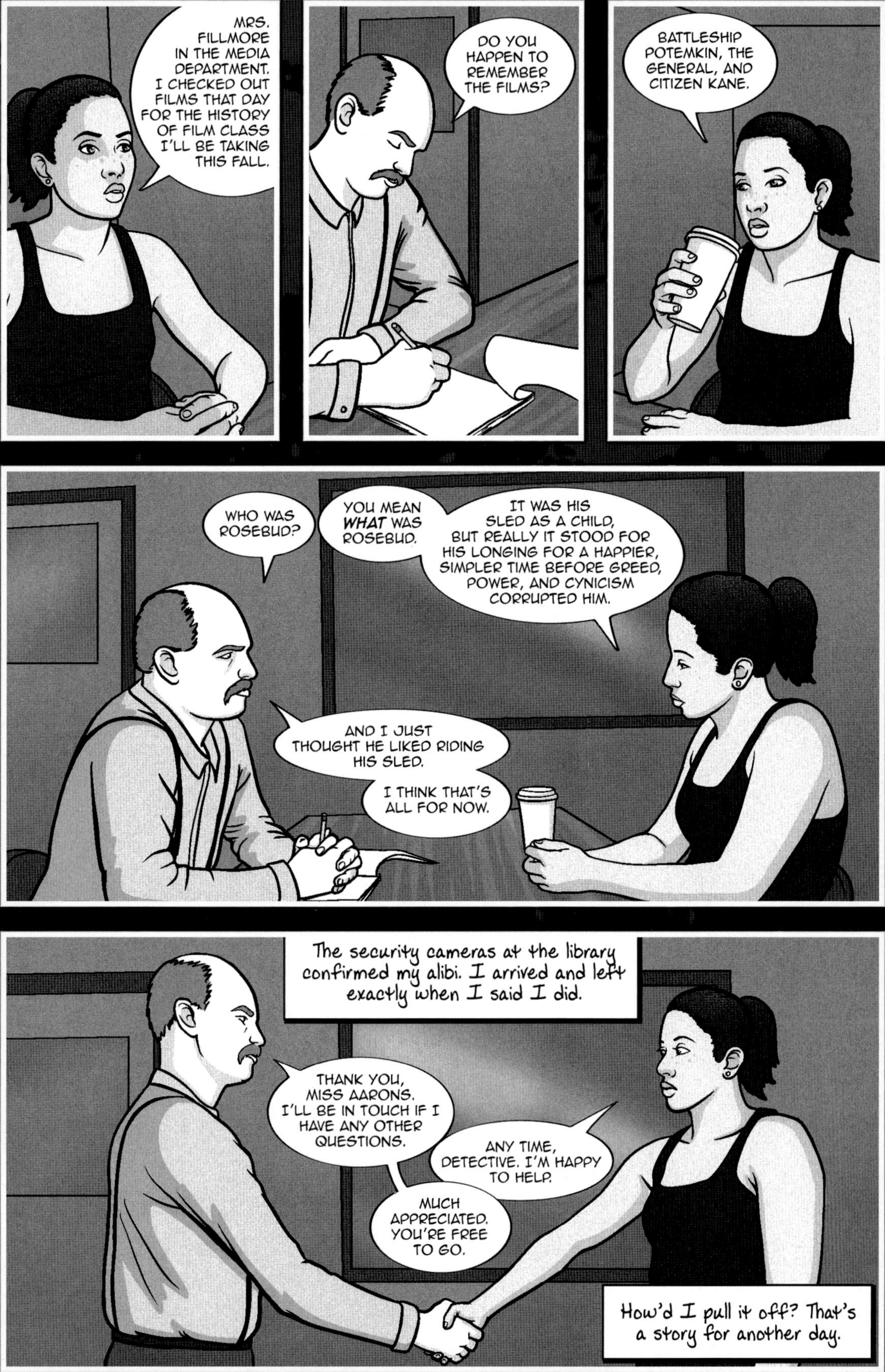
MRS. FILLMORE IN THE MEDIA DEPARTMENT. I CHECKED OUT FILMS THAT DAY FOR THE HISTORY OF FILM CLASS I'LL BE TAKING THIS FALL.
DO YOU HAPPEN TO REMEMBER THE FILMS?
BATTLESHIP POTEMKIN, THE GENERAL, AND CITIZEN KANE.
WHO WAS ROSEBUD?
YOU MEAN *WHAT* WAS ROSEBUD.
IT WAS HIS SLED AS A CHILD, BUT REALLY IT STOOD FOR HIS LONGING FOR A HAPPIER, SIMPLER TIME BEFORE GREED, POWER, AND CYNICISM CORRUPTED HIM.
AND I JUST THOUGHT HE LIKED RIDING HIS SLED.
I THINK THAT'S ALL FOR NOW.
The security cameras at the library confirmed my alibi. I arrived and left exactly when I said I did.
THANK YOU, MISS AARONS. I'LL BE IN TOUCH IF I HAVE ANY OTHER QUESTIONS.
ANY TIME, DETECTIVE. I'M HAPPY TO HELP.
MUCH APPRECIATED. YOU'RE FREE TO GO.
How'd I pull it off? That's a story for another day.

READ MORE TOP COW...

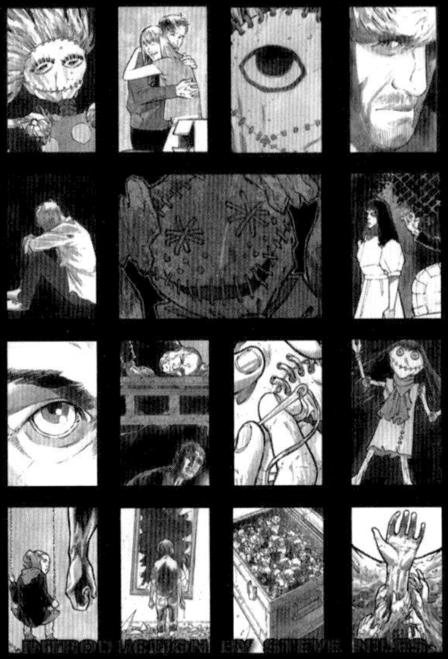

ECHOES

Writer: Joshua Fialkov
Artist: Rahsan Ekedal

From acclaimed author JOSHUA HALE FIAKOV (Tumor, Pilot Season: Alibi) and rising artist RAHSAN EKEDAL (Creepy) a disturbing story of murder and mystery wrapped in questions of sanity.

Minotaur Press premieres with a story of madness, family and death. Brian Cohn was learning to deal with the schizophrenia inherited from his father. Supportive wife, new baby on the way, drugs to control the voices. But, when at his father's deathbed, he learns that he also inherited the trophies of his father's career as a serial killer, his illness threatens to send him further down the path to madness and... ?

SUNSET

Writer: Christos Gage
Artist: Jorge Lucas

SOMETIMES ALL YOU CAN DO IS GO OUT WITH GUNS BLAZING...

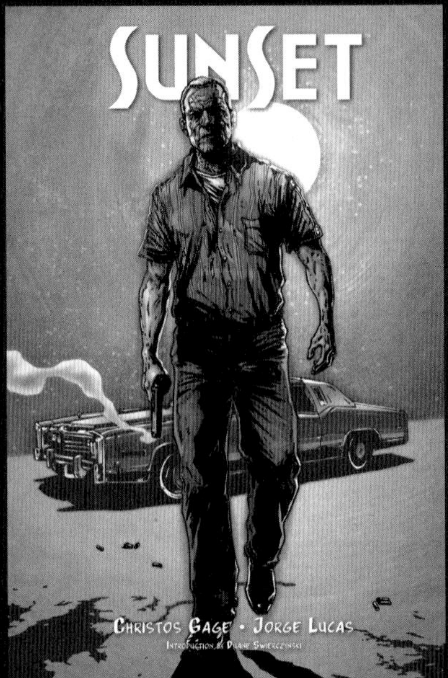
SUNSET
CHRISTOS GAGE • JORGE LUCAS

In the noir tradition of Chandler and Spillane comes SUNSET, a two-fisted tale of revenge and redemption. On the surface, Nick Bellamy looks like any other veteran retiree left behind by a modern world. In reality, Nick is a former enforcer, who stole a fortune and years of freedom from his former mob boss. Now, in the twilight of his life, Nick will lose everything he cares about except two things: revenge... and the chance to die with his guns blazing.

Writer CHRISTOS GAGE (Avengers Academy, GI Joe: Cobra) and artist JORGE LUCAS (THE DARKNESS) promise to hit hard with Minotaur Press's first original graphic novel that will make you forget all about your Prius and organic whole-grain trans-fat-free diet.

CREATOR BIOGRAPHIES

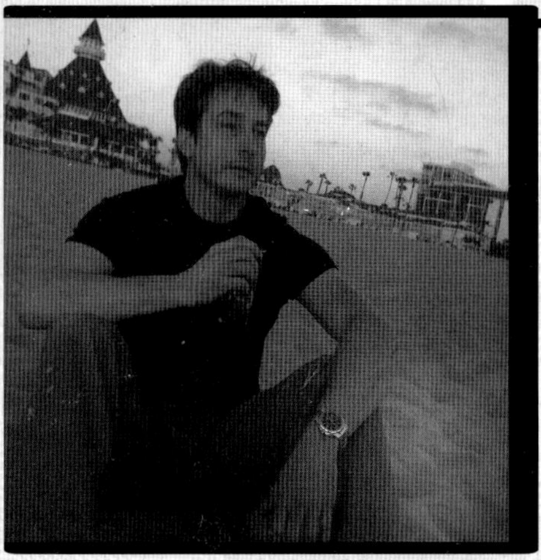

MATT HAWKINS

A veteran of the initial Image Comics launch, Matt started his career in comic book publishing in 1993 and has been working with Image as a creator, writer and executive for over 20 years. President/COO of Top Cow since 1998, Matt has created and written over 30 new franchises for Top Cow and Image including Think Tank, Necromancer, VICE, Lady Pendragon, Aphrodite IX as well as handling the company's business affairs.

RAHSAN EKEDAL

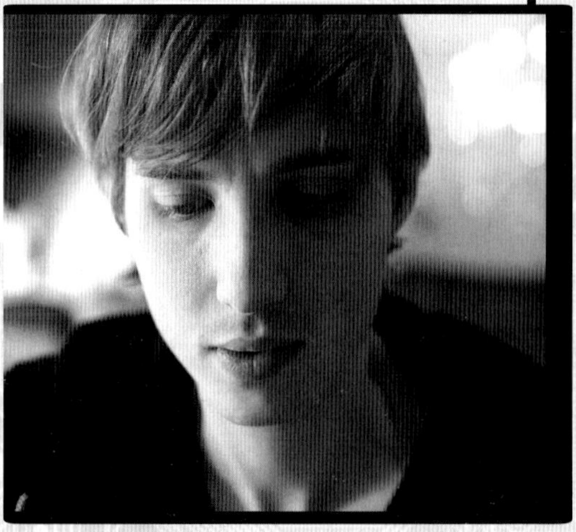

Rahsan Ekedal is an artist best known for his work on Think Tank, and the Harvey Award nominated graphic novel Echoes. He has illustrated a variety of titles such as Solomon Kane, Creepy Comics, The Cleaners, and Warhammer, and worked with many publishers including Top Cow, Dark Horse, DC/Vertigo, and Boom! Studios. He was born in California, and educated at the School of the Arts HIgh School and the Academy of Art University, both in San Francisco. Rahsan currently lives in Berlin, Germany with his wife Shannon, and their big black cat, Flash.

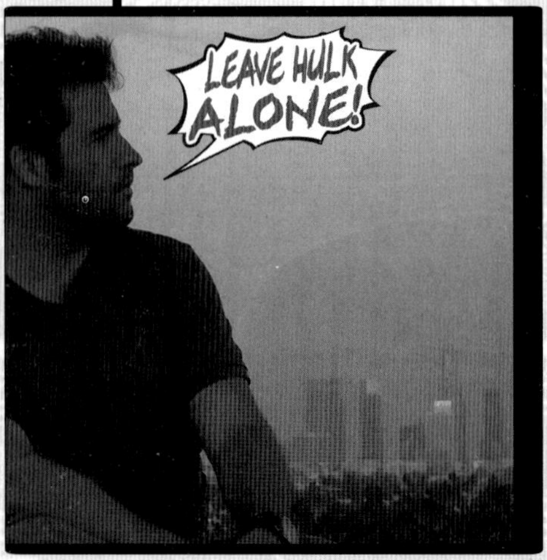
LEAVE HULK ALONE!

TROY PETERI

Starting his career at Comicraft, Troy Peteri lettered titles such as Iron Man, Wolverine, and Amazing Spider-Man, among many others. His career hit a bump in the road known as CrossGen Comics, but that's neither here nor there. Thankfully, he met a number of great creators there, which led to him lettering roughly 97% of all Top Cow titles since 2005.

In addition to Top Cow, he currently letters comics from multiple publishers and websites, such as Image Comics, Dynamite and Archaia. He (along with co-creator Dave Lanphear) is currently writing (and lettering) 77 Hero Plaza, a webcomic of his own creation for www.Thrillbent.com. (Once again, www.Thrillbent.com.) He's still bitter about no longer lettering The Darkness and wants it back on stands immediately.